hachette
BOOKS

LARGE
PRINT

THE
MOST
BEAUTIFUL

MY LIFE WITH PRINCE

———

MAYTE GARCIA

hachette
BOOKS

LARGE PRINT EDITION

Jacket design by Amanda Kain
Jacket photographs © Randee St Nicholas
Author photograph by Fabian Benhamou
Jacket copyright © 2017 by Hachette Book Group, Inc.

Hachette Books
Hachette Book Group
1290 Avenue of the Americas
New York, NY 10104
hachettebooks.com
twitter.com/hachettebooks

First edition: April 2017

Image credits can be found on page 405.

Hachette Books is a division of Hachette Book Group, Inc.
The Hachette Books name and logo are trademarks of
Hachette Book Group, Inc.

The publisher is not responsible for websites (or their content) that are not owned by the publisher.

The Hachette Speakers Bureau provides a wide range of authors for speaking events. To find out more, go to www.hachettespeakersbureau.com or call (866) 376-6591.

Library of Congress Cataloging-in-Publication Data

Names: Garcia, Mayte, 1973–
Title: The most beautiful : my life with Prince / Mayte Garcia.
Description: First edition. | New York : Hachette Books, 2017.
Identifiers: LCCN 2016054437| ISBN 9780316468978 (hardcover) |
ISBN 9780316508803 (large print) | ISBN 9781478974253 (audio book) |
ISBN 9781478948575 (audio download) | ISBN 9780316468961 (ebook)
Subjects: LCSH: Prince. | Rock musicians—United States—Biography. |
Garcia, Mayte, 1973– | Dancers—United States—Biography. |
LCGFT: Biographies.
Classification: LCC ML420.P974 G37 2017 | DDC 781.66092 [B]—dc23 LC record
available at https://lccn.loc.gov/2016054437

ISBNs: 978-0-316-46897-8 (hardcover); 978-0-316-46896-1 (ebook);
978-0-316-50880-3 (large print hardcover); 978-0-316-56025-2
(signed hardcover)

Printed in the United States of America

LSC-C

10 9 8 7 6 5 4 3 2 1

For Gia, my angel

For what we are about to see next,
we must enter quietly into the realm of genius.
—YOUNG FRANKENSTEIN

prologue

The chain-link fence around Paisley Park is woven with purple ribbons and roses, love notes, tributes, and prayers for peace. Tall poplars and elms, still naked from winter, stand over rolling brown grass. It hasn't been very long since the snow melted off, but below the cold surface, the whole place is waiting to be reborn. The sky is overcast with low clouds, but I keep my sunglasses firmly in place, because my face is a train wreck from a week of weeping.

> *There is a woman who sits all alone by the pier*
> *Her husband was naughty and caused his wife so*
>   *many tears*

I always thought it was interesting that Prince saw this sad little figure sitting off to the side in "Paisley Park," a song about colorful people and happy children. If I allow myself to get existential about it, I wonder if she is me. I hear the cool, sharp *clang* of zills, and a chill slips down my backbone. I imagine Prince sitting at the piano in those hypercreative hours just before dawn. For a fleeting moment, there I am in his mind's eye. He studies me briefly and then jots the words on notepaper, recognizing on some level this moment of truth from another time.

> *He died without knowing forgiveness and now*
> *   she is sad, so sad*
> *Maybe she'll come 2 the Park and forgive him*
> *   and life won't be so bad…*

There's a familiar Midwestern bite in the air. Springtime at Paisley Park smells like clean fog, wet fir trees, and distant city traffic. I take in a deep breath and wait to exhale. My four-year-old daughter, Gia, tugs on my coat sleeve.

"Mama, is it time to go?" she asks for the thousandth time.

"A few more minutes."

I've done my best to explain to Gia why so many people have brought so many flowers. I've told her that the man they called Prince has died.

"Prince is in heaven now?" she says.

"Yes. He's in heaven."

"With Boogie?" Gia asks, remembering what I told her when we lost our beloved golden retriever.

"Yes. He's with Boogie in heaven."

"Mama," she says, "can we get a ladder and climb up to get him?"

That's Gia. As sweet and unexpected as a raspberry.

Gia knows that I am her real mommy. Someday I'll explain to her how her birth mother and I helped the universe get that right. I'll tell her about her brother, Amiir, who was waiting for his daddy in heaven. I'll play her the songs my husband sang for our son.

tears go here
tears go here

I stroke her cheeks, which are pink and a little dry, because it's early spring in Minnesota. We've barely made it past Easter, and already 2016 has been a jarring year for celebrity obituaries, particularly in the music industry. Natalie Cole died on New Year's Eve. David Bowie passed ten days later, followed by Glenn Frey of the Eagles, Maurice White of Earth, Wind & Fire, and Prince's own protégé Vanity. Then Harper Lee, the author of *To Kill a Mockingbird*, passed away, and then Nancy Reagan and Patty Duke, and then Chyna, which shocked me to the core, because—well, because she was *Chyna* and only forty-six years old when she died.

April 21, 2016, had begun like any other Thursday. I dropped Gia off with my dad and joined the streaming LA traffic on my way to Baldwin Park Animal Care Center in the San Gabriel Valley for a dog-grooming class. We were practicing on shelter dogs, which, according to our teacher, meant there was no pressure. In my mind, the very opposite was true: I felt an intense sense of responsibility to animals in peril. I wanted these little guys to be at their most adorable when people came to check out pets waiting to be adopted. That first impression is the difference between life and death for many of these animals; it's hard for people to see them as a potential family member if they're not looking their best. I was not about to screw that up.

"If I bring my cat," I asked the teacher, "will you show me how to do it?"

He said, "Sure." But my cat, Willy, was in loud disagreement, churring and squalling as I sped down the freeway. He was being so vocal I almost missed the text from Manuela. We share a strange bond, Manuela and I. I'll get to that later. Relevant in this moment: Manuela Testolini is Prince's second ex-wife and not a person who gets on the phone a lot, so it was odd to see her brief text from the corner of my eye.

call me right away

My first thought was to ignore it until I got to class, but something pulled me to the side of the road.

"Hey, girl." I tried not to sound impatient. "What's up?"

Her voice was shallow, choked with tears. "I wanted to call you before you heard on the news. Prince is dead."

"What?"

"Yeah. I'm—I'm freaking out. I'm doing this Earth Day presentation at my daughter's school and—and he's dead. They found him in an elevator at Paisley."

There was a moment of muffled shock while the words sank in, and then it was as if I'd been sucked into a funnel cloud, everything spinning around me—the traffic roaring by, Willy yowling in the back seat, the sky falling in front of the windshield. I heard myself screaming, *"No no no no no..."*

Not him. Not like that. Not alone. Not now.

I don't remember what was said after that. I just remember both of us crying. I remember gripping the steering wheel, forcing myself to breathe, to open my eyes, to steer back into the traffic and find a way to turn around. I needed to go home. I needed to call Mama.

In the hours that followed, I felt lost in a riptide of memory and emotion, which felt more real to me than the firestorm of rumors in the press. I paced the patio outside my house until my manager, Gladys, sent me a text that simply said: *Go inside.* Attached was a grainy, zoom-lens photo of me that had just appeared online.

My ex-husband was adamant about never being seen without perfect hair and makeup. This photo was the antithesis of that. I wanted to care, but I couldn't feel anything except dry irony. I drifted inside and sat with the blinds drawn for two days. Reporters remained camped outside, pointing cameras at the windows, yelling my name every time someone stepped in or out of the door.

The story of Prince's death was repeated over and over on the 24-hour news channels. At first, the headlines were blunt: *PRINCE DEAD AT 57.* Then sentimental: *WORLD MOURNS MUSIC LEGEND.* Then speculative: *THE DRUG THAT KILLED PRINCE: WHAT IS FENTANYL?* Inevitably, they became sordid: *LOVE MACHINE PRINCE WAS CELIBATE FOR LAST 8 YEARS.* People who may or may not have known him crawled out of every crevice of the Internet, eager to comment. My phone was blowing up. Mama's phone was blowing up. There was a barrage of requests from networks and news channels and radio stations, wanting to book Prince's first wife.

Mama kept telling them, "She's not doing any press."

They kept telling her, "At the very least, she should make some sort of comment."

I had no comment. Truly. Nothing I could say about this man could be squeezed into a three-minute morning show segment. There was a story to be told, but I wanted to tell it in my own way, in my own time, not in sound bites that would be edited to accommodate their dead-rock-star narrative, and at the time, I felt too raw, too exposed. Before I could think about anything else, I needed to be at Paisley. I heard there was to be a memorial service but couldn't get any solid information. I wasn't even sure I would be invited.

"It's weird," Manuela told me. "Everything's locked down."

Prince's coworkers were like family, to him and to me, so I called Wendy and Lisa, his *Purple Rain* bandmates, and Sheila E, his longtime friend and collaborator and former fiancée.

"Come," Wendy and Lisa both said. "We've got you."

"You're my sis," said Sheila. "We are all family."

So here I am, along with family and fans and other people who knew and loved and worked with this extraordinary artist. The house we lived in—the house where we made a life together and created two babies—is gone. Years ago, in the darkest possible state of mind, he had it bulldozed to the ground and the contents burned. The elaborate playground he built for our children was torn down to make way for a restaurant so he wouldn't have to go out for food, but as I understand it, no one got the proper permits, so the restaurant didn't happen. Looking out across the land, the wealth of timber, the prime real estate, I suspect that very soon the forests around the office complex will disappear as well.

"Mommy, is it time to go?" Gia says. One-thousand-one.

"Almost. I want to take your picture."

"Mommy, no!" She groans, utterly out of patience. "Don't take my picture."

I laugh at that, because she's standing in front of the glass doors where my father stole a picture of me more than twenty years ago. He raised his Instamatic camera just as I walked out, and I scolded him, "Dad, no! He doesn't like people taking pictures here."

"Trust me," said my father, "you'll be glad I did."

The sweet sting of that memory brings tears to my eyes. He was right, of course. That photograph is precious to me now.

"Trust me," I tell Gia, "you'll want to remember all this."

I do. I want to remember it all: twenty-five years—more than half my life—of soaring highs and crushing lows, creation and loss, elation and sorrow, the sound and fury that happened onstage in front of millions of people and the silent journey only our two souls will ever know.

When I was a kid, I kinda liked his music, but my sister was the real fangirl. When I was sixteen, I saw him perform live in concert, and my world was never the same. What's most incredible to me is that he said the same thing about his world after he saw me dance. We fell into an immediate—and entirely innocent—infatuation that set us on a path neither of us could have imagined. First and foremost, we were friends. Two years later, he became my boss. Eventually, we crossed the line, and I was "his girl." From that moment forward, he molded my persona and shaped my life experiences.

Between 1990, when Prince and I first met, and 1996, when we got married, I participated in 129 performances on five world tours, plus a couple hundred aftershows and one-off concert gigs, dozens of music videos, album tracks (credited and uncredited), many national television appearances, countless photo sessions, radio interviews, and press junkets. It's a little mind-blowing to take stock of it all now, as I try to make sense of what we were to each other. Not one day since I met him, not one night out of the past six thousand, has passed without some thought of him.

He said many times, publically and privately, that his love for me changed him as a man and influenced much of the music he made during the years we were together. I never pretended I was the only woman he ever loved, but for better or worse, the experience we shared as husband and wife and as parents took us both to a place neither of us was ever able to share with anyone else.

Prince passed away so suddenly. I wasn't ready. It's been years since I last saw him, but I have always cherished what we had and honored his privacy. After his death, so many things surfaced—mysteries and questions that linger unresolved, like a frustrating unfinished octave, for me and so many others who loved him. I'm hungry to hear stories about his life that fill in some of the gaps. I honor the power of mystery, and yes, there are things I've chosen to keep private, but mystery can be a lonely place. I want to peel back the layers and let you know the man I loved—the good, the bad, the sad, and the beautiful.

I will never fully close this chapter of my life. I struggled with the idea of writing this book because, even after all this time, part of me still needs his approval. I hope that in reflecting on all that happened, I'll be able to shed some light and provide some insight as we each decide for ourselves how to best remember him.

I'll remember him as a hopeless romantic and a devoted father who longed to be the dad he never had. Only I saw the look on his face when our son was born. A moment I'll never forget. I wish I could draw it. I wish it could be danced. I'm not sure there's a way to express it in words, but words are what I can offer you now. I can laugh with you about the funny things he said and tell you about how he wore my clothes and swiped my mascara and woke up every morning in a tangle of loving arms and perfumed sheets with a little dog barking to go out and a long day of hard work ahead. I can tell you that, while we were so normal about so many things, we lived his belief that life itself should be a work of art.

Everyone who knew this extraordinary man—friends, family, and fans—has their own stories to tell, and I hope they tell them, though some will be painful for me to hear. I hope some scholar of music history will write a book that spans the incredible depth and breadth of Prince's work, all the remarkable people he collaborated with, his influence on the music industry, his lasting handprint on pop culture, and his contribution to the art of rock and roll. This is not that book.

This is *my* story—a private love story that belongs to me alone—and I need to share it my own way, just as he shared it in his. He was a private man, but through his music, he's already said more than people realize. Beneath the rhythms and between the lines, you hear the love and fate and heartbreak. It's not as easy to hear the echoes of strength and closure and hope, but they are there.

The story I'm about to tell you now is the story I'll tell Gia someday: the story of my life with Prince and my life without him, the career I forged before we met, my struggle after we separated, and how I had to make sense of it all in order to move forward. When I was younger, I thought it was the story of how I found my soul mate, the true husband of my heart. When my heart was broken, I tried to make it the story of how I found myself. But seeing my daughter outside the doors at Paisley Park, I finally understand: it's the story of how we all found each other.

At the beginning of the music video for "The Most Beautiful Girl in the World," a woman's voice cuts through the static.

You have just accessed the Beautiful Experience, she says. *This experience will cover courtship, sex, commitment, fetishes, loneliness, vindication, love, and hate.*

That's an apt description of the story I'm finally ready to tell.

Please enjoy your experience.

one

Poised a breath apart on the middle finger and thumb, the zills hold infinite possibilities, an unlimited range of nuanced sounds and varied patterns. Only one thing is certain: they will come together, move apart, and come together again. I don't remember the first time I heard the irresistible *cling* of the finger cymbals, if it was the single pierced sagat or the slotted zills, but I'm certain that it was long before I was born. If it's true that our souls travel in an endless spiral of incarnations—and I believe it is—then it makes sense to me that certain threads continue with us from life to life, from birth to birth. The zills ring with that inexplicably deep familiarity for me. Some part of me remembers the sound, and it moves me. I move without questioning it.

> *if u ever get the chance 2 travel back 2 ancient dance*

I feel that same certainty about my husband, my soul's mate. I believe—and so did he—that he was my lover in one lifetime, my brother in another; maybe we were sisters, mother and child, or even mortal enemies. At the moment of each birth, we were poised, a breath apart, destined to come together in some capacity and fated to part, knowing we would inevitably come together again. We might not immediately know each other's name each time we met, or recognize the face, but we each knew that names and faces were the least relevant aspects of the other. I recognized my beloved, though not right away, and he treasured me, though he didn't know how to keep me.

Prince Rogers Nelson was born June 7, 1958, in Minneapolis, Minnesota. His mother, Mattie, was a jazz singer. His father, John, was a musician who went by the stage name Prince Rogers. Prince spoke very little about his early childhood. He did tell me he remembered being locked in a closet sometimes. John and Mattie split up when Prince was ten, and he was like a kite without a string, sometimes living with his mom and stepfather, sometimes with his dad, sometimes crashing with friends. Prince was a skinny little kid, who topped out at five feet two, but he was still an excellent basketball player at Bryant Junior High, where he became friends with Andre Simon Anderson, who later went by André Cymone when he toured with Prince. Two things Prince would take with him from an adolescence that was as difficult as you might imagine adolescence could be for a short, skinny, black dude were his love of basketball and his friendship with André.

On November 12, 1973, while they were somewhere shooting hoops, I was born on a military base in Enterprise, Alabama, where my dad was in army flight school. My mother, Nelly, and my father, also named John, are both Puerto Rican born and raised. She was—and is—a stunner: a voluptuous, headstrong beauty. Her strict Catholic parents tried hard to keep a lid on her, but my mother was—and is, for better or worse—a bold free spirit who never did well in the role of caged nightingale. Really, it's the laws of physics; her strict upbringing made her want to rebel and get off the island. She wanted to leave Puerto Rico, so she only dated men in the ROTC, hoping for a ticket out.

Dad was a great date, handsome and kind, a former body-builder who'd won the title of Mr. University of Puerto Rico. He'd followed his father into the military and rose through the ranks to become an officer, something his own father never did. After they'd been dating for a while, Mama realized she was pregnant. And not just a little. She was six months along. Both families swooped in and basically forced them to get married immediately.

Mama still mourns the fact that she never got to have a proper wedding, which made her all the more thrilled to see me marry Prince with all the trimmings.

My dour Catholic grandmother (whose own father was black), wasn't at my wedding, but she told me on the phone, "Well, at least he's light-skinned. And he is who he is. So I'm okay with it." And that tells you everything you need to know about my grandmother.

My big sister, Janice, was born in 1969, and my parents commenced a typical military family life, moving from base to base, which my mother quickly realized was not the post–Puerto Rico life she had hoped for. When Jan was four, they decided to have another baby, desperately hoping for a boy. Dad was slated for an important test flight the day I was born. He would have been first in his class, but missed the test and came in second. Janice was thrilled to have a little sister, but when my mother heard "It's a girl!" she was so mad she refused to see me.

They whisked me away, and by the time they finally brought me in to see her, I had casts on both legs. I'd been born with severely inverted legs. An orthopedic specialist, who just happened to be there that day by a stroke of luck—or perhaps by fate—explained to my parents that my crooked little limbs would have to be straightened, first with the casts and then with painful braces that I'd have to be kept in for three years, forcing the bones and joints to develop in a normal position.

My mother was fierce about those casts, as she is about pretty much everything when it comes to the people she loves. She was adamant that my legs were going to be normal and strong. The standard three-year treatment was accomplished in eighteen months because she kept the braces—little boots connected by a metal bar—firmly on me 24/7. Family members would shake their heads, take pity on me and try to remove them, but Mama prevailed and the boots stayed on. I have scars from an infection that developed when the braces became too tight, but I can't complain about these legs of mine. They've served me well. This is probably the beginning of my ballerina's dance-through-the-agony disposition. Before I learned to walk, I learned that sometimes life requires a girl to be a tough little cookie.

My mother adored the name Mayte, a Spanish conjunction of Maria and Teresa, the Basque word for "beloved." As a teenager, she'd seen this name in a novella, torn out the page, and kept it posted on her bedroom wall for years. Janice's middle name is Mayte, but the conventional world of the late 1960s decreed that children were better off with "American" (meaning "white") first names, and that temporarily swayed Mama. When I came along four and a half years later, she figured if she couldn't have the boy she hoped for, she was by God going to name this girl exactly what she wanted to: Mayte Jannell, my middle name being a combination of John and Nelly.

When Prince and I were first hanging out—not yet

lovers, just friends and collaborators—he got it in his head that I should change my name to Arabia.

"Man, it'd be cool if your name was Arabia," he kept saying.

Prince had a way of getting people to go along with ideas like that. They'd get swept up in his genius, not just for music but also for creating characters. He'd see some unique aspect of a person, and he'd highlight that. He never bullied anyone into anything, just nicely suggested that it would be really cool if a person changed her name to . . . oh, I don't know—Apollonia, maybe. Or Vanity. How cool would that be?

The fourth or fifth time he said to me, "Wouldn't it be cool if you changed your name to Arabia?" I flatly said, "No. That would not be cool. My mom would kill me."

In my mind at the time, the wrath of Mama loomed larger than the favor of a thousand rock stars.

Mama was raised in a strict Catholic home. She dreamed of becoming a dancer, but that was not an option. She tried to enroll my sister in dance lessons, but Jan was a rough-and-tumble tomboy who would have nothing to do with our mother's ambition to either be a ballerina or raise one. Jan was the sporty one, playing volleyball and soccer; I was the girly girl, living in tutus and "turn-around dresses." (Gia is turning out to be comfortably in the middle, completely herself in a cute little dress with sneakers.) By the time

I was three, to Mama's delight, I was begging to dance, but you had to be five years old to take lessons at most studios. By this time, we'd moved to North Carolina, so it wasn't hard for my mom to locate a place near the base where no one knew us.

"When they ask you how old you are," she told me, "do this." She held up her hand, palm flat, showing five fingers, and I did exactly as I was told after she dropped me off. Whether the ballet teacher believed me or not, she must have figured I was ready, because she took me to the barre and I never looked back. Over the years, no matter how chaotic my home life was, dance was my sanctuary. It wasn't a task for me to concentrate. I never had to discipline myself to endure the practice. I loved every hour, even when it hurt. I loved feeling the music in my strong, straight bones.

Belly dancing was a big thing at our local YMCA in the mid-1970s, as big as Zumba is now, *the* thing to do. Mama started out taking lessons for fun but fell in love with it and joined a troupe that did performances and seminars. I'd watch Mama practice back then the same way Gia watches me now, utterly captivated by the rhythm of the tablas and drums, eyes big with the imagined story told by the dance, hands instinctively tracing the movements in the air. Eventually I couldn't resist; I had to get up and move behind her, the way Gia moves behind me, making a tiny shadow on the wall next to mine.

"Would you like to dance with me at the officers' wives luncheon?" Mama asked, and she didn't have to ask twice. I was so on board with that. I had every beat of the music memorized, and I had a natural affinity for the moves. The choreography was ever evolving, which is one thing I love about this art form. To dance like this gives you freedom to express yourself, but it means you have to be in the present—all of which made belly dance the perfect training ground for the work I would later do as a member of the New Power Generation.

All the other ladies were impressed that I could seriously dance. They had to give Mama her props, and she was a stage mom who ate that up. Mama made me a little costume that matched hers—a floaty dream of colorful chiffon, spangled with a galaxy of sequins and dripping with paillettes—but for me, the greatest thing about it was that I got to wear lip gloss. Please understand, people: in my five-year-old mind, lip gloss was the magic elixir that transformed a mortal being into something magical, the most beautiful creature imaginable. My desire for lip gloss was so intense, I'd actually attempted to steal a tube of ChapStick one day at the PX, prompting Mama to call for a security officer, who lectured me into terrified tears. In everyday life, lip gloss was forbidden. Dad had banned it on the premise that it might make me kiss boys. So this was my opportunity. For lip gloss, I would do anything.

Almost anything. Anything but this, as it turned out. Standing backstage, I peeked out at the audience and was overwhelmed by a stomach punch of stage fright that caught poor Mama completely off guard.

"Mayte, that's our music," she hissed in a whisper. "We're on!"

I just shook my head, unable to even form the words, *I can't, I can't, I can't.*

I stood frozen behind the curtains while she put on a fake smile and went out to wow the officers' wives on her own. Some kind lady took my hand, led me to a table, and fed me mini doughnuts and milk while Mama did our mother-daughter dance all by herself, glancing my way every once in a while to shoot me *the look.*

When a Puerto Rican mama shoots you the look, you feel it like a javelin. There was no question in my mind that when she got off that stage, I'd never enjoy another moment of peace, love, or lip gloss for the rest of my life. I sat there stuffing those mini doughnuts into my mouth like they were my last meal. And they were, for a while. My mom didn't talk to me or feed me for a week. Dad had to take over, and though he fed and cared for me with patience and sympathy, I was crushed—not because she was punishing me, but because I knew I'd humiliated her. I swore to Mama and to myself that if she ever gave me another chance, I would go through with it, and when given another chance, I did.

And I'm glad. The moment I started dancing, the tidal wave of stage fright went out and a tidal wave of euphoria came in, sweeping me through the performance, filling me with an energy I had no name for. I was quickly addicted to the powerful bliss I felt onstage. Mama and I started getting invitations to dance at restaurants and parties. We started getting a little bit famous around town. When I was seven, a syndicated news show called *PM Magazine* came and did a story about us, which was amazing, but I was starting to get a sense of myself as a dancer—as an artist—and it had nothing to do with being paid or noticed.

After we'd been performing together for a while, I told Mama, "I want to dance by myself. I don't want people to think I'm just copying you." The truth is, I wanted people to notice her when she was dancing, and when I was there, a lot of the attention was directed my way. I wanted Mama to have her hard-earned moment in the spotlight.

Dance was my refuge, as life at both school and home became more complicated. Back then, you didn't see a lot of little Latina girls in a North Carolina elementary school. Kids used to ask me, "Are you white or are you black?"

"Neither," I'd say. "I'm Puerto Rican."

They'd wrinkle their noses and ask, "What's that?"

I tried to tell them about my grandmothers on a

beautiful island that is, yes, part of the United States, but no, not a state exactly, and no, it's not the same as Mexico. The white kids didn't accept me because I wasn't white enough, and the black kids didn't accept me because I had "good hair." After school, I was always running away from somebody, making a beeline for the bus, doing my best to avoid getting beat up.

Daddy loved taking the family to a nice restaurant for dinner every once in a while, and when he stepped up to the hostess podium, he always gave the name Rockefeller. Jan and I would giggle and roll our eyes and remind him, "Daddy, we're the *Garcias*!"

"Yes," he'd say, "but if they see the name Rockefeller on the list, they'll know it's somebody important." And he had a very Rockefeller stride as he followed the hostess to our table: head up, shoulders back, friendly smile for everyone whether they smiled at him or not. I liked his Mr. Rockefeller persona. It didn't even occur to me until I was an adult that this was his positive spin on the fact that seeing the name Garcia on the list might have prompted a different level of service.

Daddy was an avid videographer, who loved the newfangled cameras that were suddenly available to amateurs and everyday folks around 1980. He'd hoist the bulky unit onto a tripod, stick a VHS tape in it, and record every performance. He also learned to play the tambourine and Egyptian tabla (sometimes called a *doumbek* because of its hourglass shape), so he was part of the act as well. From my perspective, we were having a wonderful time together, but I know now that my father and mother had been cheating on each other for some time.

Dad went to Korea for a while, and when he came back, Mom had some serious questions about a woman with him in some of the photos he brought home. He was an unapologetic flirt, and it made me uncomfortable. I used to go with him to the local pawnshops and Radio Shack to check out the latest gadgets and geek out over the amazing advances being made in video cameras and recording equipment. I remember standing there while he chatted up some nice-looking lady. Sometimes those conversations went on longer than they needed to. I'd grab his wrist and pointedly say, "Daddy. C'mon. Mama's waiting for us."

At some point, she began seeing someone else, too. My parents' relationship grew more and more strained, their bickering escalated to an uglier form of arguing and name-calling, and their marriage started to fall apart.

About that same time, a guy who was supposedly a family friend started hanging around our house, acting like the nicest guy in the world. My parents trusted him, but he violated their trust and mine. I was seven years old, so at first, I didn't understand what was happening when he pulled me onto his lap. I didn't know what he was doing or why he was doing it; I only knew it felt horrifying and bad. It made me sick inside, though I didn't know how to explain it. I felt deep confusion. I tried to tell someone what had happened, but as is all too often the case, I didn't have the vocabulary to call it what it was, and people didn't want to believe it. I did everything I could to avoid him, but he found ways to corner me. Many times he suggested that I ride in his car to get something from his office.

"You should take Jan instead," I always said, thinking that she was bigger than me, a big girl of eleven and a tough tomboy, so he wouldn't be able to hurt her.

Years would go by before we could speak of it, but he did hurt her, too. When we were both in our twenties, sitting in my apartment in Eden Prairie, Minnesota, Jan finally confided in me that he had molested her. The grief and guilt I felt about that were quickly overtaken by a surge of raw rage on her behalf—and on behalf of seven-year-old me—realizing how this man had taken my power and made me feel shame for the first time. I decided to look him up and confront him. I rehearsed it in my head. *Is this the man who violated a little seven-year-old girl? Whom I believed was a friend of the family? Whom my family trusted in their home? Who did things to a seven-year-old child that only adults do to each other? Are you that disgusting human being?*

I dialed the phone, my hands shaking, but before he

could answer, I threw the phone down. The thought of hearing his voice nauseated me. All I could do then was pack these memories away in a dark corner of my mind, and I was okay with that for a long time. But one day, not long ago, while Gia was sleeping, it suddenly struck me how precious she is—so vulnerable, so innocent, so deserving of a safe, unruined childhood—and the thought of someone robbing her of her innocence and power and peace of mind triggered another unexpected surge of rage.

I sat down and Googled the man, thinking, *I'll sue him. I'll post his name online and call him out for molesting my sister and me.* Now *I* would be the one with the power and he'd be the one with the shame. I could get revenge. If I wanted to. But as I sat there with my hands on the keyboard, thinking about what that act of revenge would mean for me and Gia, how it would affect the quiet, joyful life I was making for her, the need for it faded. I believe in karma. God will take care of this guy when his time in this world is over, and he's old now. His time is running out. Hopefully, his kids know what he is, but I know I'm not responsible for anything he did in his life—including what he did to my sister. The burden of thinking it was my fault is one more thing he had no right to inflict on me.

Seeing Gia now, I realize how very small and helpless Jan and I were amid the chaos of our parents' failing marriage, even though we thought then that we were so tough. When Mama moved out of the house, leaving us with Dad, it was a relief in some ways. The man who'd molested Jan and me stopped coming around. The constant battles cooled to an uneasy truce, and even though she was living in her own apartment, Mama was in our kitchen waiting for Jan and me every morning when we got up, and she was there every evening to make supper and tuck us in for the night. I never felt abandoned by her—quite the opposite. She was on top of things, my most loyal ally, and still is today.

In 1980, while Prince was touring with Rick James, processing his own dysfunctional childhood into a project that would become *Purple Rain* and building on the momentum from his first platinum album, Mama and I were keeping up a busy schedule of dance performances and seminars. Throughout that terrible year, I danced, and when I danced, I was untouchable. Dance was my secret power, my doorway to another dimension where there was only beauty, only music, only love.

The world of belly dancing had a hierarchy of stars, and among them, Ibrahim "Bobby" Farrah reigned supreme. He was tall and moved with a strong yet delicate danger that I liked. Sometimes, he'd start spinning, twirling faster and faster, a mad blur, and then slowly, always teasing the audience with his brown eyes. The women loved him because he was passionate, loud, and funny.

Then there was Amir, a classically trained master who'd been a principal dancer in the Russian ballet and innovated a sort of tango-belly-ballet fusion, which he performed in a bolero and tight pants that showed off his insane shimmy. Amir was everything. Every. Thing. The name itself means "Prince." He had a jet-black mustache and eyebrows, and wore a tasteful dash of black eyeliner around his soulful eyes. He had the training and strength to do things women belly dancers couldn't safely attempt, and he was the only male dancer who could keep his masculinity and not come off as cheesy. It kept me genuinely entertained. He was way ahead of his time with his amazing sense of humor and off-the-chain stomach movements and muscle isolations no woman I knew could do. He'd shimmy this impressive isolated shimmy, then pulsate his stomach muscles to the beat of the drums—and then he'd do this exaggerated stagger and gasp, as if he were out of breath, and we'd go from awe to laughter. Every movement was done with surgical precision; each eyelash told a love story.

Mama was not about to miss an opportunity for us to take classes from these two legends, so our whole family drove to Atlanta and got a hotel room for the weekend. I arrived with a terrible cold, but I wasn't about to let that slow me down. All day Saturday, we took classes. I gave it my all and fell asleep exhausted and happy. On Sunday, it was our turn to perform in the student showcases, and the whole place was buzzing because I was going to be dancing with a sword on my head. Some of the older, more established dancers objected furiously to that. I totally get it now. Who wants to have their thunder stolen by an eight-year-old? I would have probably let the adults win and skipped the sword, but with someone like Mama behind me? Oh, you better believe I danced with that sword.

"You're dancing with your sword," she told me. I didn't hear what she told them, but they were suddenly being much nicer to me.

The sword I danced with was a gift from a vendor at a previous seminar. I'd been working with it for a while, dancing for hours to the music of George Abdo and his Flames of Araby Orchestra. Most ladies dancing with a sword used a wadded rag or scarf to keep it from slipping off their heads when they did a backbend or turn. I didn't want to do that, so Dad scored the edge of the blade just enough to give it some traction against my hair. The finale involved spinning the sword forward and gracefully swooping it off. I practiced till I had a bald spot on the crown of my head.

It's second nature to me now, but spinning with a sword on your head is a very different skill from the standard pirouette. When a ballerina spins, she "spots" by focusing on some fixed point—a crack in the

mirror or the middle seat in the first row of a theater—
something immobile that keeps her grounded as she
turns. At the last moment, she whips her head around
so she's taking her eyes off that spot for only a split
second. But you can't do that with a sword balanced
on the crown of your head. I learned to ground my
balance within myself, my eyes fixed on the tip of the
sword as the rest of the world turned around me.

When it was my turn to do my thing, the buzz
amplified; Amir and George Abdo showed up to see
me dance. The celebrities never came to the student
performances. As I waited to go on, I felt the shiver of
nervousness I always feel right before I go out onstage.
To this day, I want to die just before I go on. I have
to turn around and around like Wonder Woman,
and somehow this turns me into a fearless, ferocious
dancer. Then there's no stopping me. So I turned, I
transformed, and I danced. When all was said and
done, George Abdo pronounced me the Eighth Wonder of the World and asked for our information so he
could invite me to dance with the Flames of Araby in
Boston. Mama was over the moon.

Dad always videotaped the student showcase at an
event like this and sold copies to the ladies who'd performed. A group of dancers at the Atlanta event sent
the video of their performance to a TV show called
That's Incredible!

"No thanks," the producers responded. "But who's that little girl?"

The ladies remembered that I was the daughter of the man who'd sold them the video, so the producers were able to track me down, and my parents recognized that it would be a huge opportunity for me.

Hosted by Cathy Lee Crosby, John Davidson, and Fran Tarkenton, *That's Incredible!* was a popular show that ran during prime time on ABC for four years in the early 1980s and reran in syndication for eons after that. Designed (right down to the exclamation point) to capture the *Ripley's Believe It or Not!* audience, *That's Incredible!* featured all kinds of weirdly fabulous things: intriguing freaks of nature, astonishing feats of strength, amazing performance art, and heartwarming stories that involved fate, family, and bizarre coincidences. You might see a dog who traveled thousands of miles to find its family, a dentist who tattooed teeth, coffin portraits that appeared to blink, or a unicyclist jumping through rings of fire—even a tiny Tiger Woods tapping a flawless putt into a cup—and at the end of the segment, the studio audience would shout in unison, "That's incredible!" Apparently, the producers felt that a little girl belly dancing with a sword on her head fit right in.

Mama made me a spectacular costume, and Daddy kept wanting to up my game.

"You've got to play zills," he said, so I learned to play zills and incorporated them into my act. He'd seen one of the older belly dancers demonstrate the amazing dexterity of her abs by flipping a line of eight quarters on her stomach. Dad said, "Do you think you could do that?"

"Sure!" I'd never done it, but I did a Turkish drop to the floor, ready to give it a try. My stomach was only wide enough to line up three quarters, but after a couple of hours of fierce concentration interrupted by fits of giggling, I was able to turn each coin neatly from heads to tails and back again in time with the music. This gave Daddy the idea that I should flip the quarters while playing the zills and balancing the sword on my head. I was all over this, up for anything, and spent every waking moment rehearsing with a George Abdo record.

As we flew into LA, I took in the surrealistic sight of the Hollywood sign below, feeling like someone had polished it up just for me. Everyone at the studio was so kind and welcoming, and the set ran like an on-time train. Everything was in the right place at the right time, including me. I was introduced as "the mystical, magical Princess Mayte, the world's youngest professional belly dancer," and at the end, the audience yelled, "That's incredible!"—which pretty much summed up how I felt. I could have flown home without the airplane.

The show aired several weeks later, and I experienced my first little taste of fame. This was a highly rated, prime-time network TV show, so just about everyone at school saw it. I went to the mall, and people did double takes. "Hey, are you that belly dancing girl on TV?" I got a lot of positive attention, and my classmates started to be nice to me—a welcome change from the racial slurs and bullying I'd lived with in elementary school. I started thinking, *Hey, I could get used to this.* The only downside was, because I'd been on television, some of the kids thought I was rich; they'd try to shake me down for my lunch money, so I had to start packing my lunch for school every day.

Naturally, my appearance on the show sparked a steady stream of booking requests. Mom handled the business side of things, negotiating fees and making sure people paid up. Daddy drove me wherever I needed to go and set up the sound and video equipment when we got there. All I had to do was dance, and I was serious about it. I never had a boyfriend, played sports, or got involved in other extracurricular activities. During the school year, when I wasn't in ballet class or belly dancing, I was studying. When school was out for holiday breaks, we'd go to Puerto Rico to visit our grandmothers.

Flying as unaccompanied minors, Jan and I would be dropped off at the gate, where an escort would help

us board and sometimes bump us up to first class. Even
though Jan was older, she was the one who tended to
get nervous.

"What if the escort doesn't show up? What if we
get lost?"

I'd roll my eyes and say, "We won't get lost. C'mon."

I always took control, chatted up the escort, and
headed for the Jetway.

On our arrival in Puerto Rico, we'd go to my
maternal grandmother, Nelly—maternal in the sense
that she is my mother's mother, not in the sense that
she's at all maternal by nature. Grandma Nelly had
a severe view of a woman's place in the world and a
sharp tongue to make sure there were no questions
about it. I was grateful for the beautiful dresses she
helped make for me, but I cringed, listening to her tear
Mama down with verbal abuse about her weight, her
hair, her makeup, her dancing, her life choices, and
her daughters. The "good hair" that got us beat up
at school was never good enough for Grandma Nelly,
who subjected her own head to an endless stream of
chemical straighteners and dark brown dye. She yelled
at Mama for letting me dance, but then she'd turn
around and brag to her friends that I'd been on TV.

We counted the hours, waiting for Daddy's mother,
Grandma Mercedes, to pick us up and take us to her
house. Our grandmother Mercedes was warm and

affectionate. She was a wonderful cook who could make magic from an empty refrigerator.

"We were poor when I was growing up," Daddy told us. "That's why having meat is such a big deal. Back then we had rice with beans or beans with rice."

Everyone was welcome at Mercedes's home, and whoever came to the table was fed, but Daddy and his brother noticed that sometimes their mother would sit with her coffee and cigarette, engaging in the laughter and conversation but not eating. They figured at the time that she wasn't hungry, but realized later in their lives that there was not much food, and Mercedes chose to go hungry herself rather than turn someone away.

Mercedes didn't have a living room like you'd expect to see in the States; she had a big open area with a tile floor and big gates. At night, the car was parked there and the gates were closed. First thing in the morning, she'd open it up, back the car out, and mop the floor where the car had dripped oil.

"Stay off this tile until it's dry," she'd warn, because this was my dance floor. While the sun baked the tiles dry, I'd stretch, warm up, and tape my feet to protect them from friction burn. When my grandmother finally gave me the go-ahead, I'd dance and dance. Hours would go by. I was happy, lost in my head and in the music.

Grandma Mercedes loved listening to Puerto Rican radio stations with news and classic boleros, so there was always a lot of that. Jan was into Depeche Mode, Eurythmics, and other artists. I myself was swooning over Puerto Rican teen singing sensation Luis Miguel, who was to Latina girls in the early 1980s everything that Justin Bieber would be to girls in the States thirty years later. With a father who was almost as big a stage mother as Mama, Luis Miguel scored his first hit record—*Un Sol*—launched his first world tour, and stole my heart, all by the time he was thirteen years old. I loved Menudo, that dreamy boy band from Puerto Rico, but even they could not compare to Luis Miguel.

Jan and I would be in Puerto Rico for a few weeks on our own, then our parents would arrive for a week of family visits, and then we'd have to head home. While leaving Grandma Nelly's house was a relief, it was always sad leaving the cool tile floor and rich, spicy aromas of Grandma Mercedes's place. We dreaded the day of departure, partly because Daddy was in the military and we were able to fly on the cheap if we were willing to wait around for an available seat on a cargo plane. We'd pack our bags the night before and head to the airport before dawn. Sometimes the whole day would drag by without an opportunity to board. Jan and I chased each other around and played

Rock, Paper, Scissors. We chatted enthusiastically about Menudo. We hotly debated who was cuter, John Schneider or John Stamos, and argued hard about which one of us liked which one of them better. Having exhausted that topic, we'd make up stupid songs and sing them over and over until the grown-ups got impatient and told us to shut up. Then we'd sit and read or play hangman. If the last flight took off without us, we'd schlep our bags back home and return the next day to try again, but if the stars aligned and there were open seats, we'd strap ourselves into them for the three-hour flight, next to racks of auto parts, boxes of office supplies, cases of powdered eggs, giant mysterious crates of military stuff—anything up to and including a war tank.

Once we got home, Grandma Nelly redeemed herself. Jan and I were crazy about this strange and wonderful new thing called MTV, and we begged Daddy to get cable so we could watch it, but he didn't see the necessity for that. So Grandma Nelly would roll VHS tapes, recording hours of MTV, and send them to us. It exposed us to the new stars reshaping the music of the decade—Cyndi Lauper, David Bowie, Prince. We loved Robert Palmer's "Addicted to Love" and Irene Cara's "Fame" and Madonna's "Lucky Star." They were creating something that combined music and spectacle the way live performances do, pulling music, dance, fashion, storytelling, cinematography, videography, and theater into a fabulous mash up of art forms.

In 1983, just before I turned ten, Jan and I saw *Flashdance* at the movie theater in North Carolina, and it rocked my little world from start to finish. The feverish "Maniac" sequence captured the crazy energy that took over my body when I was dancing, and though I certainly didn't let Jan see it, I had tears streaming down my face during those final soaring moments when Alex Owens dances her heart out to "What a Feeling." I didn't know at the time, of course, that Jennifer Beals had to have three body doubles— one of them a sixteen-year-old dude—in order to get through that number, and I'm glad I didn't know. Thinking it was all her made me believe I could do it, too.

I adored *Flashdance*. I used some of my belly dancing money to buy the *Flashdance* sound track and couldn't get enough of it. Dancing like a *maniac, maniac on the floor*, I wore grooves in the grooves playing the album over and over. *Flashdance* offered a PG-rated romance that a ten-year-old could embrace, while vividly demonstrating the hours of blood, sweat, and tears that go into a professional dance career. And can we just talk about the iconic Alex Owens style? All the girls were slashing their sweatshirts and incorporating leg warmers into their school wardrobes, but more than anything else, I loved Jennifer Beals's unapologetically curly hair and her *"Are you white or are you black?"* skin, the same color as mine. I dreamed of living in my own warehouse apartment with a ballet barre, sassy attitude, and pit bull named Grunt.

A year later, my little world got rocked again. Jan took Mama and me to see *Purple Rain*.

two

_____

Jan and I were instantly obsessed with *Purple Rain*, playing the album for months in our room with the sound track blaring. I was always Apollonia—minus the boobs—because I was a girly girl but brave, like Prince's love interest in the movie. Jan was learning to play guitar, so she wanted to be Wendy (or maybe she had a crush on Wendy and didn't yet know how to articulate that), but her best friend also wanted to be Wendy, so it often devolved to an argument.

"*I* am Wendy!"

"You're *not* Wendy! I am!"

Eventually, for the sake of world peace, I'd intercept and tell Jan, "You can't be Wendy. Your hair's not long enough. Be Lisa. Lisa is just as cool."

I funded the sound track purchase with my belly dancing money, and we begged to see the movie again. We loved the music, the power of Prince's performances, of course, and the style, the style, the *style*—even an elementary school kid couldn't miss it. I mean, look at the fashion in this film! Prince's ruffles, the motorcycle studs, the Wonderbra-convenient leather motorcycle jacket that Apollonia strips off at not–Lake Minnetonka.

Years later, I would stand in awe of the full costume crew who worked in a large, brightly lit space at Paisley Park. Prince's office occupied the left wing of the top floor, and Wardrobe occupied the right. Pattern makers and cutters worked on long wooden worktables under broad skylights. Seamstresses and tailors fit clothing on mannequins with Prince's body size. A stitching tailor perfected the smallest details, and the high priestess overseeing the whole operation tweaked and approved every outfit, making a sleeve half an inch longer or exchanging a silver button for a gold one. You knew you were walking out with something one of a kind and perfectly on point.

These were Prince's clothes for every day, not just performing. When I was his wife, I wore his clothes and swiped his custom-made pajamas, and when I was pregnant, Wardrobe made me several cute maternity dresses with the word *BABY* and an arrow pointing down at my belly. He had hundreds of outfits that were meticulously made, right down to the zipper pulls, which were always special and unique. He had a lot of input in the design process. He'd tear pages from magazines and instruct the designer to re-create the bodice detail from this dress and the cuff from that shirt and a collar from something Errol Flynn wore in *Captain Blood*. Inspired by the movie *Amadeus*, he had the wardrobe staff create extravagant performance pieces in velvet and lace. *The Philadelphia Story* inspired great coats and big-shouldered suits. The wardrobe staff was incredibly talented—an amazing group of people who loved Prince and loved doing what they did. Fabulous clothes were constantly being created and re-created, vamped and revamped, altered, tailored, embroidered, and deconstructed for video shoots, performances, or just moving around in real life.

There was no "casual Friday" at Paisley Park. Prince expected us to come dressed to play, and these amazing people helped make that possible for me. They also made it possible for my husband to steal my clothes—and not in a good way. If I bought a pair of amazingly cool tailored pants or a hot jacket, he'd take them to Wardrobe, have the pants hemmed up, and tell them to put shoulder pads in the jacket so he could wear them. A few days later, I'd pull on my brand-new pants, find them two inches too short, and say, "Hey! Why are my pants shrinking?" He thought this was hilarious. And somehow he rocked these outfits just as well as I would have.

The music in *Purple Rain* defined the summer of 1984. I spent dozens of hours dancing to it on my grandmother's tile floor. In Puerto Rico and back home, the singles—"When Doves Cry," "Let's Go

Crazy," and the rest—dominated radio and MTV. Prince was now a bona fide superstar. You'd hear that opening vocal grind from "Doves" as people washed their cars. "I Would Die 4 U" banged from open windows as you walked down the street.

The music spoke to me, certainly, but beyond that was the emotional impact of something very intimate Prince was able to share in *Purple Rain*: what it is for a child to witness the psychological warfare between his parents. This was something I could definitely relate to, something that connected him and me in that moment and later on, when we envisioned the sort of parents we wanted to be. We both loved our parents, but we wanted to break that cycle of crazy, dysfunctional behavior. We wanted to be a united front, committed to loving each other and creating a tight, semitraditional family unit. This vision of family is a world away from The Kid climbing in the window of his basement sanctuary, but throughout the movie and the music, you can feel his yearning for it.

I watched Prince's very first television interview (not counting one painfully awkward *American Bandstand* moment when he was nineteen) on a bootlegged MTV tape Grandma Nelly recorded in 1985, the year after *Purple Rain*. It seems unthinkable in the present age of social media. Everyone has their "platform," and fans expect to be fed a steady stream of witty banter and smiling selfies. He had a belly dancer's sense of mystery; he said everything he wanted to say through his music. So this MTV interview was a huge deal. All eyes were on Prince, who was famously reclusive, shrouded in Victorian lace and artistic mystery. I watched the tape over and over until I could practically recite it word for word.

First, the VJ introduces him, explains that the questions were being asked by his manager, and says, "Now, Prince is not alone here. The interview was shot at the filming of his new video 'America' ..." and a bunch of other stuff I'd try to fast-forward through until the video cuts to a vision of Prince looking excited, innocent, and fresh. He's surrounded by his castmates, friends, and dancers, like a landscaper sitting in the middle of a rose garden. Oh, how I envied those dancers. They sat there with serious expressions and big '80s hair and consciously casual clothes, hardly breathing, hanging on his every word. Prince wore a ruffled white shirt with a tawny tweed greatcoat, that same tasteful dash of eyeliner that worked so well for Amir, and a perfect mole in exactly the right place on his cheek. I loved that mole most of all.

He spoke softly, deliberately, choosing his words as quietly and carefully as I would later hear him choose the lyrics of a song. Long after I became one of those dancers, when I was his wife and his baby was doing slow stretches and bicycle kicks in my belly, I'd wake up and hear him at the piano. I'd pull the sheet off the bed and wrap it around myself like a sari and sit on the piano bench next to him while he found what he was looking for. You see a more formal version of that understated search for words when you watch that MTV interview. He's so young; it makes me ache to look at him. Our son would be almost that same age now, with his father's full lips and dark eyes, and I like to think he would have been as thoughtful about expressing himself.

"One thing I'd like to say...is that I don't live in a prison," he says. "And I'm not afraid of anything. I haven't built any walls around myself. I'm just like anyone else. I need love and water, and I don't really consider myself a superstar. I live in a small town, and I always will, 'cause I can walk around and be me. And..." He shrugs his shoulders inside the oversize coat and laughs a little.

"That's all I wanna be. That's all I ever try to be. I didn't know what was gonna happen. I just tried to do my best, and somebody dug it and..." He purses his lips and finishes the thought with an air kiss, assigning his remarkable existence to the kiss of fate.

He goes on to talk about how James Brown influenced his style, but when he's asked how he feels about people comparing him to Jimi Hendrix, he says, "A lot had to do with, I could say, the color of my skin, and that's not where it's at—at all. It really isn't. Hendrix was very good, but there'll never be another one like him, and it would be a pity to try. I strive for originality in my work, and hopefully it'll be perceived that way."

The interviewer says, "Some people have criticized you for selling out to the white rock audience with *Purple Rain* and leaving your black listeners behind. How do you respond to that?"

At first, Prince clowns around: "Aw, come on. Come on! Cuff links like this cost money, okay? I mean, let's be frank. Can we be frank? If we can't be nothin' else, we might as well be frank, okay?" But then he says, "Seriously... I was brought up in a black and white world, and—yes, black and white, night and day, rich and poor. Black and white. And I listened to all kinds of music when I was young. And when I was younger, I always said that one day I was gonna play all kinds of music and not be judged for the color of my skin, but the quality of my work. And hopefully that'll continue. I think there're a lot out there that understand this. They support me and my habits, and I support them and theirs."

I find it interesting in retrospect that he felt compelled to end this interview by saying, "I believe in God. There's only one God. And I believe in the afterworld, and hopefully we'll all see it. I have been accused of a lot of things contrary to this, and I just want people to know that I'm very sincere in my beliefs. I pray every night, and I don't ask for much. I just say thank you."

"I'm going to marry Prince," I told my mother. "Or Luis Miguel."

She laughed, but I was completely serious. This wasn't just a tweenager's "someday my prince will come" fantasy or the fact that I generally had a thing for guys with green eyes. This was a plainspoken certainty I felt. I had absolutely no logical reason to think that this was remotely possible, but I had seen it in my mind's eye, or perhaps remembered it from that soul-spiral—all possibilities at all times—and I knew it would happen.

Years later, this sort of premonition would be a recurring theme between Prince and me. I'd feel something in the air when he was about to call. Somehow the mailbox had a different personality when there was a letter from Prince in it. I remember watching a television special on Herb Ritts when I was a teenager, and I thought, *I'm going to shoot with him.* It was odd that I saw this at all, because we were living on a military base in Germany; there was only one TV channel, and this wasn't the type of thing we usually saw on it.

A day or two later, Prince called and said, "Wanna come to Minneapolis and shoot some pictures for *Vogue*?"

"Who's the photographer?" I asked.

"Herb Ritts."

I felt that small, satisfying *ping* you get when

synchronicity happens. This sort of thing came up all the time, and we'd laugh about it. We didn't find it spooky or illogical at all, and we never felt the need to validate it or prove it to ourselves or to anyone else. We simply accepted it as coincidence or fate, just a little shout-out from the universe, reminding us that we were exactly where God wanted us to be.

But there have been other times—moments when God seems blind and everything in the universe feels hopelessly out of sync.

In the midst of the *Purple Rain* craze, my parents officially divorced, and Daddy was transferred to Wiesbaden Army Airfield (WAAF) in Germany. It was decided that Jan and I would move to Maryland with Mama. Her boyfriend had already moved there. They'd rented a big, lovely house.

"Your room is painted pink," Mama told me. "You've always wanted a pink room, right?"

I felt more miserable every time she told us how great it would be. Daddy drove us to Maryland, where we joined Mama's boyfriend—a white guy with white hair, which threw me for a loop somehow. When it was time for Daddy to leave, Jan and I stood there at the door with our arms tight around him, not wanting to let go. And Mama stood there with big tears rolling down her face. She was clearly every bit as distraught as we were.

"She loved him. He loved her," I told Prince years later. "Why—*why*—was that not enough?"

He had no answer, but now I think back on that moment in *Purple Rain*, when The Kid's father turns to his mother with reproachful tears in his eyes and says, "I would die for you." He thinks it's the ultimate sacrifice, but in truth, it's living for someone that presents the far greater challenge.

I sat in my pink room in Maryland, not knowing what to do with myself. I was twelve years old, and I'd been dancing professionally for more than half my life. Now we were far away from the places that hired me on a regular basis, and even if Mama had scoped out the gigs, I didn't have Daddy to drive me there and manage the sound and play the tablas and just...be Daddy. When my parents lived together, they fought like cats and dogs, but they'd done pretty well as a separate but equal team, going along on parallel tracks with Jan and me securely between them.

Mama didn't have loud shouting matches with the white guy. If there was some disagreement between them, they'd go into the room they shared and shut the door. When Mama and Daddy argued, I'd be hunkered down in a corner eavesdropping, taking in every word, but I didn't even want to know what Mama and her boyfriend were saying to each other in those low, intense voices. It seemed so unnatural. Mama is Puerto Rican to the tenth power. To me, she always embodied the vibrant, loud voice of that culture. I didn't want her to tone that down for anyone.

Right away, Mama researched all the dance studios and companies in the area and decided I should take classes at the prestigious Washington School of Ballet (WSB), where Shirley MacLaine and Goldie Hawn had studied. Under the umbrella of the Washington Ballet, WSB accepted a limited number of students who were expected to work hard, be diligent about the barre, and serious about classical studies—all of which I craved. It was expensive and not terribly convenient—about ninety minutes away on Wisconsin Avenue in Washington, DC—but Mama thought it was the best place for me. She took off work early so she could take me there three times a week.

Belly dancing has always been my thing, personally and professionally, but I was a ballerina first. Dance, for me, began with ballet class, and I've always stayed grounded in it. When I wasn't at ballet, I stayed in my room, reading and dancing. My home situation was enormously depressing, and I got off the school bus one day to discover I'd gotten my first period. Awesome, right? I was already dragging through the most awkward school year of my life. Now I was in the throes of puberty as well, the only non-white kid in my class and the only girl in gym class who wasn't allowed to wear makeup or shave her legs, no matter how I begged. I absorbed several weeks of taunting and teasing—"You could braid that hair on your legs" and that sort of thing—and then I decided to take matters into my own hands.

I'd seen Mama use Nair on her upper lip, so I crept into the bathroom one day after school, read the instructions on the back of the bottle, and slathered it on my legs. Within minutes, the guilt got to me, and I quickly got into the tub and rinsed it off. When the dark hair washed away with it, part of me celebrated. The rest of me withered at the thought of facing Mama with my smooth, smooth—oh, so wonderfully smooth!—but soon to be broken legs. By the time she got home from work, I'd developed a strategy: play for sympathy, and then try to get off on a technicality.

"Mama, these girls at school—you don't know what these girls are like," I said. "And you told me I couldn't *shave*. You never said anything about Nair."

She laughed. See, she did know what those girls were like. Mean girls are a force of nature that transcends geographical and cultural boundaries. I was an easy mark, because I was different, and not just because of the color of my skin. I was that kid who always got hit in the face by the dodgeball ball. Instead of going to cheerleading practice and after-game parties, I went to ballet and ballet. And ballet. Jan, meanwhile, was that girl who could play anything—volleyball, basketball, or soccer—and quickly attract a posse of friends wherever she went. I felt more alone with each passing day.

Jan and I really didn't interact with my mother's boyfriend at all, so I was surprised to hear him rap his knuckles on my door one afternoon. I think his intention was probably some inexpert attempt to be what in his mind was fatherly.

"Mayte, this room is a mess," he said. "It's not acceptable."

My dad was a military guy, too; I understood the concept of "shipshape," but Jan and I had never been made to clean and do laundry as if we were in boot camp. I wasn't open to the idea that I should care whether my personal space was acceptable to someone else, so this didn't start well, and it quickly went downhill from there. I wasn't about to discuss things with him in low tones. Things escalated to a real confrontation, and I went a little Puerto Rican *chica* in his face. Apparently not used to being disagreed with in this way, the guy bellowed back at me, shoving me with the heel of his hand. I staggered back, stunned, and then stood in the middle of my pink room, shaking and furious. I was thinking, *Oh, he's in trouble now.* I was too afraid to say it out loud, but there was not a shadow of doubt in my mind. Mama always had my back.

He slammed the door and stormed down the hall. When I knew he was gone, I crept down to the kitchen and called my mother at work, tearfully telling her, "He put his hands on me. He is not allowed to put his hands on me." She took the story in with surprising calm, and I don't know what went on between them after that, but I never saw the guy at the house again. Within days, Jan and I were on a flight to Germany. I never even had the chance to retrieve my ballet shoes and towel bag from my locker at WSB.

Mama packed our things, closed up the house, and joined us a week or two later in Hainerberg, an ungated American community on a hill in Wiesbaden, where we would all live together for six years. Mama and Daddy's unorthodox relationship didn't seem odd to Jan and me at all. We didn't give it much thought, really. We were old enough to understand that Mama had made a huge mistake, and while we may not have had the security every child fantasizes about, we learned that mistakes aren't necessarily forever. Second chances happen. This belief stayed with me, a blessing and a curse. Thinking my husband and I would eventually remarry kept me from feeling bitter toward him, but it also prevented me from fully moving on as long as he was alive.

The summer after we moved to Germany, Jan and I went to see our grandmothers in Puerto Rico. A few weeks later, our parents showed up for the customary family visits, and while we were all hanging out one afternoon, they casually announced that they had gotten remarried.

Jan and I were surprised, to say the least. "What…

why? When? How could you do that without telling us?"

On the one hand, we were delighted that the typical child-of-divorce fantasy was happening to us—our parents were back together!—but the memories of the war zone were still pretty fresh. We worried that things were going to go back to the way they used to be. Mama and Daddy explained that it was just so she could be in Germany on his benefits. And weirdly, that made it okay. We knew they were never going to have the fairy-tale romance; it was a relief for everyone that they didn't feel the need to pretend. They cared deeply for each other, and the piece of their relationship that worked—our dysfunctionally functional family—was worth preserving. They were willing to sacrifice some pride for it and let go of the pieces that didn't work.

Life on base away from the United States was a bit of a culture shock. Because they divided the grades differently, I was outraged to find myself back in middle school while Jan went to General H. H. Arnold High School. We were free to venture out and explore the country around us, but most people seemed scared to do that. I wasn't about to be stuck at home all the time. Struggling through the language barrier that kept most of my classmates on base, I researched the schedules and took the bus into Wiesbaden, a bustling city famous for its grandly ancient architecture and natural hot springs.

In Germany, the arts were highly respected and well funded. Every town had a big theater, so I joined one and started picking up some German. Before long I was conversational, working toward fluent. Mama searched out a challenging ballet class for me and then went around to all the Turkish and Moroccan restaurants, asking, "Do you hire belly dancers?" The response was more enthusiastic than we could have imagined. Turns out belly dancing was even more popular in Germany than it was back home, so I was soon back to a steady schedule of appearances. Mama danced, too, but we were rarely at the same place at the same time.

I danced at birthday parties, weddings, and corporate events. I danced at hotels, restaurants, and convention centers. I learned the difference between the Turkish customs and the Persian customs, and tailored my style to accommodate the two completely different styles of dance and dress. The money rolled in. I usually got paid in cash, and for lack of a better idea, I kept tucking it into a little metal lockbox. If I wanted a book or a record or tampons, I just peeled a little off this wad of cash and tucked it away again. I was too young to understand or care about the money—I just loved dancing—so Daddy did all the bookkeeping.

When I had several thousand dollars sitting there under his desk, he took me to the bank to hook up my own checking account and then to the PX to write my very first check, which the cashier assumed was fake.

She peered at me over her reading glasses. "Is this real?"

"Oh, yeah," I said. "It's my check."

"Really."

"Yes!"

She looked over my head at Daddy, who had gotten in line behind me, anticipating that he might have to vouch for me. Her reaction was understandable, because walking down the street, I looked like any other twelve-year-old kid. In my costume and makeup, I looked older, and I was coming in as a professional, dancing at restaurants and events until ten or eleven at night, so the people hiring me readily believed Mama when she told them I was sixteen. Like my first ballet teacher, they either believed it or believed I could make it work. It raised only a few eyebrows each time I celebrated another sixteenth birthday.

"Wait…" the bookers sometimes said. "Weren't you sixteen last year?"

"No, no. Fifteen. Fifteen last year."

Dad was always with me, nodding and smiling, backing me up. Mr. Rockefeller. He was my wingman in all things, with me at every gig. We were a little team, he and I. While I prepared, he'd get the sound and video equipment set up and assess the audience, and we'd formulate a strategy, crackling back and forth on walkie-talkies.

"You've got a square dance floor. Wood. The good party table is on the left."

"Okay, cool."

"Birthday girl is twenty-one. Table five. Seated with parents. Grandparents. Looks like a boyfriend, a couple siblings. They've definitely had a few, but it's a family thing. They seem okay."

"Thanks, Daddy."

I stayed out of sight until I heard my music. Mama was adamant about that as a rule—and Prince always was, too. It made Mama crazy when costumed dancers strolled around and mingled with people before a performance.

"Where's the mystery then?" she'd ask in a huff. "Where's the illusion? Shattered, that's where. Destroyed! Why even bother making a dramatic entrance if you've already been seen at the bar giggling with the waiters?"

By the time I finally got to take my rightful place at General H. H. Arnold High School, the sizable chunk of money with which I'd started my checking account had swelled to more than $100,000, because I didn't spend much. I never *did* much other than go to school and dance. I did pay for my own business expenses, costumes, and dance classes. When I turned fifteen,

I got my learner's permit and bought my first car. I could have bought myself a house if I'd wanted to. (Sometimes I wish I had.) After Jan started college, I shifted some cash her way whenever she needed it, and Daddy told me, "She gets an allowance, you know."

I was genuinely confused. "Allowance? What's that?"

It hadn't really occurred to me that most kids my age looked to their parents to pay for things like clothes and a car. I liked funding my own life, but the money wasn't what made me love dancing. First and foremost for me at that age was that it was *fun*. My good friends Stephanie and Allison loved to go with me. Free food, dancing, parties—come on! What teenage girl is going to complain about that as a lifestyle?

Mama, on the other hand, was getting tired of it. I don't know if she got a little bit depressed or went through menopause or just wasn't as addicted to it as I was, but she retired, and I took over her regular gigs in addition to my own.

One of my monthly favorites was *Frauentag*—"Ladies' Day"—when the Muslim men would rent out the entire restaurant for the afternoon. Cars would roll up to the front door one after another, and wives and their children, shrouded in burkas, would come inside. No men were allowed. Only the restaurant owner was on the premises, and he remained out of the main area. When all the ladies were there, the doors were locked and curtains drawn. Then they'd shed their burkas, revealing designer dresses and shoes and fabulous jewelry. They were dressed to the nines and ready to dance, drink, and party their behinds off.

These ladies were polite but skeptical the first time they saw me. How could this skinny little curly-haired girl know anything about an ancient Middle Eastern dance form? That's a question I never could answer. Even when I tried to explain it to Prince, who had no problem with the idea of a thousand lifetimes abiding in a modern body, the best I could come up with was, "I don't know. It's just…in my blood. In my soul." And then I told him about my little leg bones when I was born—how they were confused at first and didn't know where they belonged.

Of course, Daddy couldn't go with me to *Frauentag*, but the venue always had a great sound system for my mixtapes. As per Mama's rule, I never allowed myself to be seen before the performance. These women understood the power of invisibility. I always started with my Wonder Woman turns, and then that fierce dancer in me would take over. During the first song, I'd play the zills as I scoped out the crowd, making a mental note of anyone who seemed particularly reserved, anyone with a frown on her face. At first, a lot of ladies would be out on the floor, but as they realized that I was a real dancer, they'd sit down and watch.

The second song was a ballad—veil work, sword, backbends, something pretty and a little bit shocking, something with a lot of performance value—and then we'd pick up the tempo, get them clapping, get the drums going. By then I knew who was into it and who was going to be shy. I'd go to the wallflowers and draw them out to dance with me, showing them that, yes, they could do it. By the end of my final number, I'd won them over, and they knew how to show their appreciation, if you get my drift.

Usually, I hated getting tips. On the upside: tips. On the downside: When I was little, it was always made clear up front that I was a minor, not to be touched in any way, so people threw the money on the floor, and I had to push it out of the way with my foot. After we moved to Germany, and I was suddenly sixteen, people started tucking bills into my costume. I hated it when a guy would approach, looking all sweet and kind, and then take his time tucking that bill in there, making me dodge and weave to avoid being touched. I was particularly grateful that the *Frauentag* ladies kept it classy, discreetly tipping me after the performance, respectfully tucking bills into my straps and hips.

As I became more recognized in Germany, a variety of interesting offers started coming my way, including an invitation to come in and cut a demo at a small record company based in Frankfurt. A producer saw me dancing somewhere and was certain he could make me a star. I was definitely interested in singing and acting in addition to dancing, because to be Rita Moreno—the greatest triple threat in Broadway history—is the fantasy of every Puerto Rican girl. So in I went to record my demo. Side A was a cover of Mr. Mister's "Broken Wings." The B-side was "Too Dramatic," a song I'd written myself. The words were something like, *Too dramatic, I don't know why, it's just the way that I ammmm.* I have purposely blocked out the rest. Just keep that much in your hip pocket, because it comes up again later.

I was proud of my song and excited about the opportunity, but when they decided not to sign me, I wasn't terribly upset. That wasn't the path I saw myself on at that moment. My dream was to dance in Cairo, where the top performers danced in grand hotels with fifty-piece orchestras. I knew that if I worked hard enough, I could be as good as those legendary dancers. Mama agreed, but added, "You'll need the best costumes. And those can only come from Madame Abla."

Madame Abla was a legend, the Coco Chanel of the belly dancing world. Dancers would make the pilgrimage to her shop in Cairo and leave with costumes that were meticulously made especially for them. Each one was unique in design and immaculate in fit. Starting when I was fourteen, Mama and I traveled to Egypt for ten days every nine months or so. The first day, we'd go to Madame Abla's shop on Mohammed Ali Street not far from Bab Zuweila, an ancient gate that seemed to separate modern downtown Cairo from a mystic ancient world. The narrow side streets were crowded with small shops where craftspeople made and sold musical instruments. The air was filled with laughter and music.

Madame Abla's shop was on the second floor of a shabby old apartment building near the Museum of Islamic Art. At the top of the stairs, we'd knock on the door, and an older lady in traditional Egyptian clothing would let us in. Like stepping through the looking glass, we left the dim hallway and stepped into what might have been a Parisian salon, lavishly furnished with silk brocade sofas and embroidered ottomans. Crystal chandeliers hung from the ceilings. Ornately carved bookcases held bolts of fabric and glass jars filled with every imaginable shape and size of beads and sequins. While we waited for Madame Abla, we were served *ghorayebah*—little Egyptian butter cookies that melt in your mouth—and mint tea in fancy cups from a brass cart.

Eventually, Madame Abla would sweep into the room and greet us, gracefully extending her arms. She wore a gracefully muted *galabiyya*, a traditional garment for both men and women in the Nile Valley, with her hair pulled back in a perfect bun. I wanted to contribute to the design of my costumes, so I always had a folder of sketches worked up, and Madame Abla always pored over them with great interest, gracious and encouraging. Meanwhile, I'd look through pictures of her latest designs, which were displayed in large photo albums. We'd come up with a few concepts that combined my ideas with hers, select fabric swatches and beads and thread, and then she'd stand me up and look me over, complimenting me on how nicely I'd filled out since our previous visit.

Once, I asked her, "Why don't you ever take measurements?"

"I take measurements," she said, tapping her temple next to her eagle eyes.

When we returned for fittings, we always found that this method was pretty accurate. It was a thrill to step out of the dressing room in one of Madame Abla's creations. We'd never had anything tailormade. I'd never even seen my dad get fitted for a suit. Mama and Grandma Nelly had made costumes for me, and they were good at it, but I'd never had anything on this level. Madame Abla had thoughtfully placed every detail, including an ornate appliqué on the left hip—not the right hip, as any store-bought or hand-me-down costume would have had—because I'm a lefty, and she took the time to notice that. She fine-tuned the details that made me feel polished and complete. To see myself in the mirror—a walking work of art—gave me a sense of pride and mystique that changed the way I inhabited my body and raised my dancing to a higher plane. After the fitting, she'd tell us to come back for the finished costume in a few days, "God willing." Everything was "God willing."

While we waited for Madame Abla to finish my costumes, Mama and I made an adventure of it. We stayed in a five-star hotel and ate exotic food from big high-end restaurants and tiny old cubbyhole places. We made a circle of Egyptian friends—dancers, musicians, and other folk artists—and I picked up quite a lot of Arabic hanging out with them. We spent our days visiting the pyramids and markets, wandering the Grand Bazaar, drinking mint tea and more mint tea, taking in the colorful sights and exotic aromas, replenishing our supplies of essential oils and the black kohl eyeliner that is better than anything else out there. Every night, we went to the hotel nightclubs to see the greatest belly dancers of the day along with the up-and-coming dancers and musicians.

In November 1989, on my third annual sixteenth birthday, I actually turned sixteen, so Daddy went to Egypt with us to celebrate. That night was a special occasion at the Sheraton El Gezirah. Lucy, one of my favorite dancers, was performing, followed by Egyptian heartthrob Amr Diab—who was starting to seriously blow up then and would go on to become the bestselling Middle Eastern recording artist of all time—so this was essentially like an evening with Paula Abdul opening for a pre–*Purple Rain* Prince.

In a club like this, the dancer comes on at ten or eleven and the singer performs at one in the morning. I'd been up exploring all day, but I was wide awake, dressed to the nines in a gorgeous black sequined dress, down front and center when Amr Diab made his entrance. He took a look at me, brought me up onstage, and asked me to dance. I hesitated because I felt a little overdressed, but the happy crowd cheered me on. My mother always wore a beaded scarf to add a little bling to her outfit. Or so I thought back then. To this day, she actually wears it in hopes that I'll get up and dance. When I do, she quickly grabs the scarf and places it on my hips. She always has my back, my mama. She could give stage mother lessons to the best of them.

I went up, wearing Mama's scarf over my sequined birthday dress. Just dancing for myself. Because it was my birthday. I was so happy and grateful to be celebrating in this amazing place. I started dancing at the side of the stage, small at first, but then I did my Wonder Woman turn and gave myself to the music and the moment and the wild response from the audience. I felt myself light up and realized, *Okay, it's on. I'm performing.* I didn't know or care who was watching.

Afterward, I was sitting with my parents, already overdosing on dream-come-true, when the maître d' approached us and said the general manager of the Heliopolis Sheraton would like me to come in and audition to dance in their spectacular Nubian Tent restaurant.

"Oh. I'm—I'm just here for costumes," I said. "I wasn't—"

"What time would you like her to be there?" Mama asked.

The next day was a mad scramble for an Egyptian agent and a borrowed costume. Madame Abla provided the latter, one with fishnet that covered my midsection, which is required by law in Egypt. (I know, right? Crazy.) We arrived just in time at the spectacular hotel northeast of Cairo. The lobby was a towering hall where bright-colored birds screeched from live palm trees and flew freely overhead. The audition went well, and it was agreed that I should come back in June. We picked up my costumes, said good-bye to Madame Abla, and flew home to Germany.

My heart was pounding with the possibilities.

If the hotel offered me a contract, within eighteen months, I could graduate high school, get the necessary work visa, and be back in Cairo to dance alongside some of the most honored artists in the business. For the rest of my career, I'd be able to name my price anywhere in the world. For the rest of my life, I'd be able to teach as a master belly dancer, because working in Cairo at this level—that's it. You've reached the top.

Back home, on a roll, I celebrated by triumphantly scoring my driver's license. I don't remember doing a traditional sort of driver's ed at all. I just got the license. My dad was head of transportation back then. I didn't ask questions. For the rest of my junior year, by night I danced, and by day I hurried to class, passing a large portrait of Priscilla Presley in the school's hallway. I remember thinking how cool it was that she had been going to this very same high school when she met Elvis, not even suspecting that my life was about to change in much the same way hers had.

People have tried to tell me, "You lost your childhood to dancing," but I don't see it that way at all. If anything, belly dancing allowed me to hang on to my innocence a little longer than most of the girls I knew. When I was sixteen, I was a virgin who'd never tasted alcohol—that's about as common as a unicorn among present-day sixteen-year-olds. If I can give my daughter one thing, I want to give her what I got from belly dancing: a sense of myself as precious. I respected and reserved myself—for myself, not for a man—and the side effect of that was a beautiful romance with a husband who was my first, and in that moment, my everything.

When I belly danced, I never saw it as a dance of seduction; I saw it as a dance of empowerment. That's what I try to give women now when I teach them to belly dance: that sense of self-confidence that can only come from within. No compliment can give it to you. No number on the scale. No label in your clothes. It radiates from a woman's core, and it's absolutely her own. I think that's what made Prince notice me. I wasn't onstage to turn anyone on; I was there to practice this ancient art form and make it my own. That's exactly what he wanted for every artist he worked with. Prince was a master at bringing out the best in people, and I soaked that up during the eleven years we were together. I try to bring that to every class I teach, and I see it happening: A successful businesswoman becomes more successful as she becomes CEO of herself. A teenage girl in the media blizzard of our "you can never be too skinny or too rich" culture comes away with the idea that what she is right now is magical.

Prince, from an early age, was a savant musician. He knew he was one of the greatest entertainers in the history of rock music—or the history of history—but he never felt the need to say it. It was just there and could not be denied. We shared a common belief that whatever you're passionate about, you should learn about it, work on it, do it—just let it go and let it be. And that's what I do about belly dancing. The joy I felt dancing for George Michael or for Madonna and her dancers or for any other audience is the same joy I felt dancing on the tile floor at my grandma Mercedes's home when I was a little girl. That feeling came from within, so no one could take it away from me. I knew I was good, and I celebrated that in a way that wasn't conceited or cocky. I was grateful for this body God had given me, grateful for the formal education Mama had fought to provide me, and grateful for every hour Daddy spent carting my gigantic boom box and speakers up the stairs to another gig.

Daddy did get frustrated with me every once in a while when my grades suffered, but I remember only one occasion when he tried to get tough about it.

"That's it," he declared. "You're grounded."

I shrugged and told him what he already knew. "You can't ground me. I'm booked."

As Mama and I made plans for our summer trip to Egypt, we received two pieces of terrible news: First, George Abdo called to tell Mama that Amir had died of AIDS. We were stunned by the loss of our dear, flamboyant friend. I was only beginning to understand what "AIDS" meant or what "homosexual" meant—or what "sexual" meant, for that matter. When I think of Amir, I think of talent and kindness and laughter. I remember him sitting on the floor teaching Mama how to sew a particularly lovely pattern of beading on my sleeve. To me, he was Amir, the artist, one of the most beautiful dancers I'd ever seen. That was all. And that was more than enough. I'm grateful that I had the opportunity to know and work with him.

In March, the other shoe dropped. There was a terrible fire at the Heliopolis Sheraton. The hotel was relatively new, but there were no alarms or sprinkler system. Tragically, Egyptian law didn't require those at that time. Sixteen people had been killed and much of the place had been destroyed. They didn't know when they'd be open for business again or if the Nubian Tent would ever be rebuilt.

I wasn't upset about the money, though it would have tripled my income. It didn't even cross my mind that if I'd been there, I might have been killed. All I could see was that the dream I'd worked so hard for had slipped through my fingers. It might be a year before I got another chance to dance in Egypt with an Egyptian band, and a year seemed like an eternity to my sixteen-year-old self. I was devastated and probably being too dramatic about it—*that's just the way I ammmm*—but Daddy tried to put a positive spin on things.

"You're safe. That's all that matters," he said. "We'll make the best of it. We can all go camping together in Spain."

This didn't improve things, for my taste, but Daddy pushed the plan forward.

"Look, you've only got one year of high school left. Jan's going to be living in the States. After I retire, who knows where we'll be? This is probably the last family trip we'll take together."

His genuine sadness about that made us feel bad, so we sheepishly got on board. I really was glad for that time with Jan, and Mama and Daddy seemed to be in a good, loving place with their relationship. Neither of them was seeing anyone else, so their fighting was at a nice low tide. He was feeling sentimental and happy and insisted on paying for everything, which I appreciated. It made me feel like his little girl, protected and taken care of.

"There's enough in the budget for one concert," he said. We had our choice: Celia Cruz with Tito Puente, or Prince.

"Prince," Jan said without hesitation. She'd seen him in Washington, DC, on the Lovesexy Tour a year earlier and was still in a fangirl haze about it.

I wasn't in favor of the Prince plan, because we'd gone to see Michael Jackson with Kim Wilde during the Bad World Tour, and it was a horrible experience. People were screaming and passing out, and not because they were overwhelmed by the awesome music; they genuinely could not breathe and were afraid for their lives. We were so crammed together that my feet dangled above the ground at times. I had a sweater tied around my waist, and some creepy dude tried to take it off me. That put me over the edge. I punched Jan's shoulder and yelled over the shrieking crowd, *I hate you right now!* It was amazing to see Michael Jackson live, and God bless and keep

Michael Jackson's music, but I did not want to repeat that scene.

"The Prince concert is going to be just as bad," I said. "I vote for Celia and Tito."

I offered to pay for one of the concerts, so I could skip Prince to hang out on the beach, but Daddy wasn't letting me open my wallet for anything.

"Wait. The Prince tour is called *Nude*?" Mama raised her carefully drawn eyebrow as she read the Spanish newspaper. "Oh, we're going to see Prince."

That settled it.

three

The drive from Frankfurt to Barcelona takes about twelve hours, and along the way is some of the most beautiful scenery in Europe. I loved the fairy-tale mountains and forests of Germany. As we passed through the French Alps and on to the Riviera, we heard a mix of Arabic and Spanish music that lent to the atmosphere of class and happiness. When Dad was driving, we listened to Cat Stevens, who reminded us to bliss out and appreciate the beauty in life. Finally, the freeway came close to the sea. One minute you're in France, and then—oh, you're in Spain! Easy. You find yourself on the coast of the Balearic Sea, which is always coming up with new shades of blue. The air smells like spice and salt water. You pass through busy little cities and quaint old villages, each one built around an ancient cathedral. There are very few straight lines in Spain. Curves are everywhere from the winding roads to the architecture. In everything—the people, the food, the music—there's passion.

Years later, there would be a time when my husband

and I were in desperate need of a place to run away to, and with the entire world to choose from, we decided to take our broken selves to Spain. To that cool sea air and persistent passion. From our house on the coast near Marbella, we could look out at the Rock of Gibraltar and the distant shore of North Africa. I thought Spain would take us in and cradle us while we started over again. I kept returning to the memory of that happy journey with my family the summer of 1990.

Daddy was right. It was our last trip together. The experience was sweet and a bit humbling. We did a lot of sightseeing, taking in great music and fine art and so much history. We visited Gaudí churches, climbed up and down narrow stairways, and walked cobblestone streets that reminded me of Old San Juan.

Daddy had rented an RV from the military, and I wasn't excited about it. I told him, "I have enough money to stay in a hotel." He wasn't having any of that.

"People in Spain know how to do this. They're like professionals," he told me, and it was true. At an RV park south of Barcelona, we were among a large group of campers who had ritzy setups with comfy furniture and electricity for stereos and television sets. They drank wine and played music around their campfires at night and walked to the impeccably clean shower house in designer sandals. Jan and I quickly made friends with the furnished tent people so we could hang out, play games, and listen to music in the evening after laying out on the beach all day.

As the day of the concert drew closer, I dragged my heels a bit, but Mama and Jan convinced me that the Prince concert would not be the near-death experience we'd endured at the Michael Jackson show. It was arena seating, not "carnival" (such an ironic name for it), so people would be separated in rows with plenty of oxygen instead of being crushed together like a herd of cattle. Jan and I were getting pretty tired of the camping experience by this time. With nothing better to do, we headed to the Estadi Olímpic de Montjuïc early on the day of the concert and ate a picnic lunch on a grassy hill outside before going in to get our tickets, which placed us somewhere high in the nosebleed seats. Jan immediately homed in on a barricaded area directly in front of the stage.

"Hey, look," she said. "Let's try to go to the front."

I wasn't sure that was allowed, so I was heading for my nosebleed seat where I could sit and sulk and eat a sandwich Daddy had packed for me, but Jan came running back and said, "If you come early, you get a wristband. It's limited to only so many people, so it won't be crowded. They promised. But we have to hurry."

Mama and Daddy and I followed her to the barricade, and true to their word, security did close it off with a reasonable number of people inside. There was room to breathe, and we were literally front and center as the roadies did final sound checks for the opening acts. Three backup dancers came out to look over the gathering. I didn't know it at the time, but later I'd become familiar with this routine; they were scouting girls for the after party. They eyed Jan. They eyed me. These dudes are skilled; it takes them about thirty seconds to spot a girl, determine her age, and decide whether to hand her an after-party pass. One of them started a conversation with Jan, and another started to approach me, but Daddy stepped in with a friendly smile.

"Hey," he said, Mr. Rockefeller–style, noticing the guy's army tattoos.

I don't understand how military guys instantly bro down like they do, but within minutes, Daddy had bonded with his new best friends, talking about this division and that exercise or whatever. Jan and I exchanged glances. No party invitation for us. The guys who'd come out to hit on us were now calling us "little sis."

We held our position in the front row as thirty thousand people poured into the stadium. The opening act was Ketama, a Spanish group that did funk-flamenco fusion with a twist of reggae, so right away, I was dancing. The lights were still up, and Daddy went to get us some sodas, because now we'd been standing there for several hours. Lois Lane, a pop group consisting of two cute Dutch sisters who combined girl-group harmonies with a silky sort of Eurasian jazz, played after Ketama, and then the roadies reset the stage with a big swing unit, a giant heart, and a circular ramp. I didn't know at the time that this was a minimal set for a star of Prince's caliber, but that was the whole point, he later explained.

He laughed years later when I told him, "Mama heard it was called the Nude Tour, and she was like—'we're going!'"

"Noooo," he said. "Nude means stripped down. No fireworks, no big spectacle. We're just down with the music. Nude."

Prince was all about The Reveal, that moment of *abre los ojos*—open your eyes—when the artist meets the people for the first time. During one tour, he was rolled out onto the stage in advance, tucked inside a roadie case, which he then burst out of and blew people's minds. When word got out and ruined the surprise, he had to come up with something else with equal impact, and he always did. Another time, he had me dress up as him, so when I came out, people went wild thinking it was him until I whipped my clothes off, revealing a fuchsia bikini and combat boots. And then he came out for real and they went even wilder. It reminded me of Mama's rule that you must never allow the audience to see you before your entrance. That moment is important and worth protecting.

That night in Barcelona, it began with a thick blanket of fog that covered the stage. The lights went down, and I felt a sea change in the buzzing energy that filled the stadium, as if thirty thousand souls took one deep breath all at the same time. With the rolling fog came a deep, resonating hum—the sound you'd feel in your bones if you were standing under a power main. It grew louder and deeper until I felt it sinking through my ribs into my heart. It rushed into a series of fast-cut fragments—"For You," "Partyup," "Let's Go Crazy," "Around the World in a Day," and a few others that reminded you how many hits he'd had—then a bass line, and then a rhythm, and then he was there, and he was everything. He was wearing tight pants and a scoop-neck shirt that looked almost like a unitard. They had a huge fan below him, blowing his shoulder-length hair back.

A massive roar went up from the crowd.

"I've seen the future, and it will be..."

I hear those words now, twenty-five years older (and wiser), and I see myself standing in front of him. I revisit that moment in my mind's eye, and I can only imagine the perspective from which he now sees it, a perspective beyond time. If his faith in scripture has been rewarded, "a thousand years are as a day," and his soul knows everything. He sees the grand scheme, and in the context of a thousand lifetimes, he sees this

moment when we first saw each other for the thousandth time.

I could have sworn then that he was looking at
me, but a great performer is able to make every girl
in the audience feel as though he's looking at her, and
knowing what I know now about the power exchange
between the stage and the stadium, I know that his
focus was entirely on the performance. It had to be,
because what he did over the next hundred minutes
was—there are no words—it was a marathon jumping
into a tornado swallowed by wild horses. It's impossible to adequately describe the power of Prince in
concert if you haven't experienced it: the exhilaration
of funky beats, the skill of a symphony orchestra, the
wings of a gospel choir, hard-driving dancers, hard-
rocking musicians—and all the while, he danced in
these high-heeled platform boots. This man was a
beast as a singer, dancer, and musician. I feel bad for
anyone who never got to experience it.

The highs had me jumping up and down with my
hands in the air. The lows brought tears to my eyes.
My mouth was wide-open, but I was too in awe to
scream. And this is another thing I love about Europe:
They love music and don't care how ridiculous they
look. They just go nuts, leaping and waving, which
is what I was doing when suddenly, Prince stepped to
the edge of the stage, leaned forward, and stuck his

tongue out at me. (Later on, when I told him this, he just smiled his sweetly mischievous smile.)

Out of "The Future" came the iconic chords that blow the walls open for "1999"—which had the whole place screaming along. Then came the crazy lead beat for "Housequake." He played a lot of the big songs, "Purple Rain," of course, and "Take Me with You," and stuff like that. Rosie Gaines started out as the New Power Generation's keyboardist and later stepped in with vocals when Prince was ready for a change in sound, and that night, Rosie was a wonder. She came on and killed it during "Let's Jam It" and "Nothing Compares 2 U."

They brought the long set home with "When Doves Cry"—and I was crying, too. When the stadium chanted and screamed him back onstage for an encore, he did "Baby I'm a Star"—insane Latin rhythms and dance moves with spins and slides—which segued to "Brother with a Purpose" and "We Can Funk." When he launched into "Thieves in the Temple," I felt Daddy's grip on my elbow.

"Mayte, do you hear that? It's Arabic—this music—this is your music!"

"You should be dancing to that," Mama shouted in my ear over the roar of the concert. "He needs to see you dance. Maybe he'd hire you for a music video or—"

"You guys," I shouted back, "can we please not be talking about this right now? Just enjoy the show!"

I turned my back to them and continued going completely nuts like everyone else around us until the final bars of "Respect." They brought the lights up, and people milled toward the exits in a haze. A feeling I couldn't define—love, unity, happiness, contagious energy—bound us all together, made us smile at one another, yield the right of way at the gates, and wave as we drove out calling, *"Buenas noches."* In the car on the way back to the campground, I was practically comatose.

I was completely in awe of this performer. What he'd done on that stage—that was all I could think about. And this wasn't a romantic thing. I wasn't smitten with him that way. Not yet. But I'd never experienced anything so electrifying. Everyone on the stage worked his or her heart out. Everything was perfect, but nothing came off as routine or overdone. The look of it was as finely tuned as the music. At the center of it all was this supernova of a performer who danced as hard as any of the dancers and played every instrument he could get his hands on during the hundred-minute set.

With our front-row view, I could see the straining neck muscles and wardrobe drenched in sweat. As a performer who knows how to give up everything on the floor, I knew how hard these people were working. But I could also feel how their energy fed off his. Driving down the dark highway on the way back to our campsite, I could feel that force pulling me. Not to be with him, but to be an artist. To perform with absolute commitment. To dance with absolute joy. Now I know this is what inspiration feels like. Back then, I only knew I had to feel it again.

On the way back to Wiesbaden, Mama formulated a plan, and she was sticking to it. "Mayte, that Middle Eastern music—you're going to send him a tape of yourself dancing. You should be in one of his videos."

Daddy agreed with her, but I had one foot back in reality.

"You guys are crazy," I said. "We don't have anyone's information. We don't even know where they'll be a week from now."

"I'll get the info," said Mama. "You make the tape."

"You're dreaming. It's not going to happen."

But when we arrived back in Wiesbaden, Mama did some checking and discovered that the Nude Tour was right behind us. We saw Prince in Barcelona on July 25. From there, the show was going to Marbella and La Coruna, then to Belgium and the Netherlands, and then they'd be in Germany, performing in Dortmund and then at Maimarkthalle, a huge concert and exhibition venue in Mannheim on August 8.

"We're going," said Mama. "We are *going*, and I

don't care what it takes, we are going to get that videotape to Prince."

"What videotape? There is no tape."

"You're going to make one."

"Mama, I'm not making a videotape. I have school starting soon. I have bookings. I don't have time or equipment to do it in a way that would be—It would have to be, you know, professional. Didn't you see how perfect everything was? The lighting? The—the *everything*? And you have no way to get it to him. It's a waste of time."

"All it has to be is you dancing," she said. "Just like that."

She finally wore me down, and I said, "If I have time, I'll cut together something I have. But just let me do it myself. Don't be hovering and telling me what to put in or which show or—or anything."

The night before the concert, alone in the living room, without overthinking or really thinking at all, I came up with a tape Daddy had made at a recent gig and did a rough cut with the VCR ghetto-rigged to the camera. Daddy was still in the habit of videotaping my performances so I could review them afterward and figure out ways to improve, so this wasn't anything particularly high-tech, but it showed what I could do. I let it roll past the intro and hit Record on the camera right before my entrance. I let it roll through some turns and then pushed Pause, then fast-forwarded and hit Record again as I was whipping out the sword. I let it roll for a bit of me doing backbends and floorwork with the sword on my head and spinning the sword off, paused it again, grabbed a piece of a drum solo at the end, and then out. All together, it was less than three minutes.

"That's too short," said Mama when she watched it over my shoulder.

"I don't want him to get bored," I said.

I took the tape out of the camera and tucked it in its cardboard sleeve with my business card and a brief note. Something like:

> *Hi, my name is Mayte. I saw your show a few weeks ago. I noticed you had some Middle Eastern vibe in a song you played. I wanted you to see my Belly Dancing. I hope you like it. Oh and I'm 16 years old.*

The following day, as Jan and Mama and I made the two-hour drive to Mannheim, I started to have doubts about the length and quality of my demo tape, thinking maybe I should have done something new like Mama suggested, but it was too late for that now. I could only comfort myself with the certainty that there was no way on earth that Mama—no, not even Mama with her impressive Puerto Rican Mama superpowers—would actually get that tape to Prince.

We arrived early again, intending to go straight for the barricades to make sure we'd be front and center like we were in Barcelona, but we weren't able to get in. We had to stand outside the gate for a while.

"Whoa," said Jan. "Here comes the tour bus."

The windows of Prince's bus were heavily shaded, but the band bus windows were only slightly tinted. Mama saw Prince and Rosie Gaines inside, and she started to get excited. I didn't see them, but I was happy to be there, so I smiled up at the windows and waved.

Years later, Prince told me that when he saw me standing there with Jan and Mama, he said to Rosie Gaines, "There's my future wife."

"Really?" I said when he told me.

"Yeah. I said, 'There's my future wife,' and Rosie laughed."

"What made you say that?" I wondered—and I still wonder.

"I don't know." He shrugged. "I thought I was joking."

He liked how the universe boomeranged that little joke back to him. Or maybe the universe smiled and nodded and let him think that it was a joke and not the memory of something about to happen.

As we stood there, one of the dancers doing his after-party girl-patrol duty recognized us from Barcelona, and before we knew what was happening, he was leading us through the gate to the open area in front of the stage. In the brief moment we were home in Wiesbaden, Jan had managed to twist her ankle, so she was on crutches, hobbling along. I walked after her, clutching my bag to my chest, feeling the sharp corners of the VHS tape box until Mama took it from me and started scoping for the opportunity to accomplish her mission.

The dancers, Tony, Damon, and Kirk—"TDK" as I would soon come to know them—were inside this huge warehouse sort of space, playing basketball with some roadies. We stood there watching, not knowing what else to do.

"Whoa," Jan whispered in Spanish, "he's here."

Prince was not tall, but he was muscular, and there was an aura of vibrant energy about him. He was sure and light on his feet in a way that made him seem larger than life. I had to remind myself to take my next breath, and in that split second, Mama beelined over in that direction, brandishing my belly dancing tape.

I gripped Jan's hand. "Oh, wow. Oh, God. What is she doing?"

Mama didn't get within ten yards of Prince, of course. His bodyguard stopped her and said sternly, "Sorry, ma'am. You can't be here."

She backed off but informed the bodyguard, "You haven't seen the last of me."

I was mortified. Horrified. Dying a thousand deaths. Prince observed all this before he disappeared into the sound booth. I stood there feeling like the Incredible Shrinking Woman. Mama came back to where we were standing, not bothered at all by this small setback.

"Mama," I hissed, "why did you do that? You'll get us kicked out."

"He needs to see you dance," she said with great conviction. *"Yo no tengo pelos en la lengua."*

Jan and I heard this old Spanish expression from Mama a lot while we were growing up. Strictly translated, it means "I don't have hair on my tongue"—Mama's way of saying she wasn't afraid to open her mouth and speak her mind.

"Just—please! Just be cool," I said, though I didn't even know how any of us would be able to do that in this situation.

The Dutch band Lois Lane, who had opened for him at the last concert, came out onto the stage and did their sound check. The other openers were Germany-specific; he often scheduled local or regional bands for opening slots on his tours. Something I truly loved and appreciated about Prince during the years we worked and lived together was the way he took artists like these—and like me—under his wing. When he saw talent that intrigued him, he got the artist in front of people, and his seal of approval meant a lot—in the audience and in the industry. He lifted them up above the noise so they could be noticed. Any band or artist opening for him would be seen by millions of people when all was said and done, and that gave him great happiness. He loved it when good art got the attention it deserved, so he surrounded himself with people who inspired and pushed him, and he inspired and pushed them back.

I glanced toward the basketball court, where Jan was now smack in the middle of the game, stumping around on her tragic little ankle brace and still holding her own with the boys. When I looked back at the stage, some of the musicians who would soon become the New Power Generation were preparing to do their sound check. Prince was standing there looking at me. I quickly looked away. When I looked again, he was still watching us.

"Oh, God," I whispered. "We are so kicked out."

But the basketball game continued, and for a while, nothing happened. I was doing my best not to look at the stage, telling myself that, no, you cannot feel someone's eyes on you from across the room. Eventually, he went downstairs, and the game broke up as the roadies went about their duties. Kirk, the nicest of the three dancers, came by, and Mama changed her approach.

"Excuse me," she said sweetly. "We don't know how to do this, but my daughter—she's a belly dancer. She's been talking about how wonderful you all are ever since we saw you in Spain. She would just love for him to see her work. Do you suppose you could give him this tape?"

Kirk laughed and said, "Sure. I'll be right back."

She handed the tape to him, and he took it. Just like that. I can't even guess at the look on my face as he went off down the stairs. If there ever was proof of the sturdy Catholic teaching "Knock and the door shall be opened unto you," this would certainly be it.

A moment later, he came back and said, "So I gave him the tape. He took it. He's watching it now."

"Are you serious?" I said—and again, people, the expression on my face...I can't even.

"Yeah. He saw you standing out here, so he took it."

I heard myself say something like, "Oh. Okay."

A few minutes later, the second bodyguard—the one who'd intercepted my mom on her first attempt—came back to us and said, "Hi. Prince saw your tape. He wants to meet you."

"Oh. Okay."

"I have to ask," said the bodyguard, "how old are you?"

"I'm sixteen. Like it said in my letter."

He turned to Mama and asked, "Is it okay if she goes downstairs?"

Obviously, he did not know my mom. Before the words were fully out of his mouth, she was nodding. Ecstatic. "Sure! Yes! Go!"

A side note here: Yes, I was sixteen, and he was Prince, so there was an element of *Oh, my god, I'm about to meet Prince!*, but my mother trusted me to handle myself because she'd seen me handle myself as a professional for several years in a lot of different situations. Standing backstage at the Maimarkthalle, we hadn't seen anything that looked like stereo-typical rock-and-roll tour shenanigans or substance abuse, and I was so deeply honored that he wanted to meet me.

I followed the bodyguard down a passage that seemed to have a thousand steps. The sound of our feet echoed off the cement walls. Or maybe it was the sound of my heart pounding. I remember thinking, *Oh my god oh my god oh my god this is actually happening.* We turned the corner, and Prince was standing there outside his dressing room, shaking one of those little Easter egg maracas. He looked every bit as put together as he looked onstage, but with a lighter touch, a bit more oxygen. His hair was long and had been straightened to a soft wave that touched his shoulders. His eyelashes were unfairly lovely, and his beard was precisely tailored. (He always did this himself during the years we were together; the barber was never allowed to touch it.) He smelled like the most expensive shelf in the Sephora perfume aisle. I didn't process it then, but I look back now in awe that this man wearing eyeliner, heels, and ladies' perfume somehow managed to be more masculine than the burly body-guard.

He said, "Hi."

And I said, "Hi."

I felt calm, suddenly. A peaceful feeling passed through me. Not from him. From within myself. It was that feeling that I belonged here, in the right place at the right time. I hadn't evolved enough at that point in my life to even consider the deep philosophical questions I'd soon be discussing with him—the third eye, the migration of souls, the great spiral staircase we climb up and down—so I didn't question the feeling then, but these days, when I revisit that moment in my heart, I feel this reassuring ping. *Oh, it's you! Here you are.* It comforts me to think that I'll feel it again in another time and place.

"I like your tape," he said.

"Thanks." It sounded short and nervous in a trying-not-to-be-nervous way, so I added, "I edited it. I didn't want you to get bored."

"Bored? How can dancing like that be boring?" He laughed the contagious laugh I would come to love.

"I have the whole version if you'd like to see it. And more tapes. Other tapes."

"Are you really sixteen?"

"Yeah."

"Huh." He nodded and bounced the Easter egg on his palm. "Would you like better seats?"

"Sure. Thanks." We'd spent our time trying to get backstage instead of getting inside the barricade, so we didn't actually have seats.

"We'll hook you up." He glanced over my shoulder at the security guard, who nodded. "Well, I'd like to talk to you more, but I gotta get ready for the show. Can I get your number?"

"Okay. Sure." I felt something like a fire alarm going off inside my stomach.

"Okay. I'll call you."

"Okay."

It felt like my cue to leave. The entire encounter had lasted all of forty seconds, but it felt like we'd stepped outside of time. The security guard directed me toward the stairs again and said, "Prince wants your family to sit in the VIP seats. I'll get your information after the show."

The VIP seats turned out to be folding chairs next to the sound and light boards. The show onstage was every bit as electrifying as it had been in Barcelona, but this time I saw it from the inside out. I heard the TD (the tech director) calling every cue on his headset and watched with geeky fascination as the backstage crew wrangled the boards, light banks, scaffolding— all the inner workings of a rock concert. My entire paradigm had shifted by the end of the show; I never lost my appreciation for what a crew does to make the show appear perfect to an audience. Meanwhile, my own brain was buzzing with anxiety over the details of how this was all going to work out. I'd tucked my business card in the tape box, but what if it fell out? What if they lost it? How would he get my phone number? What if he called before I got home? Daddy was there. He'd answer and go full Rockefeller. I perched on the edge of my chair, wanting to scream for seven different reasons.

As we were leaving, the bodyguard came over and asked for my number. I wrote it down very clearly on a large piece of paper and handed it to him. As the bodyguard walked away, I saw Prince run over, grab the paper, and hop into a waiting limo.

I seized Jan's arm. "We've got to go. *Now.*"

This was before the days of cell phones and voice mail. If he rang and we weren't home, we would miss the call. And we were *not* about to miss that call. Mama drove like a madwoman all the way home. When we burst in the door, Daddy was asleep on the couch.

"What happened?" he asked.

"You don't even know—" I started, and then we were all talking at once.

The phone rang, and we all turned to look at it like we were in a movie. It was like, *camera zooms in on ringing phone.*

"Oh my God," I whispered. "It's him."

Then we all dove forward to answer it.

I was all, "It's for me! You know it's for me!"

"I should answer it," said Mama.

"Oh my God," said Jan. "Somebody answer it!"

Daddy stepped in and picked up the phone. "Hello?"

It was the bodyguard. "Hi, can I talk to, um... Maaaa..."

"Mayte. Her name is Mayte." Daddy handed me the phone.

"Hi," I peeped.

"Hi. He would like to talk to you." The bodyguard didn't have to say his name. I was put on hold. I was dying. My family was dying. Moments ticked by.

"Hi."

"Hi..." I couldn't say "Prince"; I was afraid that if "Prince" came out of my mouth, I would immediately start screaming and running in circles. "Hi."

"I watched your video again on the way home, and I really liked it."

"Thank you."

"Can you come over?"

"Come over?" That wasn't the question I was expecting. I stopped breathing for a moment and said, "What do you mean?"

"We didn't get to talk much. Come over and hang out. We can talk more."

I wasn't drawing any conclusions, but I wanted to

make sure there was no room for doubt. "*My mom* and I could come over. And my sister."

"Cool. Where are you?"

"Wiesbaden."

"Ah. I'm in Frankfurt. Do you want me to send a car for you?"

"No, that's okay," I said. Because I knew Frankfurt was at least thirty minutes away for any respectable limo driver. In this situation, I could count on Mama to drive it in twenty minutes flat.

"Bring more tapes," he said before we hung up.

On the way to Frankfurt, Mama drove with a controlled urgency while Jan and I took turns hyperventilating and freaking out when we thought she had missed the exit.

Jan was in worrywart mode. "How is this going to work? We can't just walk in and say we're here to see Prince. I mean, what if they won't—"

"Everyone just stay calm," I said, even though I was still screaming inside.

Something I was about to learn about Prince: He would never allow anyone to be left hanging. If he invited someone to visit, he went to great lengths to see that they were comfortable and well cared for. When we arrived at the hotel, we saw a large black man standing out front, and because you don't see a lot of black men in Frankfurt, we immediately knew that he was waiting to meet us. We were escorted down a sky-high hallway, with windows looking out over the city lights, to the presidential suite.

From the moment the bodyguard opened the door, I felt like I was floating somewhere between the Grand Bazaar and Madame Abla's salon. The air was heavy with candles, flowers, and perfume. Plush rugs covered the standard hotel carpeting. Veils covered the doorways and were draped over lamps and light fixtures, creating a softly diffused glow.

This is called "foo foo," I learned later, and Prince had a staff member dedicated to it. Wherever Prince went, it was the foo foo master's job to go ahead of him and make sure the hotel suite would be a place where he could feel at home, recover from the dehydrating hard labor of a performance, and use what little downtime he had to rest, relax, and work on whatever he was working on next. The foo foo master would reconfigure the furniture and make sure the floor was layered in fluffy area rugs—purple or whatever color he was currently into. They used scrim and linen to swath anything that looked ordinary or sad and covered the windows with aluminum foil so it would be dark enough to sleep in the room during the day.

One all-important task of the foo foo master was to make sure that there was a grand piano in the room, which was sometimes a challenge. I remember hearing about a hotel in London where the management, given the choice of figuring it out or letting Prince stay elsewhere, had the piano hoisted up to the presidential suite with a giant crane. It was a pretty major hassle, but when Prince walked into the hotel room, he immediately sat down and played for two hours. When Robbie, the foo foo master at the time, told me about this, he was glowing. These people took a lot of pride in caring for Prince. He was conscious of the many people whose living depended on his stamina, and they understood the grueling physical and emotional demands he put on himself while he was touring. The foo foo was not about a pampered star's outlandish demands; it was about this hydraulic engine being well maintained, fed, and rested enough to pull an entire train.

To have that sense of comfort in unknown lands— this was a perk I dearly appreciated during the years when we were a couple. I looked forward to walking into a dressing room that had been preset with all the big and small things that made me feel cared for. It was lovely to check into a hotel and feel like we were coming home to our own life, at least, even if we were far from our own home in Minnesota. After our marriage ended, it took me years to get used to checking into a nondescript, neutral-toned hotel room.

That first night in Frankfurt, Mama and Jan and I stood in the center of the room, trying to take it all in. Prince came out to greet us.

"I'm glad you're here," he said. "Can I get you some-thing to drink?"

In Germany, Jan and I were both of legal drinking age, but we were incapable of processing the question. Mama said she would like some water. We sat and made small talk for about twenty minutes. He was respectful of Mama and seemed eager to let her know that nothing inappropriate was going to happen.

"I'm a night owl," he said to me. "I hope your mom understands."

"Oh, she does," I assured him. "Dancers are used to the night shift."

He asked Mama, "Would it be okay if we hang out for a while? I'll send her home in a car later."

Mama was still scoping out the situation. "You'll make sure she gets home in one piece," she said pointedly.

"Oh, absolutely."

I touched her elbow and said, "I'm fine." She saw the steady confidence in my eyes and took comfort in it. She could see that I wasn't scared or unsure; I was there to hang out with the man, artist to artist. If you were going to connect with someone in a profes-sional capacity, you would invite them to get together at either your home or your office, and when you're on tour, your hotel room is both these things. I knew she'd have my back if anything went strange, but I was equally certain that's not why I was there. Having sized things up to her satisfaction, Mama hugged me and headed home with Jan.

It was after midnight by this time, and I hadn't eaten all day, but I was wired with adrenalin and wide awake.

"Are you sure I can't get you anything?" he kept asking. "Water? Tea? Something to eat?"

I couldn't imagine eating in that scenario, or possibly ever again, but the third or fourth time he asked, it occurred to me that maybe he wanted to eat something and didn't want to be rude by eating in front of me, so I said, "Sure. Thanks." He left me sitting alone in the bedroom and came back a few minutes later with a bowl of freshly popped popcorn, which he munched on while we sat cross-legged on the floor with pillows and watched the videotapes I'd brought.

One of the duties of the foo foo master was to set up a big black roadie case that held all kinds of audio visual equipment—a TV, VCRs, cassette and CD players, etc.—that Prince would need for reviewing performance tapes, watching movies, and working on one thing or another. I was relieved to see that it was outfitted with American equipment and electrical hookups; I'd had a moment of panic in the car, wondering if he'd be able to play my American tapes in a German hotel room. I set my stack of tapes on top of the roadie case: the long version of the rough cut I'd done for him, a talent show from school, a few random restaurant gigs, and other appearances.

He graciously watched them all, asking a thousand questions: *What are those arm bands made of? Where'd your dad get those drums? When did you learn how to drop back so slow? How do you roll your belly like that?* He was particularly interested in my journeys to Egypt, so I told him all about Madame Abla and Mohammed Ali Street in Cairo. As we worked through the stack of tapes, traveling backward in time, I told him about George Abdo and Amir and the dressed-to-the-nines ladies of *Frauentag*.

"How long have you been doing this dance?" he asked.

"Since I was three. When I was eight, I was on *That's Incredible!* The world's youngest professional belly dancer."

"No way."

"Yes! Way! Here—I brought the tape." Mama would have been proud.

He fed the tape into the VCR. When it got to the bit about "the mystical, magical Princess Mayte," he paused it and looked at me in surprise.

"Wait. Your name is Princess Mayte?"

"Yeah...it was."

"Why did you change it?"

"Because I'm not a princess."

"Yes, you are." He stated this as a simple fact,

looking me straight in the eye, and I suddenly felt a flush of pride mixed with genuine sadness that I'd somehow let that go.

"I don't know," I said. "I felt stupid."

"You are! I mean, that's a cool name."

I laughed and took a few kernels of popcorn in my hand, not sure if the proper response was "thank you" or something else. He watched the rest of the tape while I sat there thinking how surrealistic the whole thing was.

"Do you do any other type of dance?" he asked.

I brought out some ballet tapes and a recent happening, which to this day I laugh about. My high school had put on a talent show, and I was known as the dancer, so the chorus class asked me to choreograph a number to Prince's "Batdance" from the soundtrack of Tim Burton's 1989 version of *Batman*. I have to laugh now, because this thing was so bad, but I was very proud of my choreography, and he was extremely sweet about it. When it was over, I ejected the tape and went back to my wheelhouse, the pieces I was most proud of, the pieces I knew would get me another contract in Cairo.

It was closing in on four in the morning—pretty late-night, even for those of us on Germany time—and I was starting to feel bleary-eyed.

"Maybe we could hang out again tomorrow," he said, and I said we could.

Before the bodyguard took me down to a waiting Mercedes, I called home and told Daddy, who was waiting up for me, that I was on my way. I rode home on cloud nine, replaying the whole incredible day and night over and over in my head. Daddy was dozing on the couch when I walked in, but he sat up and rubbed his eyes, ready to hear all the details, including the plan for returning to Frankfurt in a matter of hours. I hated to sacrifice any of the day to sleeping. I knew that the next day, my new friend would go to Sweden and then on to the rest of the world and eventually home to the States, and this strange, wonderful moment would be over.

After I'd slept for a few hours, a car came and took me back to the hotel, and when I arrived at the suite, Prince called from the other room, "I'll be out soon."

"Okay…"

I wasn't sure what I was supposed to do in the meantime. I would have been happy to sit there among the foo foo, but a very nice gentleman introduced himself as Earl and told me he was going to do my hair.

"Okay…"

I wasn't sure what that meant, but Earl looked like he knew what he was doing. As he sectioned my curly hair and blow-dried it straight, I sat upright and still, wondering if this was an audition or just something to keep me occupied while I waited. Did he not like my hair? Straightened shiny black, it did look a lot longer and thicker. Looking at myself in the mirror, I did feel a bit like an Egyptian princess. Cleopatra without the bangs.

As Earl finished my sleek new style, Prince came in and said, "Wow. You look pretty."

"I love it." I couldn't stop touching it, and I didn't even freak out when Prince took a turn. It was so smooth and silky. "I don't ever want to wash it."

He laughed and said, "Well, it's different."

Our conversation picked up right where it had left off the night before. It always did over the years. Life was so easy and comfortable when he was next to me. The anticipation of seeing him was stressful, but when we were together, it was like we'd been friends for ages. We watched a videotape of the Mannheim performance, and then he showed me raw footage and rough cuts for the "Thieves in the Temple" video, so it was my turn to ask a thousand questions: *Was that supposed to happen? Who did the choreography on this part? Have you taken ballet? How did you come up with that insane move at the end?*

"Oh, that move's from James Brown," he said. He told me a story about going to a James Brown concert when he was a little kid, and he was like a little kid when he told it, excited and on his feet, laughing and demonstrating. "In the middle of the show, my step-dad boosts me up onstage. He put me up there, I was all *slide—kick—*and the kick always goes to the splits.

It was tight. I danced so hard. And then a bodyguard came and hauled me off."

I laughed at the idea of his stepdad hoisting him onto the stage. Mama had basically done the same thing to get me into this room. Watching his footwork up close, I noticed that his shoes were specially made with a steel bar between the heel and sole to keep the bottom from breaking. I'd been wondering how it was possible for him to do some of the things he'd done onstage without breaking an ankle or two, and I was curious to know what it felt like to dance with heels like that, but I was too shy to ask him if I could try one on.

It was so refreshing to be a part of this conversation about the art and business of performing—a serious conversation about creating art out of music and movement—with someone who was a master in multiple crafts and had defied all reasonable expectations to achieve a level of success most performers don't bother dreaming about. He treated me like a fellow artist, which made me feel incredibly special and proud, but every time I repeated something like, "This is so great, I can't believe how great this is," he'd laugh this infectious laugh that came from somewhere deep inside.

Before I left, he told me I should make another tape of myself dancing.

"If I have time," I said. "I have a lot booked before school starts. Restaurants and parties and stuff."

"Send me that. The restaurant stuff."

"Okay." I knew Daddy would be rolling tape anyway. "But where do I send it?"

"I'll let you know."

I went home, not fully believing I'd hear from him again, but the next day he called, and again the conversation continued without a seam. He told me about Sweden and the new music he was working on in his head.

"I'll send it to you," he said. "Let me know what you think. And send me another dance tape."

Years later, Prince's friend and collaborator Randee St. Nicholas told me that he called her one night and asked her to come over to his place right away. It was two in the morning, but the predawn hours were always a particularly creative time for him, so this wasn't out of the ordinary. Randee arrived at his home, and they sat together on his bed, watching the belly dancing videotapes I'd left with him.

"What do you think?" he asked.

She said, "This is the one you're going to marry."

"No, no, no. She's jailbait," he said, genuinely surprised. "I'm talking about the dancing. What do you think of the dancing?"

Over the following months, he and I fell into an

easygoing dialogue that covered every conceivable topic. The tone ranged from silly to spiritual. He welcomed the opportunity to educate me on the music that meant the most to him—James Brown, The Staple Singers, Chaka Khan, Sly and the Family Stone—and in turn, I taught him about ballet and Middle Eastern folkloric tradition. We laughed a lot and told each other our stories. He didn't call me every day, but we spoke on the phone several times most weeks. It was rare for more than a couple of days to go by without a call, and I regularly received cassette tapes in the mail, along with letters and drawings, many of which I still have.

The ones I don't have—those were destroyed years later. They were burned, along with everything that was mine or that reminded him of me or of our son. In some sad, painful moment, he had it all burned, as if fire could cauterize this deep wound he couldn't close. I wasn't there to witness it, and I can't bear to think about it now. I'd rather think about that summer when I was sixteen. The warm, white popcorn in the palm of my hand. The veiled doorways and lava lamps. The sound of his laughter and the sudden certainty that I had, and had always had, the soul of a princess.

four

Dearest Arabia,

Rather than not send u a letter, I opted 4 using this strange stationary instead. Please 4give me. Thank u 4 the present from the restaurant. I have fun watching it. U're so pretty. It cheers me up if someone tries 2 ruin my day. Many do.

Today is Monday. It is now 5:15. I'm lying on a very big bed in a room about the size of the one in Frankfurt. One never knows what one is gonna encounter in life, does one? Thank u 4 coming into my world. U seem so kind and unaffected by this heartless planet we live on…

This letter makes me laugh, remembering how he tried to make that Arabia thing stick, even though I kept saying, "Sorry, Charlie. Not gonna happen."

It felt weird to call him Prince, so I never did. There was, in my mind, a disconnect between the icon I'd seen onstage in Barcelona and Mannheim and the funny, soft-spoken person I'd come to know. I confided in him things that I'd been afraid to speak out loud to any of my friends, simply because their lives were so different from mine. He confided in me things that I will never share with anyone. It's no use trying to explain the connection that existed between us. People will draw conclusions based on their own belief systems: cynics will be cynical, romantics will be romantic, people who believe in fate as a river will see how its current carried us along. I honestly didn't overthink it at the time. I simply allowed it to be.

The "strange stationary" [sic] he refers to was a regular sheet of notepaper, which would have been completely normal to anyone else in the world, but Prince had an affinity for fancy notepaper—embossed and flowery with scalloped edges and elegantly lined envelopes—designed to resemble his grandmother's notepaper.

I cherish these letters Prince wrote to me during the first few months of our strange and wonderful dialogue. I've kept them all these years in a photo album along with ticket stubs, press clippings, and other memorabilia. I look at them and see two kindred spirits who instantly recognized each other. It's clear in his letters that our ongoing conversation was an oasis for him—*U seem so kind and unaffected by this heartless planet*—a sanctuary unspoiled by sexual tension or the politics of sucking up. For me, this relationship was the opportunity to step out of my ordinary world into a rarified existence in which life itself is a work of art. It had never occurred to me that each shoe and rock and handwritten letter is an opportunity to express yourself—or it's just one more of a million little things that don't. It's up to you. But why would you choose to create a life from a pile of little things that don't actively matter to you?

This was an amazing moment in the music industry—almost as pivotal as the moment we're in now. Music videos had gained traction, making megastars of certain people, including Prince, who had a stellar sense of style on top of his music. The MTV of the early 1980s was full of random concert footage, slightly cheesy record company demos, and a whole lot of experimentation. The MTV of the 1990s had gotten a lot more sophisticated. The audience had been trained to expect visuals that were just as good as sound when it came to production values. This was Prince's world when I entered it. I wanted to learn all about this technical part of the music business, and he loved teaching me about it. Something I learned about him in the subsequent years was that work was his way of dealing with whatever was wrong or painful or disappointing in his life. He made art—musical, theatrical, and visual. He lost himself in the act of creation. That's something we had in common, so I never questioned it. I was thrilled to follow him down the creative rabbit hole. In that moment, all that mattered was the soaring sense of happiness I felt every time I received a letter from him. The more out-of-this-world it was, the better I liked it.

...If u like and if it's ok by Nellie, maybe we could fly away 2 Jupiter. I hear the food is good there. If not, u can cook. But only as a last resort. Don't bring any clothes—only your dancing costumes. During the day u can wear my clothes. We can go swimming in their ocean 2. They say all water there is pink. Imagine that. All water in Stockholm are tears. I miss u. So I cry giraffe tears.

Gilbert just called. I missed the last flight so I'll send this off tomorrow. I'll call U anyway 2night. I can't wait 2 hear U.

Love & ☮,
Prince

After Germany, the Nude Tour continued to Sweden. Prince called me from Stockholm and said, "I'm playing Switzerland this week. Do you and your mom want to come?"

"Absolutely!" My heart was already out the door.

Ten minutes later, his security person called and told me our tickets would be waiting for us at the airport. Jan and I had been bumped up to first class a few times when we were flying as unaccompanied

minors, but this was my first actual first-class ticket—
and with a Mercedes waiting to pick me up at baggage
claim. Once again, the bodyguard greeted us in the
lobby. Mama and I waited for a while, and then a note
arrived. It was written in pencil on a sheet torn from
a spiral notebook, which was unusual for him. It said:

> *Hi!* 👁 *don't look so good cuz I'm sick, but I'll
> get dressed and come get u in a little while. If u 2
> need anything, please let one of my guys know and
> they will fix u up. So happy u are here O.K. safe
> & sound.*
>
> *P ♂*

A little while later, he called and spoke with Mama.
He apologized for the wait and asked her how the flight
was, and they made small talk for fifteen or twenty
minutes, and then she handed me the phone. He said
he still wasn't feeling well, so rather than come out
to see us, he just wanted me to come in for a while.
He asked if that was all right with Mama, and Mama
wasn't going to stand in my way, that was for sure.

When I went into his room, he was sitting on one
end of a big sofa, listening to music. The suite looked
almost identical to the room in Frankfurt, thanks
to the foo foo master's magic touch. He was as put
together as he had been the first time I saw him—
meticulously trimmed beard, flawless skin, perfect

eyeliner—but he did seem a bit subdued. Something was off from his usual vibrant energy.

I sat cross-legged ("dancer style") at the other end of the sofa, and he said, "I have a confession to make. I've been having Gilbert call you because I don't know how to pronounce your name. I didn't want to say it until I could say it correctly."

I was so touched by that. People almost never know how to pronounce my name, and most of them either stomp right on in and say it wrong without caring, or they avoid it like it's a swear word. This was particularly upsetting to me when I started school in first grade, having no idea that my name was any different from Jan's. I came home upset because my teacher kept calling me "Garcia," while she called the rest of the children by their first names. This didn't sit well with Mama. I was one of very few Latin children in the class, and she wasn't about to put up with anything that smelled like discrimination. She went over to the school the next morning and told the teacher, "Unless you're going to call all the other children by their last names, I suggest you learn how to pronounce my daughter's name. I won't have her singled out." Then she schooled my teacher on how to say it, and I was used to explaining it the same way.

"Say 'my telephone,'" I said, "but stop before '–lephone.' Like Myyyyyy. Teeeelephone. My. Te—! Mayte."

"Mayte." He pronounced it carefully and correctly. He practiced it a few times, and from then on, he was the first one to step in and correct anyone—including Herb Ritts—who mispronounced it. I always loved that.

"What's the origin of it?" he asked

Rather than go into the whole story of Mama and the telenovela, I opted for the short answer. "It's Basque. It means 'beloved.'"

He seemed weary and deflated—the opposite of his presence onstage—and obviously had a miserable cold.

He asked, "Can I get you anything?"

"Don't get up," I said. "I'll make some tea. Can I make some for you?"

"Sure. Thank you."

When I brought him his tea, he declared it was exactly right, exactly the way he liked it. I assumed at the time he was being polite, but in fact, he told me for years that I was the best tea maker. "It's not as straightforward as people think," he said, and I agree; there's a precise color and chemistry to a good cup of tea with honey.

Neither of us said anything for a long while, but the silence wasn't awkward. There was music playing on the roadie box stereo, and between tracks, there was the soft hiss of a humidifier and the occasional clink of my spoon in my teacup. We sat together without needing to do anything more. Every once in a while, he reached over to rub my face with his hand, as if he were checking to see if I was actually there or just a fever dream, and I'd giggle and relocate to a spot on the floor or side chair. The quiet minutes stretched to an hour, and the hour stretched to two hours.

"On the phone you're a firecracker," he said. "Now you're here and you're not talking."

"It's because I'm dying right now. I don't know what I'm feeling."

Impulsively, I got up to hug him, but he said, "No."

"I was just going to give you a hug. I'm glad I'm here. That's all."

He shook his head. "I don't want you to get sick."

I hugged him anyway. After a moment, he hugged me back, and then we snuggled together on the sofa. The closest feeling I can compare would be crowding onto the sofa in front of the TV with Gia and our dogs. I felt safe and at home, and he seemed to feel the same way, because as we sat there together, he settled his head back, listening to the music, drifting in and out of sleep. I didn't understand at the time what a luxury it was for him to be so quiet and unguarded without being alone.

Before I left, I hugged him again, and at the last moment, we got the trajectory wrong and our noses brushed together in a way that might have led to an accidental kiss if we hadn't both pulled away and laughed.

Infatuation, from the scientific point of view, is a chemical reaction that intensifies perception and floods the body with endorphins, and Prince tried, in his way, to say something to me about this after I returned to Germany.

"I'm sending you a song I want you to dance to. It's called 'The Dopamine Rush.'"

"What's dopamine?" I asked.

He laughed and said, "Look it up."

I did look it up and figured out that dopamine is a chemical that blitzes through your brain, making you feel deliciously happy—exactly the way I was feeling at the time. My world was more colorful. The sky was bluer. The sun shone with a very personal intensity. The rain had a secret message for me. My own skin reminded me of gold and roses. It was a high I'll never forget. I was rushing on that sweet dopamine, and he was letting me know he knew it.

The "Dopamine Rush" cassette arrived. The track was part of a suite Prince had started working and reworking two years earlier in Europe and was now producing for an Eric Leeds album called *Times Squared*. I tried my best to work with it, but it was a smooth type of instrumental jazz, and something about the timing just didn't sync with my style.

"Where's my 'Dopamine Rush' video?" he asked me the following week.

"I can't dance to it," I said. "I don't know why."

He didn't question or comment on that. He just said, "Okay."

He sent me another track from the suite, an unpolished piece called "Amsterdam" that sounded sad and a little lonely, but there was an honest rhythm to it that moved me. I danced to it, only vaguely aware that this was a form of communication we were developing, a secret language in which he would tell me—or try to tell me—what he wasn't always able to say in words.

He liked what I did with "Amsterdam" and was very into the ballet videos I was sending.

We flirted, we giggled, but in the beginning, I didn't feel that I was being courted. Later on, when I was being courted, believe me, I knew it. This was not that. There was an immediate mutual affection between us, but we did not have a sexual relationship. I know this is difficult for some people to wrap their heads around. I'm not naïve about his famous appetite for sex or the fact that I was rockin' the mature body of a professional belly dancer. He never denied that the occasional impure thought crossed his mind, but the truth is, he was too wise and decent to take advantage of a sixteen-year-old, and I was a self-determined girl who intended to remain a virgin until I felt ready to be something else. There's nothing like dance to give a girl a sense of owning her own body. Because I always worked on the weekends, I had very little dating experience, and that was fine with me. Boys my age didn't understand or interest me at all. They never said ridiculously cool things like, "Charts, awards, and grades at school are a sociopsychotic illusion."

At that time, I knew about the various women in his life. I don't know what they knew about me, but it didn't matter; I couldn't see myself ever being part of that mix. I was thrilled to be Prince's friend and honored that he considered me a fellow artist. The oddly magical summer of 1990 ended. Jan went off to college in Maryland, and within days, I missed her horribly. School started in the fall, my third and final year at General H. H. Arnold High School. I hurried to class with a wink at Priscilla Presley but told very few people about the unusual relationship that had developed between my American friend and me. Only my family and my two best friends knew that this dialogue had become a huge part of my life.

After our meet-up in Switzerland, Prince and the Nude Tour had moved on to France, England, and Japan—eleven performances in twenty days—before he went home to Minnesota. As autumn went by, he continued to call me several times a week. We rarely spent less than two or three hours on the phone. Being a sixteen-year-old on the phone with a rock star, I logged each call in my diary. *He called again! We had*

a loooooong talk. He is so funny. I laughed my head off.
Now I eavesdrop on those conversations in my memory, thinking, *What I wouldn't give for just one of those
hours back...*

"Do you sing?" he asked me one evening.

"No," I answered automatically.

"Yes, you do."

"Well, just—I take chorus class. I always wanted to
be a triple threat like Rita Moreno."

It briefly crossed my mind to mention the demo,
but the fact that they'd decided not to release it didn't
exactly boost my confidence, and I wasn't sure I could
easily lay my hands on a copy of it anyway.

"I have this song I want you to sing on," he said,
"but I need to hear you sing."

"Now?"

"Yeah."

"I can't sing for you on the phone."

"No, I really need you to sing. Like this..." And
then he started singing it.

"Oh. Yeah. No. Don't do that." I was afraid if he
kept singing, I would remember who he really was,
and I was happy thinking of him as my friend. But
he kept singing, and I kept refusing to sing. After an
hour or so, per his request, I put the phone on the
floor and stood way across the room and sang.

"Why were you so scared?" he asked when I picked
up the phone again. "That was really good."

"Thanks. Can it be over now?"

"I need you to come to Minneapolis and record this song. I'll let you know when it's happening. I want you to be on it."

"What?"

"It has an Arabic vibe. There's some Arabic notes in it."

"So you want me to sing."

"Yes."

If he'd said he needed me to dance on the video, I would have gone through the roof. That was something I knew I could do well. This I wasn't quite so sure about, until he said that. Something I would learn about him over the years: He had a way of speaking things into being. He'd say, "You know what would be cool..." in a way that made people believe they could do it—whatever *it* was. He saw potential in people before they saw it themselves, and not very many people I ever saw had the will—or the lack of will—to say no when he challenged them this way.

Randee St. Nicholas is a good example. She's a photographer first and foremost, but he loved her creative eye and started asking her to direct music videos and shoot hundreds of hours of footage. When he first saw Sheila E in concert with her father in the 1970s, he told her that he and his bassist were fighting over which one of them would marry her, but more important, he vowed that she was going to be in his band someday.

Over the years, their creative chemistry had a huge impact on his work and hers. He told me more than once how much he admired Wendy and Lisa because he could lay down some kind of foundation—or even an idea—go watch a movie, and come back to find that they'd spun it out into a song that had string arrangements and chords and different colors.

He sent me tapes so I could learn the music for "However Much U Want," and I sang in the shower and in my car and in my head. The rest of the time, I was busy dancing at restaurants like Pamukkale and Taverna Aspendos and at various events. I was also preparing for an exam I would have to take in order to receive a certificate that would allow me to continue dancing professionally in Germany after I graduated. My plan was to get a work visa so I could maintain a home base with Mama and Daddy in Germany between my contracts in Cairo, but this exam was no joke. I would have to perform a classical piece, a modern piece, and a folkloric piece in front of a panel of judges. In my head, I saw them sitting, bored and frowning, behind a stark wooden table like the panel of judges in *Flashdance*.

I made videotapes of myself practicing in the cafeteria at school so I could critique myself, and then I sent the tapes on to Prince, because he always asked to see what I was doing. He began sampling the music from these tapes and incorporating them into various ideas he was working on. FedEx-ing things to him from Germany took two days and was hideously expensive, but at that time, I still had the money to spare, and he was spending a lot more than that sending cassette tapes and letters to me.

I turned seventeen in November 1990, just before the opening of Prince's movie *Graffiti Bridge*, a hyperstylized sequel to *Purple Rain*, in which The Kid makes a bet with Morris Day: whoever writes the better song gets the deed to the other guy's nightclub. The Kid's place is called Glam Slam, and Morris's club is called Pandemonium, and somehow Mavis Staples is in there, and her club is called Melody Cool. Sometimes you'll see on the Internet that I was considered for the role of Aura, but that's not true. The movie was made the year before we met. Prince told me that he originally wanted Kim Basinger, but she turned it down, and after much discussion, he cast Ingrid Chavez, a waifishly lovely unknown. When he first told me about all this, I said, "It sounds cool."

General H. H. Arnold High had homecoming, just like any high school in the States, but it was a Friday night, so I was booked, of course. The only part of the festivities I was available for was a midnight movie. They were showing *Graffiti Bridge*. The anticipation level was high, because we had all grown up adoring *Purple Rain*.

"I'll get to see it!" I told my dear friend on the phone. "I'm super excited."

I like *Graffiti Bridge*. The visuals are dark and saturated with color, and there's some good music in it. Mavis Staples kills—*kills*—a throaty version of "Melody Cool." George Clinton, Tevin Campbell, and Rosie Gaines are incredible. I see the avant-garde intentions, and I love the sentimental message about romance and art and *la vie Bohème*. I've watched it with Gia a few times, and we enjoy every campy, over-the-top minute, especially the tragic climax where Aura gets flattened by a big red Jeep Cherokee.

Critics universally panned *Graffiti Bridge*. Even today, most audience reaction ranges from "WTF?" to outrage that their beloved *Purple Rain* now had this stupid sequel attached to it. Back then, I would have loved it no matter what. I would have loved it if he'd stood there reciting his ABCs; he was my friend. At the midnight showing on homecoming night, I found myself sinking deeper into my seat, as all my classmates laughed and jeered with loud homecoming pep rally spirit. It broke my heart, because I knew what he was hearing back in the States must be this magnified a million times over.

When Prince asked me if I'd seen it, I tried to be as diplomatic as possible.

"Yes…" I hedged, "and I really, really loved… Mavis Staples! She was so awesome. Seriously. I loved that part. And the part where…the umm…

oh! 'Elephants and Flowers'! And 'Tick, Tick, Bang'! Yeah, that choreography was like...wow."

I sat there on the phone, barely breathing, not wanting to say anything that would hurt him. This was pre-Twitter, thank God, but I couldn't imagine what it felt like to put your work out into the world and get horsewhipped by the media. Prince didn't have to imagine it, of course. He'd been in this business, which can be a brutal business, since he was a kid like me. He told me about getting booed off the stage when he opened for the Rolling Stones ten years earlier at the Memorial Coliseum in LA. He was on the roster with George Thorogood and The J. Geils Band, so it was kind of an odd mix, but the Stones were known for that. Prince came out onstage wearing tiny underpants and a trench coat and started his set with "Bambi" and "When You Were Mine," which were already not sitting well with the crowd when he launched into "Jack U Off," and then things really got ugly. He tried to soldier on with "Uptown," but by that time, people were hurling beer bottles, food, and garbage at him, yelling, "Get off the stage, fag!" and the road manager pulled the plug.

Twenty-five years later, when Prince died, Mick Jagger said in a series of tweets, "I am so saddened... Prince was a revolutionary artist, a wonderful musician and composer. He was an original lyricist and a startling guitar player. His talent was limitless. He was one of the most unique and exciting artists of the last 30 years."

He must have seen all that in Prince back in 1981, because they kept him on the tour. I don't know if they encouraged him to wear pants after the LA incident, but I do know he never changed anything about himself or his music to please an unhappy audience—whether it was an audience of one or an audience of ten thousand. When it comes down to it, I was probably more deeply wounded than he was by my classmates' response to *Graffiti Bridge*.

"I'm sorry," I said with a lump in my throat. "They just didn't get it."

"Nah, it's okay." He sighed heavily. "You can't look at yourself through other people's eyes. When you're working at a certain level, you find that people live through you, and if you don't act like they expect you to, then you're the bad one."

It was an educational moment for me, how he didn't wallow in it. He was already on to the next project. Sometimes, when he was very excited to share something with me, he'd buy the package an airplane seat, and I'd have to drive all the way to the airport in Frankfurt to pick it up, as if it were an unaccompanied minor.

"You could send it FedEx," I tried to gently suggest.

"I wanted you to have it today."

"But it must have cost hundreds of dollars. To send a cassette tape. Seriously."

"Yeah, but did you listen to it?"

It was the seed of an idea for a song called "7."

"What do you think?" he asked.

"What do you think I think? I was like, *Are you kidding me? I get to hear this?* It's beyond insane."

That's as far as it sank in then, but when I listen to it now, I hear a strand of myself: a Middle Eastern vibe and an almost scriptural sort of storytelling, a mythology spun from threads of our many long conversations.

I had a lot of holiday parties in December, and I danced on Christmas for triple pay. The next day, I had a long talk with Prince, and before we hung up, he said, "I'll call you in a few weeks." But the next day he called me and said, "Can you get on a plane tomorrow?" This was something he did from time to time. There were many spur-of-the-moment excursions, starting with that impromptu trip to Switzerland, but this one stands apart in my heart. It was my first visit to Paisley Park.

It irked Prince when people asked him why he stayed in Minnesota or expressed that it was an odd place for a rock star to have a home base. "Music is music. A place is a place," he used to say to his friends, but he'd say to the person interviewing him, "The cold keeps all the bad people away." When I visited,

I finally got the joke. Germany is cold in the winter, but not Minnesota cold. Minnesota cold reaches into your chest by way of your tingling nose and tightens every muscle in your torso. It stabs your little legs. I was trying to be cool and sophisticated, but when I walked out of the terminal building at the Minneapolis- St. Paul airport, I sucked in a deep, freezing breath and screamed all the way to the limo. I was wearing a short skirt and a jacket, which was fine for winter in Wiesbaden. Not so much for Minnesota.

That was my first time in a big limo, so I couldn't keep myself from pushing buttons and exploring the fancy accessories. When I accidentally raised and lowered the window between us and the front seat, the driver asked, "Would you like me to close it?"

"Oh, no. That's okay," I said, looking around for something else to experiment on or play with.

We passed by Paisley Park on the way to Prince's house in Chanhassen. I wasn't prepared for the sheer size of it. I knew the song "Paisley Park," of course, and when I asked Prince what it was about, he told me, "It's my studio where I record and work." This was before the days of Google, so I had no mental picture of it, but I knew it the moment I saw it. It was off by itself, surrounded by rolling slopes and tall fir trees, very different from any other corporate structure I'd ever seen. The white walls and tinted glass soared like an ice sculpture above the snow-covered landscape. Once again, I felt myself consciously separating the enormous reality from the calm, quiet voice of my friend on the phone. I didn't want to lose him in all this.

The driver took a right off the main road onto a long, curving trail. Later, when I lived in Minnesota and worked at Paisley, I used to ride my bike with my little dog Mia in a basket on the handlebars, cruising along without fear that a car might come around the bend. Eventually, neighborhoods started springing up around us, but back then, there was nothing but snow and woods until we came to a guardhouse and a pair of wide gates that slowly swung open for the limo.

Prince's house was repainted a different color on a regular basis, and a new car—whatever was latest and greatest, preferably a BMW—was custom painted to match it. Things would stay whatever flavor he was into for a year or two, and then the whole thing—his whole life, really—would undergo a change of wardrobe. The last week of December 1990, the first time I visited him at the house that would eventually be our home, the exterior was electric blue and rose-hip pink. Two years later, I arrived to find it canary yellow with purple accents. You can see the matching yellow and purple car in the "Sexy M.F." video. When we were married, he had the place redone white and gold, and you can see the matching car in the "Betcha by Golly Wow!" video.

When I lived in this house, I always came and went through the garage, but guests came and went via the big front door. Prince met me in the foyer with a smile and a hug and gave me the grand tour. The living room was woodsy and masculine with a heavy oak staircase and high-beamed ceilings like an upscale log cabin. I'd grown up in modest one-story houses and small military apartments, so to me at that time, it seemed very grand, but on the spectrum of rock star houses I've been in since then, Prince's house in Chanhassen was very much a normal person's house.

In the living room, there was a lavender grand piano that looked warm and well played. Next to it was an enormous Christmas tree with all the typical decorations. In the dining room, linen-covered chairs were placed around a circular table. In the kitchen, the fridge was full of water bottles and meals made by a chef. Everything was in its place—a cookie jar on the counter, a selection of tea and honey bears in the cupboard, a supply of Tostitos that he always kept handy.

Walking down the hallway, his boots made a particularly musical sound on the terra-cotta tiles. There were metal ornaments at the backs of the ankles—a combination of the symbols for male and female—and they jingled like spurs. The distinct sound of his footsteps became so familiar to me; I still hear it occasionally in my dreams.

He took me to the guest room where I would be staying, and it was like the bedroom in *Under the Cherry Moon*—all champagne-colored silk and plush pillows, crystals, and white carpet—exactly what I had dreamed as a kid. I would be using the Jack-and-Jill bathroom between the guest room and his office, which was a serious workspace with a big, mirrored desk. It also had gold leaf and crystals and all the foo foo décor I'd seen in the hotels, along with the harlequins I'd seen in *Purple Rain*.

We went up to his room, which I immediately recognized as the room re-created in the hotels where I'd visited him. It was windowless, but carefully lit in a tasteful, sensual way that could be adjusted for the occasion. There were no windows, so it could be dark during the day. On the heavy console headboard of the bed, there were candles, beads, and more harlequins. The thick carpet, huge bed, fireplace, veils, lava lamps, dandelion lamps—they all made it feel like a genie's haven, so I found it strangely comforting to see that his bathroom was stocked with regular things like toothpaste and mouthwash, but not like a regular guy's bathroom; he had Oil of Olay, fancy soaps, and distinctly feminine perfumes.

He showed me the Wonderland that was his walk-in closet. All his clothes were organized by color, beginning with black and then brown, red, and an amazing array of purple, indigo, and blue. Coordinating shoes were lined up on the floor below, and by this time, I felt we knew each other well enough that I could let my curiosity lead the way.

I chose a pair of black boots, and we both laughed when I had to forcibly jam my foot into one. No Cinderella here. His shoe was a tight fit for me, and I wore a women's size 7. I was usually wearing flats, and most of his shoes had a generous heel, so I didn't realize for a long time that at five feet four, I was actually two inches taller than him. Onstage, his presence loomed larger than life, and in person, he had such power and charm that he somehow occupied the room with a stature that was not small, as if he were bigger on the inside than he was on the outside. Then and now, I can't imagine him being any taller. He was perfect, really. Exactly the right size to be himself.

It was about stance more than height. Something in your spine is different when you wear heels. Whenever I go shopping with Jan or with girlfriends, I stand on my tiptoes. It doesn't matter what you're trying on; it's going to look better. I dance barefoot, but I still dance on my toes, as if I'm wearing invisible heels. Prince was the same way; he always preferred to have a substantial heel to his shoe. He finally started wearing those fuzzy, flat Ugg boots that came into fashion a few years later, but even then he'd still get on his toes when he played guitar.

Our last stop on the tour was downstairs, where

there was a garden-level apartment with its own kitchen and bathroom, where people stayed sometimes. Mama stayed there once when I was having a hard time, but in general, guests were a fairly rare occurrence at Prince's house, and only a bit less rare when it was a home we shared. The apartment was mainly occupied by a pool table and game room, and there was another grand piano. This space was the studio Prince worked in before Paisley Park was built, so all the doors were those heavy wooden studio doors, and some of the walls were still covered with soundproofing. This was where he and Susannah Melvoin, Wendy's twin sister, wrote "Starfish and Coffee" together.

At the time, I just thought the place was very cool. It didn't occur to me until much later that he'd had a lot of women in that house before me. And after me. At least one during me. But that's a matter for the sad woman sitting on the pier, not for the fresh-faced seventeen-year-old. See, people, this is the inconvenience of all lives existing at all times: we cross paths and trip over each other occasionally. I don't know which self to follow, because so many memories—so many versions of myself—existed in this place at different times. I was both a child and a mother in this house, a beloved wife and an unwelcome ghost who haunted the place until he tore it down.

Prince was sensitive to what these walls had

witnessed. Maybe that was the reason for the habitual wardrobe change the house underwent—at least on the outside—every year or two. Right before we got married, he had the entire place revamped to welcome me home. He very carefully and consciously made it *our* home with lavender carpet that I loved and our entwined zodiac signs at the bottom of the stairs. Our family symbol—a combination of his symbol and the letter *M* combined—was mounted on the wall and inscribed on the sinks in the master bathroom. The drawer pulls and closet knobs were fancy gold *M*s that formed a heart. All the furniture was new and reflected a home in which children and Christmas trees and dogs and family would be the natural next step. He spent a lot and paid great attention to detail. When he carried me over the threshold, slung over his shoulder caveman-style, it was like coming into a completely new house. A huge delivery of boxes arrived, and he was very excited to show me.

"It's our china," he told me. It had been specially made with an imprint of his symbol combined with an *M*.

It seemed rather overboard, but it was such a lovely gesture that I hated to point out, "But we never eat at home."

"We will," he said. "I'll make you some eggs." And he did.

After the grand tour, he asked if I wanted to eat.

I was too overwhelmed to imagine eating, but I said, "Sure."

We went to the garage and got into a Jeep Cherokee with deeply tinted windows. I wasn't usually one for tinted windows like this (driving his tinted-out BMW in LA not long after this, I hit a curb and flattened two tires), but he loved driving around in his car, knowing he could see out but no one could see in. It wasn't exactly incognito; everyone in Chanhassen knew it was him, and he'd honk and wave. For a moment, they'd be startled—*Hey, why is this car honking at me?*—and then they'd realize it was him. Who else would be driving around a small Minnesota town in a turquoise or canary yellow BMW?

Instead of going somewhere to eat, we drove around listening to *Diamonds and Pearls*, his first album with New Power Generation, and talking about the music. He took me to Lake Calhoun, which was frozen solid. I'd never seen people walking around on a lake like that. There was an arboretum near his house, so we went there and listened to the whole album again. He drove into Minneapolis to show me the city, which was all decked out with holiday decorations, and then we went back to Paisley Park.

This was the week between Christmas and New Year's, so the building was closed, and there was no one else there when he unlocked the door near the stairway that led to his office. We went to the main lobby, which felt like a cathedral, and visited the white doves, Majesty and Divinity.

"Are they boys or girls?" I asked.

"One of each," he said. "I got them when we were building this place."

His office was like another whole house, and a lot like his office at home. He went there when it got late—or early—and he just needed to close his eyes for a little while before heading back into the studio. The skylights and stained-glass windows filled the place with natural light. The kitchen offered the standard fare: Tostitos, an assortment of Celestial Seasonings teas—mostly the spicy, cinnamon ones, Earl Grey, something with a tiger on the box—and plenty of honey in plastic bears.

He showed me Studio A and Studio B, where music was recorded, and Studio C, which was like a dance studio. We went to the soundstage, where movies and music videos were filmed and tour performances rehearsed, a space taller and wider than any military airplane hangar I'd been in.

"Wow. This is big," I said, and my voice echoed somewhere in the dark high, high overhead.

He didn't work too much that trip, but I could tell he was having a hard time being away from it. I wandered around by myself, exploring for a while, paid another visit to the doves, and played with Paisley, the building cat who'd been there since Paisley Park opened. I went back to the studio to quietly observe as he continued to finesse the music we'd listened to in the car. The jet lag was starting to catch up with me, but I was only there for two days and didn't want to nap away any of my time.

I'd brought music and a belly dancing costume, because it was strange to me that he'd never actually seen me dance. (No, videotape is not the same.) Somewhere between my Wonder Woman turn and the final *clang* of the zills, I felt a shift in the energy of the performance. I'd always danced as an act of personal power, not seduction. This was the first time I was more focused on the person I was dancing for than I was on myself. The sensual undercurrent took me by surprise. I noticed when I stopped that he had taken a pillow from the sofa and was holding it in his lap.

"You should go change," he said.

I went to bed fairly early and woke up in the *Cherry Moon* bed. We made pancakes, and we loafed around a little and then went to the movies. *The Godfather III* was playing, and he was very into the whole *Godfather* saga. He brought me up to speed on the way to the theater. "See, Michael Corleone meets this girl—half Greek, half Sicilian," he told me. "And Apollonia is the most beautiful girl he's ever seen. He's struck by what they call 'The Thunderbolt'—meaning he immediately has this passion for this woman, this longing that only she can satisfy. So he marries her—she's a virgin, and it's a very big deal—and then she gets killed by a car bomb."

"Oh, no!"

"Yeah. And he remarries—Diane Keaton—but she ain't no thunderbolt, and his hunger for revenge ends up destroying the whole family."

"So in *Purple Rain*—that's why you called her Apollonia."

"Originally, I wanted Vanity to do it. She said she wanted a million dollars. I said that wasn't possible, and she said, 'Then I'm not in it.' That was it. Broke my heart. I started watching audition tapes. No. No. No. *Hell* no. Then I get to this one. 'Yes. She's cool.' Opening day we hid under the table at a hotel like little kids. Just got kind of freaked out."

"Why?" I asked.

He shook his head. "It was such...magnitude. But that was a long time ago."

"Seriously," I said. "I was eleven when I saw it."

"Eleven." He made a sound that was slightly pained. "She had to say it."

Our tickets had been purchased ahead of time, and we waited for the lights to go down before we crept to our seats. I was holding our bucket of popcorn in my lap, and as the previews were playing, he dumped a box of something into it.

"Hey! What was that?" I whispered.

"Goobers," he whispered back.

"What are Goobers?"

"They're chocolate-covered peanuts. Don't tell me you never had Goobers."

"I'm a ballerina. My junk food vocabulary is limited to baklava and pancakes."

I scooped up a handful of popcorn with Goobers, and I have never looked back. To this day, when Gia and I go to the movies, I can't help myself. I have to throw Goobers in the popcorn. I don't dump in the whole box of Goobers like he always did, because all that sugar would send Gia bouncing off the walls, but I love how excited she gets when she discovers one.

"Mama! You gave me a Goober!" She squeezes my arm in the dark, and I think of my dear friend and what it means to be hit by The Thunderbolt.

*See the man cry as the city condemns where he
   lives
Memories die but the taxes he'll still have 2
   give...*

Within weeks of Prince's death, the estate announced that Paisley Park would be open to the public as a tourist attraction, and just the other day, I read that Warner Bros. would be releasing the first of many recordings from Prince's infamous "vault" at Paisley Park. This thing actually is a vault, like in a bank, filled with fully mastered music, most of which has never been heard outside the studio. I'm conflicted about this, because I've heard some of the music, and it's amazing. It should be heard by the world. But during his lifetime, he fought so hard to keep it out of the corporate pipeline. He loved the evolving technology that would make it possible for him to sell music—or give it away—directly to fans.

I understood the need to pay the enormous cost of upkeep on Paisley Park, but it bothered me, and I didn't even know what that meant—the "estate." Family, I suppose. Half-siblings. Omarr, whom I came to know over the years, and his sister Tyka, the first person he named when I asked him, "Who are the people you truly love?" But I'd mostly heard Prince speak of his coworkers as family—Sheila E, Morris Day, Wendy and Lisa, and his other bandmates—and I came to think of them as my own extended family as well.

five

The first time I went to prom, I went with a punker who wore a dress. You have to have some kind of weirdness to interest me. We weren't dating, just friends. I think I may have loaned him my eyeliner. The last prom I went to, I went with my friend Papu, a big Hawaiian kid, who was very understanding about the fact that I could be there for only thirty minutes. Just long enough for us to have our picture taken. My parents were waiting outside to take me to a gig. Prince thought this was hilarious.

That last year I lived in Germany, I was the go-to belly dancer in Wiesbaden, Frankfurt, and Mainz. I had friends at school—mostly my chorus and drama people—but I was known as a good girl. I didn't go to games or pep rallies. I didn't even eat lunch at school, because I spent half the school day at the state theater, taking ballet classes that were counted as class hours, which allowed me to graduate a year early. All I wanted to do was dance in Cairo. Only my good friends Stephanie and Allison knew where I'd been over the holidays. I liked keeping a low profile about it. The letters and tapes were deeply personal. I didn't like the idea of being questioned about it. I didn't like the assumptions I knew people would make.

The night of the thirty-minute prom, I was also double booked to dance. The first gig was a slight departure from my usual belly dance/flamenco fusion. This was a full-on flamenco thing—a showcase for belly dancers supporting other belly dancers—which I'd agreed to do months earlier. By the time I realized that prom was that night and my professional certification exam was the next morning, advertising had gone out, and Mama was getting nervous about the time frame. I was the hardest working belly dancer in the show, and she was worried that I'd perform some underprepared dance and not look good for the belly dance community.

She'd always had more of a Spanish flair, so she took an old costume of hers, altered it to fit me—a gorgeous red dress with a red bolero. I had studied and watched the dance but never got into the *zapateo* part of it, but I tried on the outfit the night before prom and loved it. I asked her to let me have the big Spanish *peineta* that women always wear with a huge flower and a *manton*, the lace Spanish shawl. The more stuff I asked for, the more nervous she got.

"When are you planning to rehearse this?" she kept asking.

"I've been visualizing it," I said. "When I'm in bed and working on ballet and talking on the phone."

She did not find this comforting and was anxiously waiting in the car while I did the prom drive-by. On the way to the show, she and Daddy kept trying to talk to me, and I kept saying, "Please! Just be quiet and let me listen to this music. I have to memorize this drum solo."

I love a good drum solo, by the way. Nothing is choreographed, but when I know the drums, I have a basic plan. Nothing excites me more than a live drummer. Not knowing what the other person is going to do creates a tense energy between dancer and drummer, and I love that. I didn't know it then, but this was exactly what would happen when I was onstage with Prince, particularly during his famous after-concert shows, when he'd leave a huge stadium performance and head for some small club where we would all jam our butts off for two hours or more. One night in London, he slayed an extended version of "Peach" for over half an hour while I danced around him like a Turkish darvesh on steroids. When it was over, he spiked his guitar like a football, grabbed my hand, strutted backstage, and just fell out flat, spread-eagled on the floor. He was in ecstasy.

Getting into my costume for the showcase, I trusted the drums to take me where I needed to go, but I was worried about a strained muscle in my foot. One of the male Egyptian belly dancers saw me backstage trying to stretch my feet by stepping on a bottle and asked me what was wrong.

"I've been preparing for a ballet exam," I told him, "doing a lot en pointe."

He said, "I'm Ali. I'm a massage therapist. Let me take a look at it. Maybe I can help."

At first I said no, because I never liked to be touched like that, especially by a man. Even now, a friend will try to gift me a massage—not happening. (But thank you!) In this case, I was desperate, so I sat down, and he took my foot between his hands. Within minutes, the pain was gone. I don't know what he did, but I've never forgotten the experience. It was such a relief, and as the pain disappeared, a fresh infusion of energy replaced the tension I'd been feeling. I finished preparing, putting my hair up and drawing a bold curl on my face. Mama took one look and was more scared than ever, but I laughed and told her, "Go sit down already. It'll be fine."

The moment that music kicked in, I was lost in that energy, and a passion that can't be choreographed took over my body. There was a moment when I caught my mother's eye just as I did a deep backbend and released that updo she was worried about, letting my long hair flow down as I came up. I smiled, because her face was priceless—complete awe at what she was seeing. To this day, she says it's her favorite performance of mine.

People loved it and wanted to know who'd choreo-graphed it. I had to tell them, "No one. And I couldn't repeat it if my life depended on it." It was something that came out in that moment and only that moment. If I tried to replicate it, it would never be the same.

But there was no time to revel in it. I had to get to my regular gig at a local restaurant. After that, I went home exhausted and ate a huge plate of spaghetti, knowing I'd need the carbs to get through the exam the next day.

Along with about fifty other girls in tutus and pointe shoes, I registered for a master class, which was grueling but doable because my ballet teacher was strict and had prepared me well. I warmed up and waited my turn to perform my classical piece. When I finally walked into the room, I had to laugh. It was exactly like *Flashdance*, right down to the long table of grim-looking judges and an old-school turntable off to the side. I put a cassette into the tape player instead, but my finger was trembling just like the girl's was in the movie when I pushed Play.

After I danced, I waited outside with the rest of the girls, expecting someone to come out and tell us to either leave or prepare for the next round. Instead, someone came out and said a list had been posted. Everyone was either really good or really bad. You either had your certificate or you were out. While everyone was freaking out around me, surging for the list, I sat there thinking about the years of stress fractures and no pizza or brownies or going-out nights. I had sacrificed a lot to be a ballerina. Now, for the first time in my life, I was getting scared, because a lot of girls who'd sacrificed and slaved for the same goal were seeing that their best wasn't good enough, and it was heartbreaking.

As the group thinned, I made my way forward and saw my name on a sheet of paper. *Congratulations*, it said in German, *you have passed. No need to do the rest of the segments as the judges could see through your classical routine that you have all the technical work to perform any of them. Best of luck. Please allow a few days for your certificate.* I drove home on cloud nine and ate a cookie to celebrate. When my dad pulled up in the driveway, I ran out and jumped into his arms like a four-year-old. He and Mama were so happy for me. They'd sacrificed for this, too. The certification would keep me in Germany as a professional dancer if I wanted that, but I knew I could make better money in Cairo, and when I was done with Cairo, I'd be able to go anywhere in the world and teach. The dancer's diet is sort of symbolic: As a ballerina, I'd be killing my hunger with tomato juice and coffee, carrots in my pockets at all times, in order to stay stick thin. As a belly dancer, I'd be making bank and eating baklava, trying to maintain an extra fifteen pounds. No brainer.

Prince called that night, and I told him the whole saga.

"This is big," I told him. "Now I can go anywhere as a dancer. I can do anything."

I'd filmed myself practicing all three components of the exam, and unlike the German judges, he wanted to see them all, plus the magical flamenco moment and everything else I was doing. He loved the classical and belly dance best. The music he was sending me was more and more in sync with the rhythm I could dance to, and I started seeing the classical dance moves he was instinctively doing onstage. *Entrechat quatre*— a classical ballet term meaning "interweaving" or "braiding"—is when a dancer jumps up, exchanging feet quickly, *front back front back*. When I noticed him doing that, I said, "Hey, that's ballet! Where did you get that?"

"Baryshnikov," he shrugged. No big deal.

Before graduation, I made a short trip over to the States to visit Jan at the University of Maryland. She was in her element, soaking up college life, hanging out with a nice crowd, and working as a DJ and standup comic. But I knew this wasn't for me. I didn't even bother taking my SATs. In May 1991, I graduated from high school, seventeen going on thirty. I was a lot more grown up than many adults I've known in my life. I'd been running my own business in a pretty big way for several years, traveled all over the world, and studied my craft with diligence and self-discipline. I had done a lot, seen a lot, and been through some pretty intense life experiences.

Legally, however, I was still a minor. Prince seemed to operate on a plane of existence where age didn't matter. He always said he didn't count birthdays because he didn't count days at all, and then he'd add with a sly smile, "That's why I look the same as I did ten years ago." His legal team was not so existential about it. Prince wanted me near, but since I was just seventeen and a half, they drew up a power of attorney document, making Prince my legal guardian for six months. After that, I'd be eighteen, a legal adult. Meanwhile, the document with my father's signature allowed me to travel by myself to LA and Minnesota, work on film and recording projects, and participate in performances at all hours of the day or night. The agreement was pretty open as to what these projects and performances might be, but Prince got on the phone with Daddy and told him, "She'll be safe. You can trust me."

"I know where to find you," said Daddy, and he wasn't completely kidding, but he and Mama had faith in my ability to keep my head on straight. They knew that the opportunity to work with Prince could be a game changer for my career.

I was completely oblivious to all this at the time. This document came as a complete surprise to me just a few weeks ago. Blew my mind a little, to be honest. But maybe it does explain, in part, how protective Prince was in those days. He was careful not to get my hopes up or encourage any expectations on my part. The first time he flew me to LA, he'd mentioned he was doing a music video for "Diamonds and Pearls," but I thought I was just going to be there to hang out like we usually did. That was exciting enough for me. As I flew into LAX from Germany, I remembered flying in for *That's Incredible!*, seeing the Hollywood sign for the first time, knowing with that hazy sixth sense, *I'll be back.*

Prince's security people met me at the airport and said, "Hey, Martha."

"What? Why are you calling me Martha?"

"You're Martha George," they told me. "He wants you on this video, but if they find out you're seventeen, you can't do it. Your dad said it's okay, but there's a union thing and paperwork, so...you're Martha."

Okay, I figured. *I can rock Martha.*

The "Diamonds and Pearls" music video was an elaborate vision that cost a bundle and was being directed by Rebecca Blake, who also directed "Kiss" and "Cream" for Prince. (She'd also done a few music videos with my old heartthrob Luis Miguel.) When I presented myself to her, she said the polite but dismissive things directors say to you at a cattle-call audition you're not nailing. Later Prince told me what she'd said to him: "I don't think she's sexy enough. I don't think she's got that thing."

Hard to hear. But good to know.

"I cannot believe she doesn't see what I see," he said, "but...okay."

He trusted her judgment, and I can't argue with the final results. The music video is a thing of beauty with gorgeous locations, grand pianos, dancers, musicians, children, bubbles, a chase scene—it was a huge, huge production. I was pretty crushed not to be a part of it, but I took it like a professional. It was still thrilling to be in LA, visiting Prince at his house and helping him make breakfast the next morning.

He asked about my parents, and I said, "They broke up again. Sort of."

"How do you sort of break up with your wife?"

"They're still living together, but they're both seeing other people."

"Huh-oh. That don't work."

"They love each other, but together—I don't know. It's a strange relationship. I keep saying, 'Would you guys please, please break up?' I think they're waiting until I leave home, but I can't take the fighting. It's just like when I was a little kid. Arguments and jealousy and...just that lack of respect for each other."

He squeezed my hand. "My parents were like that, too."

He slid eggs off the griddle onto our plates, and

while we ate, he told me a bit about his own battle-field childhood. He told me that when he was around seven years old, his mother came home from a shopping trip one day with her shirt inside out, because she'd been trying on clothes and was in a hurry to get home. His father jumped to the conclusion that she'd been out cheating on him and went ballistic. As he was telling me about the violent scene that unfolded, I could see how deeply it still affected him. You see some allusions to it in *Purple Rain*. You see the house where he grew up witnessing a more vicious—and sometimes violent—version of what I grew up with, but not everything you see in the movie is literally autobiographical. His father didn't have a gun, and his parents split when he was a little boy. His mother remarried, and Prince went to live with his father, but that didn't last long. He was basically on his own when he was twelve.

This was the first of many conversations we had about his father over the years. Before we were married, I asked him, "Will I ever get to meet your dad?"

"I don't know," he said. "We had a falling out."

"About money?" I guessed, because if there was one thing that caused friction between my dad and me, it was money.

But Prince said, "No, it was about music. He kept sending me cassette tapes just pounding on the piano and maybe after an hour, he finally hits three beautiful notes, but I gotta listen to a whole tape of that pound-ing for these three notes? I think he lost it."

At the end of the day, we both loved our parents and saw them for the beautifully flawed people they were. The best we could do was try to understand life from their perspective and be grateful for what they gave us.

"My mom grew up without any affection," I said, "so she's not a very affectionate person, but she's smart and witty and incredibly strong, and she has a strong faith. Daddy's the opposite: emotional, an atheist— which I don't get at all. I'm like, 'How can you think that? Don't tell me you haven't seen any miracles in your life.' It's a soul thing. We have these deep dis-cussions, and he goes with me to almost all my gigs. He's my best buddy, but sometimes—I mean, would you believe he brought his girlfriend along to a Frank-furt gig when I was fifteen? We're on our way, and he stops off to pick her up, and I'm like, 'She's coming? Excuse me?' "

"Ah, nah." He cringed. "That's not right. There's a thing called discretion, man. There's a thing called savoir faire."

"I made her sit in the back. And he had to pay for her drinks."

Prince really cracked up laughing then, and it felt like a win when I was able to really crack him up. He loved to make other people laugh and embraced a good laugh when it was available to him. And this rental house in LA had a good kitchen for laughing. Just the right amount of reverb off the tile backsplash and big windows. We shared many mornings like this in various houses he rented in LA. During the years when we were a couple, every once in a while, when it got unbearably cold in Minnesota, too cold for the good people and the bad, he'd prod me awake and say, "Let's go to LA." California seemed to be full of light and air, and breakfast together felt like the safe haven of love and pancakes neither of us had when we were children.

Prince hated that I was bummed out about not getting cast in the "Diamonds and Pearls" video, so he took me shopping on Melrose Avenue, which back then was a cool street where you could get all the up-and-coming designers. Prior to that day, my only experience of shopping was at the mall: part utilitarian, part social function.

"Trust me," he said, "you don't want to go to the mall with me. Last time I went to a mall, I took half the people with me. Not good. There's screaming and craziness. People get hurt."

His idea of shopping was a "fast and plenty" approach. We drove down Melrose in the limo, and at each place, either a bodyguard would go in first to prepare the store for Prince's arrival or Prince, who was faster than anybody else, would bolt in and out before the people inside knew what was happening. So I followed suit. No time to check price tags. Just scope out the coolest clothes, grab whatever we want, and hand it to his security on our way out.

"Do you like this dress?" he'd ask me, holding up something I wouldn't wear in a million years. My day-to-day clothes were mostly leggings with oversize shirts and maybe a jacket. But wanting to be a team player, I'd say, "I don't know. I think so?" He'd smile and hand it to the security guy. When I really did like something, I didn't have to say a word. All I had to do was smile and he'd hand it over. We laughed at the crazy stuff—bondage bras and leather—but it was a little early for that sort of thing.

There would come a time later on when I would lead these expeditions on my own—and Prince would usually end up wearing the clothes I bought for myself. When I was in the band, Melrose was my go-to place for short skirts, tiny tops, cool boots, and punky sweaters. It was the King's Road of Los Angeles. I became the shopper because when he wasn't wearing custom clothes, he wanted to wear a jacket or stylized pants, and the best styles (and sizes) for him were usually found in the women's department. I got used to buying suits, knowing that he was going to take them for himself and put in shoulder pads or dude them up in some way. He's the only man in the world who was really able to make that work—and work well.

He walked through one shop after another, scooping things off racks—dresses, skirts, sweaters, jackets, and sneakers so I could play basketball with him—and people followed behind us, paying for everything.

"It reminded me of that shopping scene in *Pretty Woman*," I told Jan.

As the limo pulled away from the hotel, taking me back to the airport, I looked over my shoulder crying. Another *Pretty Woman* moment. I felt like that every time I left him, like I was leaving my other half. It was so comfortable to be around him. He could be incredibly funny and had the capacity for such tenderness. He could also be mean, I soon discovered—but so could I, so even *that* was weirdly okay with me. It made him human, and he seemed to like and respect me more when I checked him on it. He had more than enough women putting him on a pedestal. He needed someone who wasn't afraid to tell him the truth and work hard and play hard. I couldn't beat him at basketball, but I could lift him up, and my legs were so strong, I could get a wrestling lock on him and make him say "uncle."

I started making frequent trips to Paisley Park. We recorded "The Max," "Blue Light," and "When God Created Woman" all in one marathon session. I hung out on the soundstage watching the Diamonds and Pearls Tour show coming together. I sat dancer style on a long black sofa in the studio, watching and listening to him work, doing my best not to nod off. When I was in Germany, he called almost every day, and I continued sending him videos. Lisa Bonet was directing a video for him, and after she also declined to cast me, he wrote:

MAYTE!
What a kickin' tape! Ballet is cool, but when u dance like that…SISONd⅄H! Thank u. 👁 keep all your tapes in a little secret section in my house. Only 👁 know where they are.
Believe it or not, Lisa thought u were 2 pretty 4 the part in the video. The girl she picked is tall and strange-looking with short hair. Such is life. But 👁'm sure we'll work 2gether on something. 👁 miss u 2 & hope 2 see u soon!

That summer, I saw the movie *City Slickers* and fell in love with Billy Crystal's rescued calf, Norman. I announced to my dad and everyone else, "I'm not eating beef ever again. I'm going to be a vegetarian."

"What if I make beef?" said Daddy.

"Make it. I'm not eating it."

I felt myself taking ownership of my life in big and small ways. When it came time for my regular visit to Madame Abla, I told Prince, "I think I'll stay in Cairo for three months or so. I need to gain some weight and improve my Arabic and get my next contract hooked up."

"Wait a second," he said. "You're going to Egypt? Can I send a film crew with you?"

Without asking questions, I said, "Sure." I didn't know it at the time, but he was already envisioning a compilation of music videos that would become *3 Chains o' Gold*—his operatic answer to "Bohemian Rhapsody"—and all he really knew about it himself was that it had something to do with me and what I was doing as a dancer and the story all this was beginning to tell inside his head. All this time, he'd been sampling from the tapes I sent, beginning with me as a little girl with a sword on my head on *That's Incredible!* He didn't know exactly what would happen if he sent Randee St. Nicholas and a well-equipped crew of a dozen or so people with me, but he knew it would be something beautiful.

"Just do what you do," he told us, and that turned out to be the most brilliant direction he could have given.

Randee went everywhere with me, asking a million questions about the people and the pyramids and the art of belly dancing. We hired someone from the hotel to take us out of the city, but the guy turned out to be a bit shady and made off with the passports of everyone on the crew. As they followed me around Egypt—my

Egypt, not the one you get from the double-decker tour bus—Randee picked up on how this place had always fed my soul, even before I understood what that meant.

She put me in a little black jumper Prince had bought for me that day on Melrose, added a sheer white veil, and had me dance on the pyramids when no one was around. (That footage ended up in "Damn U.") She asked an old man to come over and talk to me, and before she started shooting, she said, "Pretend he's telling you something that breaks your heart." The moment I heard his voice, tears started coursing down my cheeks. We just kept creating these moments and images and sending them to Prince, who was completely open to whatever we sent. He'd already sent me early versions of "7," but for the most part, we didn't know what our work was inspiring on his end. We had as much faith in him as he had in us.

We'd been hearing disturbing rumors about someone breaking into the hotel rooms of American women, robbing and raping them. One night, I was getting ready for bed, and a man walked into my room. I was seriously shaken up about this later, but in the moment, I felt only a rush of adrenaline—*oh hell no!*—and I whipped out my sword. The astonished guy took off running, and I went after him. Someone from the crew opened her door when she heard the noise. "I just remember you chasing him down the hall," she said to me recently, and she sounded kind of astonished by it herself.

If you listen closely to "7," you hear the swooping sound of a sword cutting the air, and you see me in the video, brandishing my sword with both hands on the hilt. I love that stance in contrast to the way I am when the sword is balanced on my head, turned by just the tip of my finger. It's a fitting symbol of a woman's great power, I think. There's the posture, the balancing act, but there's also a sharp blade of badass when needed.

In November 1992, I turned eighteen. I was officially my own woman, and it felt good. Prince was working hard to prepare the Diamonds and Pearls show, trying not to be distracted by the Arabic vibe and Egyptian imagery that seemed to be speaking to him.

"My heart's already there," he told me, "but my head has to do this thing right now."

Ideas for "7" and "The Sacrifice of Victor" were taking shape but would have to wait for his full attention. This was the way he always worked. That's how he was able to shrug it off when something didn't sell as well as he'd hoped or the critics trashed him; by the time that particular thing was released to the public, he was already on to the next thing creatively. He wanted me to be on call, essentially, so I'd be close by when he did have an opportunity to work on the new stuff, and to be totally honest, he wanted me to be available to hang out more often, so he asked me to come to Paisley Park and stay for a while.

I didn't expect to stay at his house. It was semi-cool for a female friend to visit now and then, but not to camp there on an ongoing basis. At first, I stayed at the Sofitel, then they moved me to a nice little prairie house at the Country Suites, but I couldn't even make a cup of tea there, so they got me an apartment and rented furniture.

I asked his assistant, "How long is he expecting me to stay?"

"I don't know," said the assistant, and handed me the key.

It was an odd arrangement, and I knew how it probably looked from the outside.

"What are you doing there?" Jan asked, and I didn't have a solid answer.

I was determined, personally and professionally, not to miss a call from Prince, but he always seemed to hit me up when I was either in the shower or taking out the trash. I'd come back and see that I'd missed a call from a Paisley Park number and I'd scream. I felt like a prisoner, waiting for those phone calls, and I hated that, so I bought a long phone cord I could stretch all the way out the door while I dodged down the hall with the garbage. That wasn't enough, so I dipped into my dancing money and bought a cell phone, which was not a small expense back then. The bill was insane, but essential to my sanity. Some days when I felt like I was about to lose my mind, I'd go into Minneapolis and take a ballet class or go to the mall and smell perfumes.

I pride myself on my nose, by the way. I have a knack for matching the perfect scent to the right person, and not long after this, I was buying all of Prince's perfume (Dune, Samsara, Carolina Herrera, and Yves Saint Laurent) and cosmetics (all MAC, until he started stealing my Dior mascara). He loved the essential oils I brought from Egypt. These days my favorite is rose oil with vanilla. He would have happily stolen that.

When he called, no matter what I was doing, I acted like I was doing nothing.

But he always knew. "Where are you?"

"Ballet."

"Cool. I just wanted to make sure you're okay."

In January, he sent me to New York to do a photo shoot and press training.

"Why me?" I asked.

"You're the princess," he said. "I want you to be that princess."

And he wasn't saying it in a method acting "if you see it, you can be it" kind of way. He wanted me to tell people that I was a princess from Cairo, because he was certain that, in a previous life, I had been one, and at this moment, that version of me was more real to him than any other.

"But what if they ask—"

"Just smile," he said. "They won't be able to breathe."

Something had been shifting in our relationship since I became my newly emancipated self. I was an interesting adult instead of a charming kid. Our odd little friendship deepened with every long conversation. The connection was becoming more personal. A different kind of flirtation began to go both ways. I was his muse of the moment, and he was becoming more obvious about the things he was trying to communicate to me through his music.

He realized that she was new to love, naïve in every way, he wrote in "The Morning Papers." *That's why he had to wait.*

Speaking for myself, I was in love, but I was no fool. I was driving a rental car and living with rented furniture. After a few months, I asked him, "Am I ever going home?"

"Going home?" he said, genuinely surprised. "But...you're in the band."

"I need to go back," I said uncomfortably. "I can come back if you want, but I feel weird not working and being able to buy stuff I need."

Being part of the New Power Generation was an exciting concept, but apparently it hadn't crossed his mind that while these things I was doing for him were fun, creative things I loved doing—other people actually *paid* me to dance for them. At Paisley Park, I wasn't getting paid; I was just…I didn't know *what* I was.

"I hear you talk about girls wanting money from you and agents calling and 'getting rates,'" I said. "I'm not that person. I need to know that you know that. I was never that person with my parents. Why would I start being that person now? If that's what it's about, then I'd rather go back to Germany. I have my work visa, and I can get another contract in Cairo."

"But you're going on tour."

"Am I?"

"Yes," he said. "We just haven't gotten to that part of the show yet. Why do you think you're here?"

"I honestly have no idea."

The next day, someone came from administration with paperwork to put me on the payroll. My heart sank. I was to receive a salary of $300 a week. I could make more money belly dancing for one night than I would get paid for a month at Paisley Park.

Okay…suck it up, I told myself. My rent was being paid, and I still had a healthy stash of money in my American checking account. I was determined to prove my worth, stick out the tour, and do my best until I couldn't any longer, and after that, Egypt would still be there. I knew it wasn't the most financially prudent decision I've ever made, but by this time there was no use denying my strong feelings for this man. I didn't really expect that to go anywhere; I just wanted to hang out with him as long as it felt right.

But just to reality check myself, I called Daddy and asked him what he thought.

This was the first time he'd seen me not know how to deal with a situation, so he flew over to see me a few weeks later. As I came out to greet him, he took my picture, and I rushed over to scold him. Taking pictures at Prince's home and studio was simply *not* done. I had a Polaroid when I was pregnant, because I wanted to take pictures of my blossoming belly, but for years, there was almost a phobia of cameras in Paisley Park. Truthfully, there was something liberating about knowing there were no cameras around. There was also something very sad and lonely about it. Given the choice, I'd have to say I prefer the selfie-obsessed culture of connection that lets me see the people I love and share photos of the camera-loving puppies I rescue. I'm that mommy who Instagrams every finger painting and will archive every first day of school from kindergarten through college on Facebook Memories.

"Your dad got a little crazy when he talked to my manager," Prince told me later.

"Oh, no..."

"I think he must have read a book about the music business on the flight over."

"Oh, dear…"

He told me the over-the-top demands my father had tried to float. Daddy even had the nerve to ask for a point on the records, which was like asking for 20 percent of Prince's cut. I about fainted, but Prince laughed and said, "Don't worry. Parents can be like that. I get it. He sees me writing songs about you, and he wants to make sure you're not being taken advantage of."

I didn't get a raise, but I was grateful that my dad got to see where I worked and hadn't done anything to screw it up. I called Mama and said, "I need you to send me my things. I'm going to stay for a while."

The New Power Generation—also known as NPG—was a movable feast of incredibly talented people who functioned as Prince's backup band and the core of his filmmaking talent pool from 1990 until 2013. There was never really a job opening in NPG; if Prince saw something that intrigued him, he found a way to bring it into the NPG experience. If he sensed someone would be better off somewhere else, he cut them loose—even if the person was himself.

When I became part of the group in 1994, NPG was a fairly new development, but they'd found a groove that worked for them. Now here I came—a solo performer who'd always done whatever I wanted to do—and no one quite knew where I was meant to fit in. We didn't pal around a lot while we were rehearsing for the Diamonds and Pearls Tour, but we bonded onstage and became a unit that Prince accurately referred to as family.

The drummer, Michael Bland, was a musical genius with perfect pitch, as was Sonny T. Prince would test Michael on it, and I never heard him miss. Sometimes I'd get on the bus and grunt some discordant noise, trying to stump him, and without fail he'd tilt his head to the side and nail it. "I'd call that a C sharp. Or an elephant fart. One or the other."

Tommy Barbarella, named after the Jane Fonda movie, played keyboards. Also hair. His hair was long and wavy and key to his showmanship. I'm amazed he didn't rupture a disc in his neck flipping and swooshing it. Tommy is also a musical genius. There was a lot of that going around at Paisley Park. During my time with NPG, he was usually shredding the keytar, which is kind of like the love child of a keyboard and a guitar, also known as the Purpleaxxe, which was actually invented and patented by Prince. (Fun fact!)

Rosie Gaines was still playing keyboards and contributing vocals that moved ceilings and walls. Sonny T. played bass, Levi Seacer played guitar, and there was a horn section. I hate to make it sound like "a movie star...and the rest," but so many people came and went over the years, I can't begin to list them all here, even if I did remember all their names. I will say that every one of them was unique and brilliant. There was never a member of NPG who failed to blow my mind in some way.

In Prince's mind, there was never a hard line between the visual and the musical; it was all one. We all came together—dancer, drummer, keyboard, lights—to transport the audience into an experience that was already a reality inside Prince's head. I think that's part of the chemistry that made him a megastar; he brought all this game along with his musical genius at the perfect moment in music history—the moment when "video killed the radio star."

All of which is to say, Prince saw his dancers as part of the band. He always talked about the impression James Brown's backup dancers made on him that time his stepfather lifted him up onto the stage.

"On my way out," he said, "I saw some of the finest dancing girls I've ever seen in my life. I respected that. He influenced me by his control over his group. His dancing girls. His apples and his oranges."

I think a lot of people heard that in some sexual way—like the dancers were his harem or something—but Prince's dancers were more likely to be men. Way before I entered the scene, during the shooting of *Purple Rain*, Prince walked into the bathroom and found Tony, Damon, and Kirk breakdancing on the tile floor. He was so impressed, he highlighted them in the movie (look for them up in the balcony during "The Bird"), and the dancing beast TDK (aka The

Game Boyz) was born. For the next ten years, they toured with Prince, did music videos, and contributed a lot to the general fun and mayhem that went on.

Lori Elle and Robia LaMorte, aka Diamond and Pearl, were Prince's mascots at that moment. They were on the *Diamonds and Pearls* album cover and featured heavily in the touring show. It didn't take long for me to wise up to the fact that Lori and Prince were romantically involved.

We did the music video for "The Max" with me belly dancing with my sword on top of the piano, and then we produced a commercial—"Introducing Mayte"—and we continued rehearsing for the tour. This was such a blast for me. I loved being part of that energy that had taken my breath away when I saw that very first show in Barcelona, but there was a bit of an adjustment period.

I always wore bright red lipstick, because (little dancer secret) it provided a focal point that helped me spot myself in the mirror, and I always showed up stylish and put together, because that's just me. But on one off day I arrived wearing sweatpants, and Prince made me go home and change. I was annoyed and humiliated, but he knew how to get me laughing again when I came back in spandex. I did understand where he was coming from. He never left the house unless he was done up pretty.

"Marilyn Monroe never left the house without full

makeup," he told me, as if no other explanation was needed.

Sneakers were for basketball, period. He always showed up for rehearsal in high heels, makeup, good hair—the works. There were no jeans, ever, around Paisley Park in my era. He wore a jean jacket on "Sign o' the Times," and I tried to give him a hard time about it, but he said, "That's custom. That's different."

Bottom line: You never ever saw him looking wrong. Knowing this, I felt a cold shiver down my spine when I read in the Minneapolis *StarTribune* that when his body was found in the elevator at Paisley Park, "Prince was wearing a black shirt and pants—both were on backward—and his socks were inside-out."

This made no sense to me. The sheer irony of it broke my heart all over again.

six

The Diamonds and Pearls Tour was a great introduction to touring life for me. Even though I was in only a few numbers, I was on the soundstage for every rehearsal, soaking in everything I could learn. It was fun. We were doing what we loved. I never woke up saying, "Oh, God, we gotta go to rehearsal." I did get lonely, though, when Prince was gone out of town or too busy to hang out, and we hadn't quite figured out my role in the whole Paisley universe, so I had a lot of downtime.

I loved coming and going from Paisley Park every day. Rehearsals for the tour were in full swing, and in the studio, Carmen Electra was working on an album. Prince went to LA for a few days to produce something for someone, and before he left he suggested that Carmen and I hang out while he was gone. Carmen hit me up to go see a movie. I was surprised to learn that she was nineteen, only a year older than me.

She picked me up in Prince's black-on-black Jeep Cherokee with the severely tinted windows, and as we drove to the movie theater, she said, "Every time I get in this car, people honk at me. I don't know why."

I glanced at the dashboard. "Maybe it's because your brights are on."

I reached over and clicked the headlights to low beam, and she giggled.

"Oh my God! I was wondering what that was."

We both got a huge laugh out of that and ended up having a great time. After the movies, we drank tea in my apartment, and the conversation was eye-opening. I hadn't realized that she and Prince had a thing, and it had never occurred to me before how challenging it was to be his girlfriend. He traveled constantly and worked insane hours. His girlfriend couldn't call him. Didn't even have his number. He called. You answered. But he was good about checking in with people and had an uncanny sense of timing—at least he did in my experience.

When he called me later that evening, I asked him, "Are you dating Carmen?"

"No, no. She has a crush on me," he said. He was so good at this. One could easily take a very cynical view of the way he was with women, but for the most part, you gotta admit, the women weren't complaining.

It was a one-time hang with Carmen. I didn't see much of her after that. She was sent off on tour to promote her album, even though the reviews weren't great. Something I eventually learned: Prince's top girlfriend was always in Minneapolis. When you came to Minneapolis, you were the girl on her way in. When you left Minneapolis, you were the girl on her way out.

This would have been a valuable piece of information for me to keep in my own hip pocket.

My first show with Prince was at the Tokyo Dome in April 1992. I was incredibly grateful and excited to be part of it. Before the show started, I peeked out at the Jumbotron. Playing on a continuous loop were ads for Carmen Electra's forthcoming album and Prince's single "Sweet Baby," then the symbol that would later become his name landed on the screen, followed by "Introducing Mayte," with footage of me walking in Cairo.

Before every performance of New Power Generation—or any version of Prince that I was around—we all gathered in his dressing room to pray. No matter what else was happening, we came together and joined hands. He'd ask for God's hand on us, that He would give us strength and send angels to protect us from injury, that the Holy Spirit would lift up the music, that the audience would be blessed and happy and safe from harm. It was a powerful ritual, centering, and we never took the stage without it.

The Tokyo Dome was filled almost to capacity— an audience of forty-eight thousand—and the torrent of energy that came from the crowd made me feel like a fork in a light socket. I'd spent two-thirds of my life onstage, but this was a whole new level of performance high. The show started with a stirring rendition of "Take My Hand, Precious Lord" and ended with "Peter Gunn" and visited some of his hugest hits along the way. For two hours, Prince sang, danced, shredded guitars, and played the piano, when he wasn't dancing on top of it or leaping off it to land in splits. He knew how to read the crowd, and he gave everything, which made all of us want to give everything right along with him.

I started the show out of sight below the huge love symbol set piece that rose up in the air to reveal me standing there in my belly dancing outfit made by Madame Abla. Wardrobe made Prince a yellow and purple outfit to match it. Both were gorgeous one-of-a-kind creations, but his could be dry cleaned. Because of the hand beading on mine, it required special care. So they both got progressively more shopworn, but mine was getting seriously ripe as the tour went on.

One night as we headed for the stage, he said, "Getting sick of that outfit yet?"

"It could walk out there on its own," I said. "I could be taking a nap."

He laughed and nudged me, elbow to elbow. "You're funny."

Every night, I'd feel a rush of adrenalin as the giant symbol set piece lifted up over me and the roar of the crowd hit me like a hurricane. I danced to "Thunder," and then I dodged offstage for a quick change to a chiffon dress with ballerina tights and pointe shoes while the roadies whipped down a piece of Marley flooring for me to dance on. I danced to "Diamonds and Pearls" and then I had forty-five minutes to change again, touch up my makeup, drink some water, and get back onstage for "Cream."

We were in Japan for a week, and while we were there, we filmed "The Continental" music video, which has footage from the Cairo trip with Randee along with live concert footage from the Tokyo Dome, some B-roll shot on the bullet train in Japan, and a whole lot of bedroom footage I had nothing to do with. Many of his music videos came together in this sort of collage, which is why we never questioned dressing up or standing on a bridge or riding around on a carousel. I don't think he knew himself when a lot of these images might come in handy; he just knew they would. If you watch the "Sweet Baby" video, you see me walking around Minneapolis, riding a camel across the desert in front of the Great Pyramids, and goofing around on a carousel with Prince, but it all makes sense somehow in the story of a girl going out into the world to find herself.

After Tokyo, we went to Australia and did fourteen shows in twenty days. We had a two-week break and then hit Europe—Belgium, the Netherlands,

Germany, Ireland, England, Scotland, back to Germany and the Netherlands, and then France. Somewhere after Brisbane, they all started to blur together, and I started getting the standard tour jokes about not knowing what city you're in or even what day it is. The tour manager would usually remind Prince before he went out onstage, but every once in a while, he'd say something like, "You look so fine, Copenhagen!" and the tour manager would be in the background yelling, "Ghent! We're in Ghent!"

Touring at that level requires tremendous endurance, speed. The one thing that kept us going was the music. We'd look at each other, and we'd be in the zone. That all went out the window when we got off-stage two hours later, dizzy from hunger and dehydration. My head was reeling. *What just happened? How long did we perform?* We'd stumble back onto the bus and wait to see if there was an aftershow, which would mean another two hours onstage.

We could tell there was going to be an aftershow if the sound people rented extra equipment, because the equipment from the show would have to be boxed up immediately and sent on to the next city. Extra equipment meant we were gearing up for a second shift. Sometimes we all went along to these aftershows. Sometimes he just wanted me to come and dance while he played guitar. Sometimes he'd go by himself, and I'd get the call at five in the morning to come over and see what he did. We'd sit with our feet up, munching popcorn and watching the videotape on the roadie case like we did when I was sixteen. We'd fall asleep at seven or eight and wake up a few hours later to do it all again.

There wasn't much downtime. We'd travel, get to the hotel, head to the stadium, go to a dressing room—always a familiar place, thanks to the foo foo elves—then do the show, do the aftershow, crash for a few hours, and travel again. Huge eighteen-wheelers hauled the set and gear. There were three buses: one for crew, one for the band, and one for Prince. I was officially on board the band bus, but I often traveled with Prince. It was comfortable and easy when we were together, but the fact that we were close put some distance between me and the rest of the band. When the tour started, the dancers were already there, doing this whole thing that he created and everyone liked. When it was clear that I was not leaving, people started questioning why I was there. I was questioning it myself!

As the tour headed across Europe, the German producer at that little record label in Frankfurt (*toooo dramatic*, remember?), caught wind of the fact that little ol' Mayte was now onstage with Prince, and they quickly released the single I'd made when I was fifteen. They didn't ask my permission, and they certainly didn't send me any money. I didn't even know about it until some members of the band got hold of it and started playing it in the hotel hallway one night, singing along at top volume.

"Too dramatic! I don't know why; it's just the way that I am!"

Hilarious. I couldn't deny it.

Less amusing was the fact that I was now touring with the biggest rock star in the world, my first single was out there getting airplay, and the janitor at the record label made more money than I did.

One morning in Australia, I went for pancakes with a male band member. Back at the hotel, I saw I'd missed several calls from Prince.

"Where have you been?" he asked when he finally got hold of me.

"Eating some pancakes."

"With a guy?"

"No, just—"

"With who?"

I told him.

"That sounds like a guy."

"Yeah, but not like—wait a minute."

I didn't understand what he was getting at. I wasn't his girlfriend, and even if I was... But that didn't matter. He was displeased, and people around him, including me, wanted him to be pleased. I could see this poor guy sweating like there was a hammer over his head, even though he'd done nothing wrong. Not surprisingly, no one wanted to hang out with me or even talk to me after that.

The hotels were booked on the ABC system: Artist (something swank with a presidential suite), Band (something less swank but still upscale), Crew (something budget conscious and close to the venue). I stayed in the same hotel as the band, but Prince would call me sometimes to come and hang out with him. I'd go over to the Artist hotel and watch movies and talk and laugh and make him laugh until I was tired, and then I'd ask one of his security people to take me back to the Band hotel.

One night as I was on my way back to my room (I won't even pretend to know what city we were in), I passed a room where the door was ajar, and some of the people from the band were inside talking and laughing. I stood still, close to the wall, listening to the jumbled bits and pieces of the conversation.

What's this belly dance thing he's got going on? Why is she here?

I couldn't tell who was saying what in the mix of male and female voices, but I could tell they were talking about me. I suddenly felt profoundly stupid with my Wonder Woman turn and my ballet work ethic. When the music is my music, I'm dancing it, but there was very little of my music in this show. I was in only two or three numbers. He had me here so I wouldn't go to Cairo. And somehow I was the last person to know it. He kept talking to me about "7," saying, "I'm already there, but I have to do this."

…and I was like, oh my God, she stuffs her bra!

My jaw dropped. Seriously? Diamond and Pearl turn out to be middle school mean girls? They were laughing at me. And sadly, I didn't have my sword handy.

"Mayte…" One of the horn players passed by on the way to his room. I walked quickly toward my room, and he hurried along with me. "What up? Why are you crying?"

"I just heard what everyone's been saying about me."

"No. They didn't mean it like that."

"Yeah, right." I went into my room and shut the door.

Prince called me a little while later, and he could tell I was upset. I didn't volunteer the story right away, but he nudged for it in a way that made me feel like I was gossiping with a girlfriend rather than ratting out my coworkers.

"What exactly did they say?" he asked. I was embarrassed and didn't want to tell him, but he said, "Don't make me fish for it. Just tell me."

"They said…they said I stuffed my bra."

He cracked up laughing. "So?"

"Yeah. Hilarious. Because I didn't get tortured enough in sixth grade."

"Are you laughing or crying right now?"

"Both."

"Stop crying," he said. "They know their time is limited. I've moved on."

Not long after that, while I was still trying to make sense of what I was to him and where I fit in, he wrote to me:

> *Our souls are the same. But our flesh is different. If we trip on things—material and worldly—then we will always trip on these things. One of the main reasons 👁 love and worship u is because u don't have a history. And what's more beautiful is that u don't desire one. 👁 can't begin 2 tell you how many women are jealous of u because they know u're a virgin. They don't want u around because they feel less than u. Their souls aren't advanced enough 2 know that deep inside—beneath their 'history'—we are all the same. Anytime someone 'tripped' on your presence was because of jealousy or fear. U had something they wanted. And whenever u 'tripped' with them—that's when u were unhappy.*

My relationship with Prince during the Diamonds and Pearls Tour quickly became a lot more stressful than the giggling phone calls we shared while I was living in Germany, living on my own terms and making bank as a belly dancer.

Understandably, he wanted everyone to look the way they did in rehearsal. That was the vision, and it needed to stay that way throughout the tour—as you would expect in any touring show. Costumes have to fit the same way at the end as they did at the beginning, which was easy for him because he was working up a sweat for 100 minutes plus the aftershow several times a week. I started to feel subtle changes in my body, because I'd stopped taking hours of ballet every day and danced only a few numbers in the show. I had access to a gym, but I never went, because my cell phone was useless in Australia and Japan, so I was glued to the hotel room phone waiting for him to call me. I was still in good form, but without the daily workout, I had to activate ballerina diet mode, eating leaves while Prince ordered fettuccini Alfredo and ate it standing up.

My makeup artist at that time had a fixation with whipped cream and soda and cookies, which she kept next to her station. Prince never walked into makeup—ever—because he had his own setup in his dressing room, but one night while I was getting my makeup done, there he was. Everyone was silently freaking out, standing very straight, trying to be cool. He had come in to see me, but the look on his face changed as he approached the station where I was sitting.

He eyed the whipped cream and said, "Is that yours?"

I would not have ratted this girl out, but to her credit, she stepped up and said, "No, no, no. That's mine, sir."

He looked at me skeptically.

"I'm not eating it," I said.

He left without saying anything else. Twenty minutes later, the tour accountant came in and said, "I'm so sorry. I'm embarrassed to say this, but I have to dock your pay this week."

I don't remember if I was even able to form the word *"What?"*

"I know. I can't believe it," he said. "In twenty years, I've never been asked to do this, but...it's not my call."

I went back to the dressing room I shared with Lori and Robia, raging and crying. "I'm not going to let him humiliate me like that! I'm not putting up with it!"

They seemed shocked, but not because my pay was being docked; I think they were appalled that any girl would talk smack about Prince. As word got around, I did get some sympathy from Rosie, but everyone else kept their distance. I had no money to call Mama, and this made me feel even farther from home.

The ballerina in me took control. I pulled myself together and went out and did "Thunder" and "Diamonds and Pearls" and then went back to the dressing room for a moment alone while the girls were dancing onstage. I put on my next costume and went to the side stage, out of sight from the crowd, and danced there for the rest of the show. Sometimes I did ballet barre, sometimes belly dancing. I'd look over once in a while and catch him watching me. He'd smile. I ignored him, thinking, *I hate you right now.*

I hadn't eaten a decent meal in three days, but I was dancing, and I was dancing for myself, which felt good. This became my regular workout night after night, and it didn't take long for my body to regain its rock-hard, quarter-flipping tone. What I didn't know at the time was that this was the best thing I could have done to train for what lay ahead. It took a few days for me to get over the humiliation, and he was wise enough to give me some space. The next time he called me to come to his room and hang out, he was fishing to see if I was upset about it.

"Did the accountant talk to you?" he asked.

I said something like, "Yep. Don't worry about it."

I wasn't about to argue with him, but I swore to myself that I would never let him or anyone else ever make me feel that way about my body again.

The funny thing is, later on when I was pregnant, I gained eighty pounds, growing more gigantic by the day, because I was being careful about exercise and retaining a lot of water. My husband never said a word about my body except to tell me, "You're beautiful."

The tour ended, and we all went our separate ways.

Another hazard of the touring life: proximity burn. We were ready to take a break from all that togetherness. Prince went back to Paisley Park. I went to visit my parents, and when I returned to Minnesota, someone from administration called me into the office and told me, "Now that the tour is over, you'll be taking over the rent on the apartment."

This floored me. I was still making $300 a week, and between the phone bills and body makeup—not to mention frivolous expenditures like food, utilities, transportation, and taxes—my healthy stash of dancing money had dwindled to almost nothing. For the first time since I was eight years old, I had no money.

"Come home," said Mama. "You can still go to Cairo."

"The thing is..." I didn't know how to explain this thing that was evolving between my dear friend and me.

My employer, I had to keep reminding myself.

We weren't exactly dating during the tour; we went out almost every night with forty-eight thousand other people. But we had become more than friends. There was gossip and crosstalk about it, partly because he came into a rehearsal one day when Carmen was there, and he shook my hand. Prince didn't shake hands with people, and he hated it when people tried to shake hands with him. He couldn't afford to collect germs and get sick, but more important, his hands were his instruments. He felt naturally protective of them. Everyone in Prince's inner circle knew this, so when he offered me his hand, it meant he felt the need to touch me, and the rumors started rumbling.

He never volunteered any information about where things stood with the other women in his life, and I didn't ask. There was a sort of shorthand: If a girl had a bodyguard, that meant, *Don't talk to her. Don't look at her. She's mine.* So Carmen had a bodyguard before the tour. And now suddenly I had a bodyguard, too. I didn't press him for answers, but I didn't jump into bed with him, either. We did more than shake hands, but there was a line neither of us was ready to cross.

Sexual chemistry was a huge part of Prince's creative force, and it was a place he'd retreated to at the most painful moments in his life. I understand what he meant when he talked about a person's "history," and I'm glad that mine began with him. I wish his had ended with me—and he did try, I think—but that didn't happen. Making peace with what did happen is an ongoing process.

During the "Most Beautiful Girl" days, after we'd become intimate but before we were engaged, Prince wrote to me:

Mayte,
👁've never wanted 2 know someone 4 the rest of my life... "👁 want to know u 4 the rest of my

life!" 👁've never hated to see anyone cry before...
"👁 hate 2 see u cry!"... U are a child of God—an
angel, and 👁 worship you! 👁 thank him 4 u—
always!... 👁 didn't meet u by chance. 👁 don't
live day 2 day. 👁 try 2 see the future. It gives me
hope. 👁've never wanted 2 talk about babies. "👁
want 2 talk about babies with u!" If u frown at
me—u will frown at your babies. Beautiful people
are a dime a dozen. Flesh. 👁 don't want 2 watch
them grow old. "👁 want 2 watch you grow old."
It's my destiny. 👁 have no choice. 👁 only have u.
Minneapolis is my home. 👁 brought u here 2 live
with me. This is your destiny. Until u choose oth-
erwise. And u will have 2 leave me, because I will
never leave you.

👁 will never leave u. 👁 will never leave u. 👁
will never leave u. 👁 will never leave u. 👁 will
never leave u. 👁 will never leave u. 👁 will never
leave u. 👁 will never leave u. 👁 will never leave
u. 👁 will never leave u. 👁 will never leave u. 👁
will never leave u. 👁 will never leave u. 👁 will
never leave u. 👁 will never leave u. 👁 will never
leave u.

As he repeats these words over and over on the last
page of the letter, his perfect handwriting becomes
larger and wilder, as if he's trying to write in the middle of an earthquake.

Toward the end of our marriage, I kept that letter among the things I treasured most. I needed those words of commitment and passion from him, and he was no longer able to speak them. One day, I saw him walk over to a girl and shake her hand. And I knew.

Let's just be straight up about it: he had a lot of women, and a few of them were very important to him. He had little respect for certain girls, but they had their role in his life, and they used him as much as he used them. Welcome to rock and roll. The thing is, he could make any girl feel like a princess—for a moment, anyway. A perk of his creative genius, I suppose.

Prince did have tremendous respect for the women with whom he collaborated. Creative chemistry is a powerful thing. Romantic relationships were bound to grow out of some of those collaborations, and I think it made him genuinely sad when those relationships didn't end well. As for me, I was his wife and the mother of his child. What we had was unique, and I cherish it. I bear no other women in his life any ill will. I worship Sheila E; she's a golden goddess. It never occurred to me to be jealous of Apollonia because when she had her brief relationship with Prince, I was just a little kid. My feelings about Manuela are more complex, but she's apologized. I said to her, "If it wasn't you, it would have been someone else." But the pain is there.

There was a post-apocalyptic moment right after Prince's death when we were all kind to one another, but it didn't take long for the side-eyes and not-so-subtle digs to pop up on Facebook and Twitter. I deliberately do not engage with any of that. I'd rather be like Michelle Obama: when they go low, I go high. I never wanted to be part of that mix back in the day, and I certainly don't want to be part of it now. When I hear one of his old flames say, "I feel like his widow," I'm sad for her, because in so many ways that matter, I feel like he's still with me.

seven

The last dress Madame Abla made for me before she died was a sheer coal-black gown with gold coins. Each coin was sewn on by hand and perfectly placed so they jingled with a soft, eerie music like distant wind chimes when I danced. When Prince saw it, he loved it so much, he had the wardrobe people call up Madame Abla. She sent them some extra coins, and they made a jacket for him in the exact same style. Usually when I arrived at work, I went in through the back, up the elevator, and through the kitchen to his office, so I was surprised when he told me to meet him in front of Paisley. I'd been feeling a little bummed because he hadn't called me for a day or two. My heart turned over when I saw him open the door to give me a big hug, proudly wearing the jacket.

"Nice." I jingled his sleeve.

He kissed me and said, "Yeah, I know. Some hot belly dancer was wearing a dress like this, so I had to have a matching jacket."

Madame Abla's dress can be seen in *3 Chains o'*

Gold, an ambitious collection of music videos that come together in one film, directed by Randee St. Nicholas, Paris Patton, and Prince. The songs became the ♀ album, and the story about a great love affair between Prince and Egyptian Princess Mayte was spun off in a comic book. Woven through the film and its music are all the elements that occupied his mind in that moment: an enhanced form of story-telling that was operatic and held nothing back, the idea of one soul being born into the same circle again and again, his growing fascination with the sound and style of Egypt, and his growing fascination with me.

Before Prince was in love with me, he was in love with the idea that we'd known each other in previous lifetimes. He loved that I was completely open to that idea and willing to spend hours with him, imagining in rich detail the joys and heartbreaks, the births and deaths, and the ultimate meanings of our past lives. One result of all that was *3 Chains o' Gold.* Another result was everything that's happened in my life since.

The basic plot of *3 Chains o' Gold* begins with the assassination of Mayte's father. Convinced that only Prince can protect her and her three sacred chains of gold from the assassins, she searches him out and they fall in love. The epilogue ends with his rebirth "marking the beginning and ending of cycles of creation" and the announcement that from this time forward, his name will be the unpronounceable symbol ♀, "for in the dawn, all will require no speakable name to differentiate the ineffable one that shall remain."

I love the word *ineffable*—though I admit, I had to look it up—and the idea that for some things, there are no words. As I tell this story, I find myself falling back on words that can't begin to express what certain moments have meant to me: Profound. Amazing. Beautiful. Love. These words are said so often, they've lost their power.

During this hypercreative era, Prince was searching for other forms of self-expression. A lot of that stuff in the vault at Paisley Park was created during this time. I never quite understood my role in all that until years later when I heard him tell someone, "Mayte made me more open. She makes it easier for me to talk to God." *Rolling Stone* referred to it as "an existential time in Prince's life," because this is when he started actively questioning everything about the way the music industry interacted with artists. Ultimately these questions led him to change his name to the unpronounceable love symbol, but that didn't happen overnight; it was a place he came to after a long, difficult soul search.

The footage you see in *3 Chains o' Gold* was shot over the course of almost two years, beginning with scenes Randee and I created together in Egypt in 1991 when I was fresh out of high school, and ending with the filming of "7" on an LA soundstage in 1993. Prince continued to work on the pieces during and between the Diamonds and Pearls Tour and the Act I and Act II tours the following year, which is a testament to his unbelievable stamina, because touring—how can I describe it? The most fun you could ever have while putting your entire body through a meat grinder? There were good times and bad.

When we set out on the Diamonds and Pearls Tour in April 1992, I was still well funded by my belly dancing money, but by the time we started Act I in March of 1993, I was broke and paying the rent on my empty apartment in Minnesota. What little money I had left I used to pay my phone bill, because Mama's voice on the other end of the line was my life raft at times. Sometimes I splurged and got a salad or a basket of bread with Thousand Island dressing from room service. There were times I was hungry enough to sneak food from room service carts in the hotel hallway. I learned that tea with a lot of honey kept me sustained for a long time, especially when I put the whole honey bear into the bottom of the mug. That would be my breakfast, lunch, and dinner.

On show nights, I couldn't eat anything before I danced, because I needed to feel light, but afterward, if there was still food on the crew's craft service table, I'd quickly wrap up a little meal to go and stow it with my things above my seat on the bus, so it would be there when I came back ready to dig in. Like clockwork, Prince would call me just before we boarded.

I'd get on his bus silently praying, *Please, tell me we're eating.* I was reluctant to ask him to feed me after the pay-docking incident.

That summer, we were in Minnesota shooting some footage for a music video, and Prince asked me to decorate a video cassette cover that he wanted to use as a prop. I went to Michaels crafts and spent my last few dollars on beads and chains. I took them home and put the thing together, and then I sat there, looking at my empty refrigerator. My empty stomach. My empty bank account. I started crying, and I cried all the way to Paisley Park. It took every morsel of nerve I could scrape together, but shaking in my boots, I walked up to him and said, "I'm leaving."

Prince was startled, because in the time we'd known each other, he'd seen me in pain, he'd seen me sick as a dog, he'd seen me frustrated and upset, but he had never seen me cry at work.

"What's going on?" he asked, and I let him have it.

"I could be in Cairo right now, making a thousand bucks a night. Instead, I'm here, living on Triscuit crackers and water and spending money I don't have to buy foo foo for you. I'm going home. And then I'm going to Cairo. Maybe later on, if you—"

"Hold up, hold up," he said without raising his voice. "I don't even know how much you make."

"Three hundred a week," I said. "And my rent is six hundred a month."

He winced like I'd kicked him in the shins. "Let me make a call."

"I don't want you to think I'm that person who's—"

"You're not that person. Relax." He got on the phone to the business office, and his voice was tight with irritation. "Can you tell me how much Mayte is making?" There was a pause while he listened to the person on the other line. "Okay. I need to see a list of what everyone else is making, too."

The following week, my pay had been tripled. Daddy was proud of me for standing up about it, and I was glad to think that the net result was a significant pay raise for everyone. I knew Prince wasn't being miserly; he had so many people doing so many things for him, it was impossible for him to know what was going on with all the people all the time. Sometimes an individual he cared about had to step up and say something, and people weren't always willing to do that.

I felt like an idiot that I hadn't said something eighteen months earlier, but I was glad I'd proven my worth as a dancer. Being Prince's friend—or girlfriend—was not enough to keep you employed by him. I'd seen that during the Diamonds and Pearls Tour. After a week in Japan and three weeks in Australia, Carmen and her band joined the tour and opened for us in the Netherlands and Germany. They showed her video for "Go Go Dancer" before her set, and I thought the set was good, but the reviews weren't what one dreams of, and Prince wasn't happy with the audience reaction. As we were setting up for the first show at Earls Court in London, word went around that Carmen's slot had been omitted. The Pasadenas and Shakespeare's Sister replaced her the following week in Manchester and Glasgow. Indra and Trio Esperanza did a couple of shows in Paris. Other than that, the tour played out with no opener. Carmen went home, and at the end of the Diamonds and Pearls Tour, Lori and Robia were let go, too.

"Had to happen," was all Prince said about it to me. "But I'm gonna ask Morris to join NPG."

Morris, aka "Mr. Hayes," had been around for a while. He replaced Jimmy Jam in The Time and was co-founder of the house band at Prince's nightclub, Glam Slam, in Minneapolis. He'd been in Carmen's band on the Diamonds and Pearls Tour, playing keyboards, including a bulky Wurlitzer that sounded like a whole orchestra in his hands. He's one of the funniest people I've ever known. Prince was always saying he should do comedy. Morris was one of Prince's most durable musicians and a longtime friend who stayed with him for twenty years. He was grateful and kind, and I never heard him complain or backbite on anybody.

Over the years, Prince worked with a lot of different artists, and that constant evolution was part of the rare energy he created. I always operated on the assumption that my employment was seasonal, but I hoped my season would last awhile. And more than that, I hoped our friendship would survive whatever professional ups and downs fate had in store. Romantically, I wasn't counting on anything. There was flirtation, but nothing below the belt. He kissed me one night when we were in Australia, and I let him know I didn't hate that, but I had no desire to be part of the harem. I remember a big party in London where Carmen was wearing a super cool little outfit with these sexy great boots, and Lori told me, "I turned down that same outfit when Prince bought it for me. Now Carmen's wearing it." This took the "bitch stole my look" drama to a new level. Ain't nobody got time for that, but my hormones were in high gear. When Prince sensed my frustration, he just said, "Good things come to those who wait."

I was glad when Christmastime rolled around, and Paisley Park became the ghost town it had been the first time I saw it. This time I was one of the people going home for the holidays instead of a *Nutcracker* mouse tiptoeing in when no one was there but the Prince and the Christmas tree. Mama and Daddy were in Puerto Rico, so I went there, too. Prince went to Miami to get away from the cold, but after a few days, he called me and said, "I'm coming to Puerto Rico."

"No, you're not," I laughed.

"No, really. I am."

The idea of him rolling up in the 'hood where Grandma Mercedes lived was kind of ridiculous, but the following morning, there he was. It was so strange to hear the *jangle-click* of his boots on the tile floor where I'd danced to his music when I was a little girl. Somehow the sound made me feel even more at home there. He met my grandmother and all the relatives, chatted with my parents for a while, and then went to his hotel. I went over to hang out with him that evening and found him sitting on top of the piano in his hotel room, looking out over the ocean.

"I can't stay long," he said. "These mosquitos are eating me alive."

"They do that." I climbed up and sat dancer style beside him, breathing the ocean breeze coming in through the open balcony doors.

"I've been sitting here thinking about it all day," he said. "I'm going to change my name."

"To what?"

He indicated the cover of the album we'd been working on.

"But...how do you pronounce that?" I asked.

"You don't."

"Ah. Okay."

He smiled and touched my chin. "I bet you're the only one who won't try to talk me out of it."

We sat on the piano lid talking as the sun went down and the stars came out over the ocean. Years later, in our wedding program, he wrote:

All alone, staring at the ocean, he implores the heavens 4 an answer—
"What is the symbol? What does it really mean?"
A voice says to him, "It's your name."

He told me he'd heard this voice before, when he was writing "Purple Rain," and he knew not to question it. I asked him where he believed the voice came from. "Was it God or an angel or some part of the subconscious?"

"Maybe all those things," he said. "Maybe the Holy Spirit. Maybe my own spirit."

...sometimes freedom moves in mysterious ways and in the end it's "whatever peanut butters your jelly." Most understanding of all is Mayte—his true soulmate, who simply says with a smile, "👁 never called you Prince anyway."

After the holidays, I went back to the Minnesota ice and snow, and we spent the rest of the winter making music videos. A lot of acts were doing live shows and direct-to-video compilations. Renting videos was still a thing then, and the market for music videos was hot. We were always filming bits and pieces, scenes and images that appealed to him even though he didn't know how or even if they would ever fit together. Some were done on location in Australia, Japan, and LA—running on a beach, holding hands at the zoo, that sort of thing—but most of the work was done on the huge soundstage at Paisley Park.

One day there was a big hydraulic lift with a glass chamber on the set. Prince kept changing wardrobe, going up and down in this elevator sort of thing with fog machines billowing all around it. None of us had a clue what he was doing, but he looked cool doing it, so we just went along. The song "7" had been produced the previous year, and the way *3 Chains o' Gold* was unfolding, it was a natural climax for the story. Warner Bros. was getting behind the production of this music video in a big way.

"Let's put some money in it," Prince said, which was more about energy and time and thought than it was about finances.

We shot "7" on a massive soundstage in LA. I wore my spectacular yellow Madame Abla outfit, which had been properly cleaned by this time, thank God. Both our costumes were reproduced in miniature for seven little boys and seven little girls who danced with us on an elaborate set that featured the model city of gold. (You can see Prince and me and our merry little group of mini-me dancers on the cover of the ♀ album.) Everything I can think of that I most love in this world was in that video: these beautiful children; Prince; the rich, Arabic-inspired music; belly dancing with my sword; rocking my beautiful dress; doves— oh! I got to kiss a dove! Where do you even go for dreams after you *kiss a dove*?

I loved that Prince played an acoustic guitar in this music video. It was so rare to see him playing an acoustic guitar on video or onstage. People expected to see him shredding a sparkly Stratocaster or one of his many custom-made guitars—his iconic Cloud guitars made by a luthier in Minnesota and the purple Love Symbol guitar made by a German craftsman. But when he was at home or in a hotel or on the tour bus, he often played an acoustic guitar like the one Jan played when we were kids. The sound was soft and organic in contrast to the urgent blare of an electric guitar.

"The acoustic guitar is my favorite," I told him. "I like that little squeaking sound when you slide your fingers up and down the neck. It's so personal."

Between takes, he played it for the children. We spent half their union-allowed time laughing and monkeying around with them. Prince got a huge kick out of seeing me with those kids. The director rolled film on a lot of that and recently sent me some of the unedited footage: Prince watching me dance with the little boys and girls, taking my hand, leading them toward the golden city. He's looking at me in a way he had never looked at me before.

"There's so much love there," she said. "You can see it."

And I do see it. We look like a happy family. There's lightness in the way he walks away at the end, after he's let go of all his crap and slain these seven selves who didn't know how to be with us.

...words of compassion words of peace...

I can't explain it, but we changed during that shoot. There was a moment when I looked at him with tears in my eyes. All I could say was, "This is everything I love." He hugged me close, and then we went on with the job at hand, but something was different.

One of the last shots we did was a close-up of his face close to my stomach as I did hip-work and abdominal undulations. The director called it, and we were getting ready to go home. Prince leaned in to my ear and said, "I think it's time."

"What do you mean?" I said, like an idiot.

"It's. *Time.*"

"For..."

"For you to get on birth control."

People, here again, my face. I can't even guess what that looked like.

"Oh." A nervous giggle bubbled out of my mouth. "How...how do I do that?"

"You go to the doctor."

"Right. Right, of course," I said, not wanting to tell him that I'd never been to the gynecologist and was terrified at the very idea. I won't go into the thousand deaths I died making the appointment, enduring my first Pap smear, and forcing myself to present the prescription at the drugstore, because I was almost twenty years old at that point, and I'm sure the twenty-year-olds reading this are doing some hard eye-rolling right now. You have to understand, I wasn't ignorant, but I'd had a traumatic childhood experience that made me extremely protective about that part of myself. I was grateful—then and now—that God sent me someone who was sensitive enough to be cool about it, even though he didn't fully understand exactly why I needed so much extra time and patience.

A week or so later, I wrote in bold letters in my journal: **February 9, 1993—not a virgin.** And I drew a winking smiley face in the margin. It was a big deal to me. So that's all I'm going to say about it, other than this word of advice to twentysomethings: Patience pays off.

One day not long after that, I saw a precious little black Yorkie pup in a pet store at the mall, and I was powerless to resist. She was the size of a hamster, and the shop owner said she'd grow to about twelve pounds. She was skating around on the slippery linoleum floor, not able to get any traction with her soft little paws. Her eyes were bright and full of friendly mischief. I took her home and named her Hena, because I'd seen an Arabic movie and loved the way the women did the henna on their hands while they were hanging around the harem—a scene that almost hit a bit too close to home.

When I called home and told Mama all about Hena, Mama said, "Mayte, take her back. Take her back first thing in the morning. Don't get attached."

I gave the classic answer any almost-twenty-something would give: "I'm an adult, Mama! I can do whatever I want."

But right after we hung up the phone, I thought, *Crap. I'd better take her back.* Prince was a bit of a clean freak and probably wouldn't want a dog around. He had Paisley the cat but never wanted the responsibility of a dog. I would be going on tour again soon. I hadn't even thought that far in advance. But when I looked into her little face, I just couldn't part with her. Not yet. I decided I'd keep her until it was time to go on tour and then send her to stay with Mama, who was living in Puerto Rico at the time. After the tour I could go to Puerto Rico and fetch her, and wherever fate was planning to take me next, Hena could go with me.

The Act I Tour started in Florida in March 1993: twenty-five shows in five weeks across the continental United States, plus a couple of nights in Canada and who knows how many of those after-concert jam fests. When Morris Hayes came in to replace Rosie Gaines on keyboard, I missed her ballsy vocals, but I loved Morris and the direction in which NPG was evolving, including more of the rhythms and vibes that brought out the belly dance/flamenco-fusion style that was second nature to me. Prince encouraged me to explore and take chances—as he did with everyone—so my role in the Act I Tour expanded. More stage time, being involved in almost every number, meant I was working harder and learning more, and I loved that.

It was up to me to bring the female energy. We opened with "My Name Is Prince" and "Sexy M.F."—like kicking down a door—and then we kept that insane pace going for over two hours. Through most of the show, I was The Girl, dancing hard and loving it, kneeling to kiss his guitar, feeling wild and sexy and free. Some of the choreography was the same as it was when Lori and Robia did it, but I brought my own style to it, and it worked. The staging of "7" was created around me, beginning with a long Arabic solo and ending with Prince's cryptic declaration: "To whom it may concern: You must come to your senses. There are no kings in this world, only princes."

It was a different experience touring with Prince as his girlfriend. From the time I was little, I had always tried to perform at my highest possible level, but now I knew that anything less than an 800 percent effort would reflect badly on him. It was lovely, however, riding along listening to music he loved. He introduced me to Kate Bush and Miles Davis and so many others I still love. And, you know, I didn't exactly hate staying in the A hotels with the full-on foo foo.

My love/hate affair with room service took an ironic turn. When I was broke, I'd scavenged people's leftover bread and Thousand Island dressing from carts in the hallway, because if I ordered my own, they would charge me ten bucks for the bread. When I was with my rock-star boyfriend and money wasn't an issue, they'd offer it for free, but I cringed at the thought of ordering it because it reminded me of my past. I loved getting breakfast at the start of a busy day, but to sit in a room and order food is so weird to me. Get out and greet the day, already! But of course, that was out of the question for him. When I'm traveling with friends now and someone suggests room service, I don't mean to stare daggers at them, but all we ever did back then was room service. Dinner out was extremely rare and took a lot of planning, which is why dinner out is so special to me, and I cherish a light breakfast out in the sunshine as one of life's great simple pleasures.

In the old days, I'd hang out with him till the wee hours, but except for my initial visits, I never spent the night, even when things progressed to making out. After "7," I started spending the night with him and riding with him to the next venue. As we traveled, I was on the bus with him. It was lonely at times, but I didn't miss the drama, and I rather enjoyed being put on a pedestal, the cherished object of all his famous and infamous romantic tendencies. He was particular and very protective of me, but I never felt like there was a lid on me or that he was trying to make me do or be anything I didn't want to do or be.

This was my first real boyfriend, so I was tripping on all the emotional ecstasy most girls get out of their system in high school. Prince loved that I was so in love with being in love. I'd never had my heart broken, so I was open and unjaded. Any old trick in the romance handbook—a candlelit bubble bath, rose petals on the sheets, a sexy handwritten letter—none of the novelty had worn off for me. I was thrilled with all the small gestures of affection, and he enjoyed being appreciated. There wasn't much drama between us, but I discovered that, if anything, I danced better when I was mad, so we always ended up laughing it off after the show. Somewhere around this time, he wrote a song called "Courtin' Time" that came out later on the *Emancipation* album, and I was touched to hear an instrumental version on a concert video just a few years ago.

> *baby, now you're gonna know*
> *what it's like when a boy truly loves a girl…*

But all that was off-hours. Our working relationship didn't change. He wasn't one for showing affection in public until after we were engaged, maybe because he liked to keep people guessing, but mostly because when he was working, he was lost in the music and entirely focused, moment by moment, on the work. Raquel Welch could have been standing there naked and he'd never notice. Prince consciously surrounded himself with coworkers who were able to find and maintain that same laserlike focus. Take a look at what he's doing on that stage. (He kept most of that stuff off the Internet when he was alive, but now tons of footage is spilling onto YouTube.) Performers can and do get hurt when they're operating at that caliber. Everyone has to have his or her head in the game.

About six months after Prince died, I performed "7" in a tribute concert put together by his family. I was horribly nervous about the way it was coming together. People seemed to think we could do all this without a lot of planning and rehearsal. And they were right. I was silly to worry. I should have remembered: These people are the best. No one could walk in, rehearse for one day, and put on a show like NPG, because all of us had been trained by this man who took each unique talent and pressed it to the next level.

The Act I Tour ended in April 1993. We'd be at home in Minnesota for the summer, rehearsing for the Act II Tour, so before we started, I went to Puerto

Rico to see my parents and fetch Hena. When I got there, I found the most spoiled dog in canine history. She was dolled up with a little fountain hairdo, ribbons, and charms. Basically, my mother had replaced me with her. When I put Hena in her little carrier and put her in the car to go to the airport, Mama looked so stricken, I couldn't bear to take Hena away from her.

"Mama...keep her. She's yours."

No argument from either of them. They lived happily ever after for many years.

Back in Minnesota, I walked into the first rehearsal and was stunned to find that the band was like a skeleton crew. Several people had been let go, including Tony, Damon, and Kirk, who'd been with Prince for almost ten years. Kirk came back later on as a drummer, and Prince tried to orchestrate a soft landing for them all with *Goldnigga*, an album that gave them a way forward without him. Truthfully, I wasn't a huge fan of it—particularly the song "Johnny," which is this crude song about condoms. The first time I heard it, I wrinkled my nose and said, "What's up with that? My father's name is John. Your father's name is John. I don't like that."

I couldn't understand why Prince would let TDK go. To me, they seemed like such an integral part of his vision for the band. When I asked him about it, he said, "I don't want guys onstage with me. Just you."

"Just me? I don't get it. Why would you change it when—"

"Because it changes. It will always change. Maybe next year I won't have a band at all."

"Okay, but from a technical standpoint—how do you expect me to do all that myself?"

"You'll learn," he said.

He'd already lined up a series of choreographers to work with me for five weeks. After that, sink or swim, we'd be on tour again.

I trained hard for the rest of the summer, moving in ways I've never moved before, thinking about who I could be as a dancer in an entirely different light. In a strange way, hip-hop and belly dancing are natural cousins, because of the muscle isolation that's necessary to both, so nothing about the choreography felt weird. The only thing that scared me was the stamina it would take to motor through that two-hour show as the only dancer onstage.

One day during rehearsal, Prince looked at me and said, "You know what would be cool?"

"What..."

It always worried me a little when a sentence started this way.

"I was just thinking about this dancer with bangs like—"

"No," I said. "You don't want to see me with bangs.

I tried bangs when I was twelve, and I feel like I'm still kind of emotionally scarred from it. They won't lay down straight. As soon as I start sweating, they curl up into weird little devil horns."

"You'd have them chemically straightened. They'd be straight."

"Maybe," I hedged. "I guess they'll grow back."

The next day, I flew to LA to have a particular hairdresser cut and straighten my bangs, and much to my surprise, I loved the look. I couldn't wait to get home and show Prince. When I stood in front of him, feeling like Bettie Page and Bette Davis and Joan Crawford rolled into one, he studied my face carefully.

"Wouldn't it be cool," he said, "if they were cut like a V?"

"What do you mean?"

"So they'd come to a point here"—he touched his index finger just above the bridge of my nose—"at the third eye."

I suppose it's a demonstration of my trust in him. I let him take me over to the hair salon at his house. (Yes, of course he had a hair salon at his house. Doesn't everyone?) He stood me against the counter.

"Close your eyes and stand very still."

It was a strangely sensual experience. I felt his slow, deliberate breath on my face and then the bright coolness of the sharp scissor blade on my forehead, one side and then the other.

"Okay, take a look."

I opened my eyes and turned toward the mirror. He was right.

My eyebrows naturally go to kind of a zazzy place, and I had them plucked and penciled to accentuate that, but now the subtle but distinct V created a cooler, edgier version of me—a look I'd never seen on any other girl. Probably because I was looking at a woman.

The Act II Tour started in England in July 1993: twenty-seven shows in twelve countries in less than seven weeks. I'd never worked so hard in my life, and the harder I worked, the more fun it was. Prince was very competitive and liked to see us compete with each other, so every once in a while, before the show, he'd call out, "Funk Night!" This meant that whoever did the funkiest thing would get a bonus of a thousand or maybe three thousand dollars, sometimes even five thousand. So we were highly motivated to get out there and get funky. People did crazy things, often prompted by Prince's come-on: "Wouldn't it be cool if..."

I remember somebody climbing high into the scaffolding one night, scaring the daylights out of everyone. Tommy Barbarella used to fly around on a wire harness.

"Wouldn't it be cool," Prince said, "if somebody just like, *shaved their head* onstage?"

Mr. Hayes stepped up for that one.

During the Diamonds and Pearls Tour, I wasn't onstage all that much, so Prince was always suggesting to Lori and Robia, "Wouldn't it be cool if somebody did a stage dive at some point in here?" They were not super into that idea. I'd see them gingerly approach the edge of the stage, tentatively lower their bottoms toward the crowd, and then retreat. Toward the end of the tour, I think at least one of them did it, but not very enthusiastically.

When Act II rolled around, I was out there onstage with a lot more opportunities, rocking the world in a bikini and combat boots, and I started plotting how to get that Funk Night cash. It took me a while to top those guys, but I saw my big chance one night in Berlin. The band was on fire, the crowd was in a state of frenzy, the lights were blazing purple and white and blue. I took a deep breath, started running about twelve feet from the edge of the stage, and dove out over the crowd. Like that old saying: *Leap and the net will appear.*

For a moment, I flew like an eagle. I corkscrewed in midair so I was facing the ceiling, my arms over my head, my body parallel to the earth. And then I hit the floor like a bag of wet cement.

What up, Germans? Geez!

They looked down at me like, *Was ist das?* as cartoon stars circled my head. I was back onstage dancing within thirty seconds, the undisputed winner of Funk Night, but the next day, I was as stiff as the Tin Man, and for weeks, I had to cover the deep green and blue bruises with body makeup—along with all the other bruises I'd sustained during the most demanding, rewarding, infuriating, exhilarating days and nights of my life so far.

The next time I impulsively launched out over the crowd, the people below the stage caught me, lifted me up over their heads, and sailed me back onto the stage again. I was laughing, weightless, totally borne up by their love for what Prince had made of the New Power Generation. He'd created a symphony that was more than musical; it was visual and visceral and theatrical.

"You're not a backup dancer," he told me. "You're part of the band. Your body is the instrument."

By the end of the tour, I was stage diving like the black swan, and it became my thing for the next few years. I learned to look down first and gage the depth of the reliability pool. If the people down front looked stony or stupid or weak in the triceps, I waited for some burly types to push their way forward. Stage diving is not for sissies. I got pretty banged up sometimes, and one night in Paris, some guy ripped off my shirt. But that's rock and roll. All in a day's work, right?

Looking at moments from all this on YouTube or the old concert videos, people don't always appreciate the hard physical labor that goes into performances like these. It looks so effortless. Underneath our clothes, our shin splints and bruises told the real story. I was always slathering body makeup from my toes to my collarbone. It left a sticky amber ring in the hotel bathtub after each show. I can't imagine what house-keeping thought I was doing in there.

We didn't talk about the pain we were in. Prince didn't complain, and I didn't see him taking anything other than vitamin B injections, which I refused at first but welcomed later on as the wear and tear of touring life set in. Later on in his life, when we were no longer together, I heard rumors that Prince had had hip replacement surgery. This wouldn't surprise me at all. And I wouldn't blame anyone for turning to some kind of pharmaceutical pain relief if they've given as much of their body and soul as he did every time he stepped onstage.

eight

"Have you ever been hypnotized?"

"Not that I know of."

"You would know."

"Not if there was a posthypnotic suggestion. Like, 'You will not remember being hypnotized' or something like that."

"Truth. Good point."

"Why do you ask?"

"I want to hypnotize you. Lay still. Listen to my voice."

"I listen to your voice all day."

"This'll be different."

"How?"

"You'll be in a trance. You'll travel through time to past lives. You'll speak deep truth from the subconscious mind."

"I don't think that works on me."

"Not if you keep messing around, girl. Lay still."

"Okay, but—"

"*Shhhhh*...breathe in...breathe out...let go of

the tension in your forehead... let go of the muscles in your legs... feel your mind become pure energy... feel your body fill with light..."

He stroked my face, speaking softly, whispering me into a deeply meditative state. He liked to call it "hypnosis," and it was a kind of hypnotic spell, I think, but not like a Vegas act or clinical "stop smoking" type of hypnosis. The first time he tried it on me, I couldn't stop giggling, but then I gave myself over to it, and I liked it. I closed my eyes and watched the natural kaleidoscope inside my eyelids.

"Tell me your name."

"Mayte."

"Princess Mayte?"

"Yes."

"Where are you?"

"Cairo."

"What are you doing?"

"Waiting."

"For what?"

"For you."

When I was in this altered state, as we went there more and more often, I could answer his questions without weighing whether I should tell the truth. I could spin long Scheherazade-style stories that seemed to come from a part of my brain I'd never accessed before. In those clear, quiet hours just before dawn, I'd lay beside him, completely relaxed, no ballerina mask hiding my emotion, no showgirl costume telling me who I was supposed to be. I'd let myself go and freely speak to him. It was weirdly therapeutic for both of us. This was the only time he'd let me talk without interrupting me. He listened, 100 percent attentive, and I felt safe. There was an absence of the whipped-cream-paycheck power imbalance. Whatever came to light, there was no blame or shame or lack of faith. Sometimes it felt like a child's game. Sometimes it was a connection even deeper than sex.

"Have we known each other before?"

"Many times."

"Where?"

"Many places."

"How did we find each other?"

"Before your soul set off to live its first lifetime on earth, my soul said to your soul, 'We need a plan so that you'll recognize me when you see me. Everywhere you look, you'll see reminders. At first you'll think it's coincidence. Then you'll know it's fate.'"

Together we explored universes and lifetimes and emotional truth. Under his hypnosis, I could finally speak about the family I wanted to create—forgiving and trusting, not like my family—and that's something I couldn't say to him in real time. When he was ready to bring me back, he'd snap his fingers next to my ear and say, "When you wake up, you'll know that you are loved and safe and warm."

Afterward, he'd tell me what I'd said, and he never tried to alter my words or use them against me. This gave him a way to tell me everything he couldn't say in real time. It gave him a way to be honest with me about the family he wanted to create, about his fears and struggles. He could speak about other women in his life and what they meant to him, knowing that I wasn't going to pop off or judge.

We still loved the simple act of hanging out together, watching old black-and-white movies and talking about the mysteries of the universe and the unexplainable power of love. These long conversations had deepened to a more spiritual level as we became closer. He asked me about the angels in the room, and I described them in detail. We talked about the possibility of our two souls having met before and where that might have happened. He was fixated on the idea of Egypt then, maybe because of the music taking shape in his head—and sometimes the music took shape because of the conversations.

He once wrote to me:

> *Whenever* 👁 *imagine what my work would look like had* 👁 *not met u,* 👁 *must admit—it's quite a different picture. It's not better or worse. It's just different.* 👁 *regret nothing except whenever* 👁*'ve made a compromise because* 👁 *felt u wouldn't understand.* 👁 *know that u don't mean*

"Princess" Mayte, age 7, in the *That's Incredible* days.

My business card from my professional bellydancing days in Europe—I attached this card to the tapes I sent backstage to Prince.

Mayte
06121 - 74616

Me as a young balle-rina, shortly after I met Prince—this was the sort of photo I'd send him dur-ing the "pen pal" stage of our relationship.

One of Prince's typi-cal letters to me, in his lovely script (and unique spelling).

MAYTE!

What a kickin 'tape!
Ballet≈cool, but when u dance like
that... SISONAH! Thank u. 👁 keep
all your tapes in a little secret section in my
house. Only 👁 know where they are.
Believe it not, Lisa thought u were
2 pretty 4 the part in the video. The girl she
picked is tall and strange-looking with short hair.
Such is life. But 👁'm sure we'll work

1992, outside Paisley Park. My dad finally came to visit me in Minneapolis after the Japan Australia tour, to make sure things were good. I was embarrassed and upset with him at the time, because I knew Prince was quite protective about cameras in his home, but now I'm happy he took it.

In Cairo with Randee St. Nicholas in 1991 — I didn't know how much my life was about to change.

This was one of the first times he appeared with me publicly — I was shocked he invited me to this public event with him.

That's my outfit he's wearing—one of many he "borrowed" from me and made his own. I had bought it in New York, and it disappeared soon after I put it in my closet.

He had this photo of me framed and next to his sink.

The wardrobe designer for the tour would take a Polaroid of me in my costume, to show Prince for approval. I smiled because I knew he'd see it, but my smile also said if I liked the costume or not. On very rare occasions, I would not smile.

Just goofin' around in one of my pregnancy sweaters—yet another thing he swiped from my closet.

He would tease me into laughter during a photo shoot, and then get serious in seconds. We hadn't yet become intimate during this shoot, but you can see the chemistry between us.

He was ticked off during this shoot; his bags had been lost, and he was forced to wear black pants with orange striped shoes—not the outfit he'd planned on. They promised to airbrush his shoes to match his pants, but as you can see they didn't. Afterward he told me, "Now you know why I'm so picky about getting photo approval."

The famous V-shaped bangs that caused a thousand girls to reach for their scissors. He has "South Bitch" written on his cheek (we were in Miami).

Our wedding
program.

COiNCiDENCE
or
FATe?

Me and my dad on
my wedding day. This
picture was taken right
before it was time to
put on my wedding
dress. Prince had just
arrived, and my dad and
I were both happy and
relieved.

The CD he made for me
on our first anniversary,
with his hand-drawn
illustrations.

The day we got Mia.

My mother took this Polaroid of me and our new dog. I sent it to Prince, and he said next time he wanted to go roller-skating with me.

My husband decided he wanted to announce our pregnancy to the world in his typical dramatic style.

This is the only photo I have left of my pregnancy showing my belly—a Polaroid taken in our backyard. I cherish this image.

December 1996—our son would have been two months old. I had lost the weight, and I looked OK from the outside, but I was dying inside.

Our last public outing together in Paris. I was so upset, but he was wearing my necklace (bearing my zodiac sign), which gave me a little hope.

This shot was taken by Steve Parke at our house in Spain for *Vogue*. This was the last time my husband visited our house, the same trip that he tried to get me to sign an annulment of our marriage.

I took this "selfie" of us during that same Steve Parke *Vogue* shoot. You can see the distance between us.

Then, Prince (behind the camera) turned the lens on me himself. All I can think when I see this picture is how sad I look.

e parke

The gates of Paisley Park
when Prince died.

Doing the tribute concert in Minneapolis in June 2016 was one of the most difficult nights of my life—but also cathartic. So many of the important people in his life came together to celebrate his extraordinary life. I was honored to be there.

Me and Gia—my light, my everything.

2 make me feel that way but there again—it's a fact of life. 👁 *accept it as the very reason* 👁 *must love u because* 👁 *care about your feelings. In the past* 👁 *could do a movie and kiss the leading lady and not care what another woman would think. That's what time it was. But these are the people* 👁 *'m not with 2day! What words do* 👁 *use 2 make u realize what u mean 2 me? If* 👁 *imagine holding another it would only reinforce the fact that no one fits my arms the way u do.*

During those years, our chemistry onstage combined with our chemistry in private, and the result was something neither of us anticipated. We incorporated props and set pieces and costumes as if we were performing an opera. We didn't know where any given idea would take us; we just kept going with it, working the choreography that gave the music a story we could communicate to an audience, and people loved it.

In 1994, there was no official tour, and in 1995, there was only the Ultimate Live Experience Tour in Europe, but we were always working. During those two years, in addition to recording three albums—*Come, The Black Album,* and *The Gold Experience*—New Power Generation did hundreds of one-off concerts, dance parties, aftershows, and television appearances.

Prince and I talked a lot about music, but we

didn't talk much about the music business in those early years. I was his oasis from all that. I'm not sure I would have understood it at the time, anyway. One of his crew people told me years later, "Everything was great until *Purple Rain*. Then he got everything he ever wanted, and he didn't like it." That made sense from my perspective.

The Warner Bros. situation was brewing and getting closer to the surface. The basic issue was a dispute over when and how Prince's music should be released. He had a strategy that didn't jibe with the label's, and it bothered him that someone else had the clout to tell him when he could and could not put his own music out there. He didn't have a personal beef with anyone at the label—or with the idea of record labels in general; he recognized that record labels are great for most artists. But Prince wasn't like most artists. He had his own massive studio where he could do anything the label's studio could do. He needed the relationship for distribution, and he was becoming more and more uncomfortable with what he had to give up on his side of that deal: commercial control of his music. When he recorded under the umbrella of the record label, they owned the master—the physical finished version of that song. In Prince's thinking, the logical counterpart to "master" was "slave."

This all came to a head in 1994 because of a disagreement over when to drop the ⚥ album and in what order the singles should be released. The studio wanted to release "7" as the first single; he wanted "My Name Is Prince" first. Ultimately, they did go with what he wanted, but "My Name Is Prince" only got to #36 on the Billboard Hot 100; "7" rocketed to the Top 10 and peaked, coincidentally, at number seven. I don't think he was bothered by the fact that this made it seem like they were right and he was wrong; it was the fact that the decision was open to discussion at all. He felt he'd earned the right to call those shots, and from my perspective now, I have to agree with him.

One day I rode to Warner Bros. in the limo with him because he was going to a meeting that had him feeling stressed. I waited in the car, making a few calls. When he came out, he had *SLAVE* written on the right side of his face.

"So...that went well," I said, hoping to make him smile.

"It definitely changed the tone of the meeting," he said.

Honestly, even now, I have only a general idea of what this was all about, and at the time I was completely confused by it, but I could tell there was something weighing on him when we came home from the Act I Tour. He hadn't told me the details of all that yet. He did say that he'd signed a $100 million deal for ten albums—which was a lot more than some other major stars were getting. He was a long way from delivering the ten albums and already beginning to feel trapped, because he had this mountain of unreleased material in the vault, but they wouldn't let him release it.

He said an exclusivity clause in his contract meant he couldn't just go off and be a member of someone else's band—an idea that made him happy, in theory—so he developed a character called Tora Tora who had a whole life of his own. When you see him with a scarf or a veil of chains over his face, that's Tora Tora. And in the middle of all this, MTV kept asking him to do *Unplugged*—and he really wanted to do it—but again, there was no negotiating ownership of the master.

During a rare moment of downtime, I invited Mama to bring Hena up for a visit. I didn't tell Prince that Mama was in town, because he would have thought it was rude to call me to come over while she was visiting, and I didn't want him not to call me to come over. One afternoon when I hadn't seen him for a few days, he called me sounding overwhelmed and sad, not saying much but not wanting me to hang up.

"What's wrong?" I kept asking.

"Nothing."

"Should I come over?"

"No," he said. "I'm sick. I don't look good."

"I don't care about that."

"I care."

He sounded hollowed out and foggy, and that

scared me a little. He didn't get sick very often. And this felt different. We sat together on the phone without talking for a while, and then I said, "Hey, remember Hena? The little dog you saw in my dressing room in Florida? She's um...she's visiting me. Let me bring her over. She'll cheer you up."

I wasn't at all sure this was true, but I hoped it would be, and it was the only way in I could think of at that moment.

Prince surprised me when he said, "Yeah. Bring her over."

I hustled Hena into her car carrier and booked over there as fast as I could. I was startled when I saw him. He was in his pajamas, which wasn't totally unusual at that hour of the afternoon, but he kept his eyes away from mine. He seemed vulnerable and weirdly...loopy.

"Are you all right?" I asked.

"Yeah. Not feeling well."

I want to be clear: In all the years we were together, I never actually saw Prince doing drugs. He didn't want me to see it. I'm sure he knew what my reaction would be. I didn't drink or do any kind of drugs, and I didn't want that in my life. I knew Prince loved port wine, but he wasn't a big consumer of anything except sex and music, as far as I knew. He had a black bag that always seemed to be close at hand—like a gym bag, not too man-purse-y—but the contents were pretty tame: candy, vitamins, makeup, a Bible, and a big wad of cash. He had incredible amounts of money, and he always seemed to have plenty on him so he could send people off to get whatever it was he needed. He was still young—in his mid-thirties—and never complained about fatigue or pain. Sometimes on tour, he got vitamin B_{12} shots, and so did I. For me, that was enough to keep my energy and immune system up to the task of traveling and performing. I never had any trouble sleeping because I was dog tired. I thought it was the same for him.

But there were a few disturbing incidents that happened while we were together, and this is one of several occasions when he told me he was "sick" or that he had a "migraine." Looking back, I can see it was something else. I didn't see it then. Maybe because I didn't want to.

I set Hena down, and she wagged over to him, wanting to love him on pure instinct. We sat quietly for a while. Every now and then, she'd put her paw on his face or nuzzle his hand, and eventually he brought her up to his lap.

"You should go," he said. "I don't want you to get sick."

"Are you sure?"

"Yeah, but...do you mind if she hangs out for a while?"

"Sure," I said. "I can come and feed her in the morning, but you'll need to take her out later tonight."

"Yeah. We'll be cool."

The next morning, when I arrived to feed Hena, Prince seemed like himself again, but I could tell he'd had a long night. He rubbed Hena's head and said, "She's an angel. No matter how bad I was feeling, she'd come and put her paw on me."

"She's very intuitive," I said.

He nodded. "It gave me a whole new respect for dogs."

"Will you be all right if we leave?" I asked.

"Oh, sure. Of course. But hold up a minute." He handed me a sealed envelope. "I need you to take this to the office."

When I took the envelope, I didn't ask what was in it. I guess he could see the curiosity and concern in my face.

"Don't worry about it," he said. "It's just in case—just take it to them. They'll know what to do."

This was not the only time he asked me to do that, and on each of those occasions, I got a distinct vibe that the envelope—which I never opened, of course—had something to do with the future of his music. That's why it was so strange to me when I read that he had died without a will. I know for a fact that he was on top of his business concerns and did think about a time when someone else would be curating his creative life's work.

He wrote to me:

> *This was the year 👁 grew up. Part of me wants 2 be alone 4 a while, not away from u, just alone with me. There is a difference. Wherever 👁 am, whatever 👁'm doing—👁 think of u. Always. Hypnoparadise. 👁'd like 2 go away and make serious plans 4 the future. 👁've never felt so adult in my life. Now, there are a lot of things 👁 have 2 deal with. My Paris apartment, the property on Melrose 👁 pay rent monthly on, the Love 4 one another concept, the renting or sale of the L.A. house (since we'll be on tour). 👁 hope u can grow up a little more with me as well. Cuz 👁'm gonna need your support as much as your love these next few months. We've gone thru so much 2gether. And yet it seems like we've just started. I look forward 2 everything…*

In an effort to throw him a bone, apparently, Warner Bros. allowed him to release a single as a one-off aside from his contract. "The Most Beautiful Girl in the World" is a song that was particularly important to him. I know of at least three women besides me who believe it was written specifically for them. I hope every woman who hears it thinks it was written specifically for her. Because it was. Take a look at the music video. You won't see me in it. You'll see a collage of girls and women of every age, race, and body type. This was his love song to all of us.

There's a nervous bride, a woman sweating through childbirth, women working, women mothering, women making a difference. A gorgeous black woman (played by Nona Gaye) is elected president of the United States. A fabulous redhead slays onstage and then drags off a carefully styled wig to show her actual close-cropped hair. At the end, we see education pioneer Marva Collins, a teacher who used her retirement savings to start a small school for low-income black children labeled "learning disabled" by the Chicago public school system. Set against this song, it's undeniable: every one of them—every one of *you*—is perfectly and uniquely stunning.

> *. . . this kind of beauty has got no reason 2 ever be shy*
> *. . . this kind of beauty is the kind that comes from inside*

It was a pivotal moment in his career, because he was able to release the single as an independent artist on his own new NPG label in a distribution partnership with Edel in Europe. (Yeah, *that* Edel. Too dramatic, right?) The single was an international hit, his first UK number one hit—the only one during his lifetime—and number three on *Billboard*'s Hot 100 in the United States. With this one song, he was able to prove that he had the answer to the big question everyone kept asking when he talked about living outside a label: What about distribution? The song was remixed for the *Gold Experience* album, released by NPG with Warner Bros., but the handwriting was on the wall. With the successful release of the single, he had proven that it was possible and important for an artist to take ownership of his or her work, creatively and commercially, and he was already reaching out to artists like Chaka Khan to jump ship and follow him.

"The Most Beautiful Girl in the World" was the first recording officially credited to ♀ instead of Prince, and this threw people for a loop. In 1999, he told Larry King, "I had searched deep within my heart and spirit, and I wanted to make a change and move to a new plateau in my life, and one of the ways I did this was to change my name. It sort of divorced me from the past and all the hang-ups that go along with it."

Suddenly people didn't know how to refer to him in the media. They came up with the Artist Formerly Known as Prince, which he didn't love because, to him, it felt like a cheat. Some people tried to shorten that to TAFKAP, and he particularly hated that because it was a double cheat. It's interesting to see how people wrap their heads around it—or not—and how their handling of it reflects how they feel about artists in general. I mean, is that allowed? Do we get to play with entity and identity that way?

But I think that's exactly what he intended. I think he wanted to take it from your mouth and place it in your mind or take it from your mind and place it in your heart. Instead of verbalizing a word inside your head, maybe he wanted you to feel something that was uniquely him, to breathe in both artist and art and be with that for just a split second. So I would ask you to bear with me and do that here so I can honor his wishes. Up to this moment, he was Prince; from 1993 to 2000—legally, professionally, creatively, and spiritually—he was ⚥.

Prince's decision to have his name legally changed to ⚥ was a much bigger deal for the rest of the world than it was for us. As our relationship evolved over the years, the man I knew was always separate in my heart and mind from the stage persona, so I'd never addressed him as "Prince" anyway. He once told Oprah, "I'd drop my tea if I heard 'Prince' coming from the kitchen." People kept asking me, "But what do you call him?" and the truth is, I didn't call him anything. Every once in a while, I'd call him "hon" or "honey," which made him laugh for some reason, or I'd call out, "Hey!" which also amused him because his stepdad's name was Hayward.

Most of the time, if I was still and looked at him for more than a second or two, he'd turn to look at me. Perhaps that connection is how the unpronounce-able is pronounced: it's a look, a touch, a stillness. And it went both ways, even after we were no longer together. One night after our divorce, I was at the Say-ers Club in LA, and I felt him there standing behind me. I turned to look for him, but I didn't see him. I did notice, though, that the guitar pedals were set up exactly the way he liked them. Someone told me later that he'd come in to jam with the band that night, but when he saw me sitting there, he didn't feel like playing.

His given name was Prince, so he didn't mind when his longtime friends and family called him that, but Prince—the recording artist owned by War-ner Bros.—was someone else entirely. And the Artist Formerly Known as Prince was something the media invented because that was the easiest way to talk about him. He didn't want it to be easy for them. He wanted to make people think about their own identity and about the people they idolize and the concept of being and doing "whatever peanut butters your jelly." He wanted people to know he had changed.

"In the Bible," he said, "what happens when a per-son changes? God changes their name. Abram became Abraham. Sarai became Sarah. Jacob wrestled with the angel of the Lord and became Israel."

Prince opened the original Glam Slam nightclub in Minneapolis in 1989 so he'd have a place to go when he wanted to go nightclubbing without causing a stampede or when he wanted to jam with people he liked. The place was named after a song on the *Lovesexy* album, and over the next several years, he opened up Glam Slams in Los Angeles, Miami, and Yokohama.

After the Act II Tour, he asked me to help him reimagine the Glam Slam experience in Minneapolis with a concept we called Erotic City. He gave me a lot of fantastic unreleased music to work with, and I created vignettes with hanging ladders that appeared to be standing into space, a go-go dancer in a birdcage, and a huge skrim where tricks of light created suggestive silhouettes and reality-bending projections. Dancers came down from the ceiling and through the walls. I did a whole thing with a chandelier on my head.

In mid-January 1994, I filmed the show and flew to LA where he was working at the moment, staying at a house he'd bought on Heather Way. We watched the show together, and he was very excited about it. Afterward, he needed to go back to the studio, but I was exhausted, so I went upstairs and crashed. I was sound asleep at four thirty A.M. when a 6.7-magnitude earthquake gripped the San Fernando Valley for twenty seconds that felt like two hours. I huddled on the bed for another twenty-five minutes as aftershocks rumbled through the house. I heard things falling and breaking. And then I heard the front door.

"Mayte! Mayte!"

"I'm up here!" I called back, because I was frozen in place, terrified to step into the dark. He bounded up the stairs and pulled me into the kind of hard hug where you feel muscles and bones. He kissed my face and neck, asking over and over, "Are you all right? Are you hurt?"

"I'm okay. What's happening out there?"

"It's bad," he said. "Light poles were falling. I couldn't get through. There's no cell service. I was so worried about you."

The next day, we flew out of poor, beat-up LA, back to Minnesota, a place that gets cold but remains firmly in place. On the way home, we watched the video from the Glam Slam show again.

"I'm impressed," he said. "I want you to do this in Miami."

I was excited about that until he told me the first step was for me to fly down there and fire everyone currently playing and dancing there. I did not want to be that person, but this was an opportunity for me to step out of his shadow a little and take a leadership role in creating something very cool. Besides, I already had a secret plan to rehire most of the dancers after I fired them.

I arrived at Glam Slam Miami a few weeks later with a forced smile on my face and did what had to be done. When the dirty work was over, I went to work on a show for a celebration of ♀'s first birthday on June 7, 1994. Nona Gaye hosted a simulcast at the LA Glam Slam while we performed live in Miami. He didn't fall back on any of the old Prince music for this event; it was all about the new music he was creating as ♀—fresh, fire-in-the-belly funk, for the most part.

The night of the birthday party, about a thousand people milled in the street outside the club. Advance ticket sales were big. Unfortunately, fake ticket sales were even bigger. The situation got real as people realized not everyone was going in. Fights broke out, and several people were arrested for disorderly conduct. At half past midnight, security just stepped back and waved everybody in. When my friend and I saw what was happening, we just looked at each other like *here goes nuthin'* and stepped out on the stage.

"Hold on to your wigs," he said, and the place went crazy.

In January 1995, Prince received the American Music Award of Merit. It was a huge honor for him and a major performance for New Power Generation, but beyond all that, it gave ♀ a chance to "put Prince to bed," as he put it. He was proud of everything he'd accomplished as Prince, but by now he was fully invested in this reinvention of himself. He wanted to play live, but the show organizers wouldn't let him. They wanted him to lip sync so there'd be no surprises and because of union laws.

"I'm not going to fake it," he said. "If they want lip sync, I'm not using a microphone."

He took pride in the fact that he wasn't pretending, but he was still going to deliver a stellar experience for the live audience and the millions of people watching. You can see on the video that he's brazenly chewing gum, as if to say, "Yeah, we all know I'm not singing right now, but look at this."

This performance was entirely about the visual. "The Purple Medley" directed by Jamie King involved multimedia technology, a giant staircase, glowing rock walls, fireworks, and Tommy Barbarella flying through the air playing the Purpleaxxe as the climax of a live show that would be broadcast all over the planet. Fifty dancers—many of them from my Glam Slam show—rehearsed in LA while the New Power Generation rehearsed at Paisley Park.

At dress rehearsal the day of the show, he pulled me aside and said, "Tell everybody not to go full-on during the rehearsal. The censors are watching to see if we do anything offensive."

He nodded toward a woman who was sitting out front. Narrow eyes. Straight mouth. Uptight. Definitely had the look of a censor. We rehearsed the whole thing, modifying the moves or just standing there

during the parts that might have been deemed bor-
derline. We left out the part where the backup dancers
whipped off their panties, but she did not look like she
was buying it.

Before we took our places for the live broadcast, we
gathered in ♀'s dressing room to pray, as we always
did, but as everyone else headed for the stage, he
caught my wrist and said, "Hold up." Opening his
ever-present black bag, he pulled out a huge wad of
cash and handed it to me. "Stuff this in your bra.
I want you to pull it out and count it. You'll know
when."

"Hmm." I took the cash and tucked it into the
front of my shirt. "Do I get to keep it?"

"Nope."

Nona Gaye introduced him, reading the inscrip-
tion on the award he was about to receive. "He has
proven himself the ultimate showperson. A daring
composer/lyricist, an electrifying singer/performer, an
outstanding arranger/musician, master of more than
two dozen instruments, a visionary producer, creator
of fourteen platinum albums, a motion picture star,
and entertainment entrepreneur..."

Hard guitar chords opened the door for the danc-
ers' company. (And Carmen Electra! I almost forgot.)
Everybody was all out there, panties to the breeze.
After a medley of Prince hits, there was a light change.
The backdrop was lettered in gothic print:

Prince 1958—1993

A woman's voice: *Welcome to the dawn. You have just accessed the gold experience.*

A man's voice: *On June 7, 1993, Prince departed from this earth, his name changed legally to an unpronounceable symbol. Ladies and gentlemen, the Artist Formerly Known as Prince.*

People went nuts when they saw him dancing at the top of the staircase. It took them a minute to realize that it wasn't him. It was that ingenious moment of reveal he always crafted for a live show. He'd actually been lying flat on the floor with a black sheet over him. He'd been brought on, hiked over the shoulder of one of the dancers earlier in the medley, and because the move was repeated by several other dancers, no one noticed. He sat up abruptly, swung his leg around into a split, scissored up to his feet as if gravity ain't no thang, slicked his hair back, and launched into "Billy Jack Bitch"—and he did all this with a nonchalant, gum-chewing savoir faire that had the whole place screaming with adoration. Epic reveal. People still talk about it.

I met him on the grand staircase for " 👁 Hate U," and the choreography was all lyrical romance until *"Take off your clothes."* Then I stripped off my skirt, and by the time it was all said and done, I'd poured water down my shirt, beaver-shot the crowd with a little peekaboo between my knees, and did an inverted split with my legs in the air. A lot of stuff didn't make it onto the live broadcast, but I managed to slip a few tricks past the censors while making my ballet teacher very proud and inspiring thousands of girls to go out the next day and cut their bangs into a V just like mine.

As the rest of the dancers were peeling themselves off the floor, he tipped his head close to mine and said, "Cool?"

"Mm-hmm!"

I gave him a quick nod and a smile and stepped back so he could do the acceptance speech, which included a long list of genuine thanks to everyone from Wendy and Lisa and Sheila E to Muhammad Ali, Joni Mitchell, and Martin Luther King Jr. There was probably some tension in the air as people wondered if he was going to make some statement about his dispute with Warner Bros., but his parting word was a pointed comment "to everyone sweating NPG's financial bankroll."

I pulled the cash out of my bra and started counting it.

"Like an Eskimo," he said. "Chill. It's all good. Peace and be wild."

Meanwhile, work continued. When I get sick or exhausted, the first thing to go is my voice. I can hold up as a dancer longer and stronger than I ever could as a singer. I was starting to get scratchy while we rehearsed in Denmark during the summer of 1995 and was full-on barking as we went on to perform in Germany, London, Italy, and Spain. Nonetheless, I loved being out promoting, finally feeling like a full-fledged member of the band. I'd worked hard to come up to speed: jazz, hip-hop, modern, lyrical—you name it, I could dance it. I felt confident and respected, and because I had such great respect for my bandmates, that meant a lot to me.

We were multitasking performances and promotion, so the last week of July, ♀ went back to LA to produce an album for someone while Sonny, Morris, and I stayed in Barcelona to do some press for the upcoming release of the New Power Generation album *The Gold Experience*. My love and I kept missing calls from each other because of the time difference. He finally caught up with me for a brief conversation, but he sounded sad and vacant—the way he did when he had a "migraine"—and I felt an unsettling nudge in my gut. I wished I could be there for him, mostly because he needed me, but also because I was young and insecure, and I knew there would always be someone else on hand who'd be there for him when I wasn't.

"I wish we could talk longer," I said. "Do you want me to tell them—"

"No, no. Go do what you need to do."

I reluctantly hung up and went up to the rooftop

patio to meet Sonny and Morris, ready to do my part on the press junket. The idea is to post up in a nice-looking location where TV crews and photographers and freelancers do short interviews one after another. The whole day was booked this way, just like the day before had been booked in another city, and the following day was booked somewhere else. Sonny and Morris are so hilarious, they made it fun, and I was good at playing The Girl, but I couldn't shake this weird feeling.

I told Morris, "I need to go downstairs for a minute. I won't be long."

I just wanted to call him back and say, "I love you." When I got to my room, the desk phone's red message light was blinking. It was his security dude: "Hi, it's Aaron. He wants to talk to you again. Give me a call."

When I called back, Aaron put him on immediately, which was pretty unusual. He was never one to sit by the phone. That was my job.

"You're supposed to be sleeping," I said. "Are you okay?"

"I'm fine."

He was quiet for a long time, which was not unusual at all. Sometimes he just needed to sit with that connection for a little while. I was happy to do that under normal circumstances, but I had these people waiting for me on the roof, so I said, "You know where I am, right?"

"Barcelona," he said.

"It's so beautiful here, and oh—they have fresh apples in the hotel lobby."

That made him laugh for some reason.

"I want to talk to you," I said, "but they're waiting for me. I just came down to tell you that I love you. And I'm here for you."

"Thank you."

We hung up, but something kept me sitting there for an extra second or two, and it only took that long for the phone to ring. When I picked it up, there was a long pause.

And then he said, "Will you marry me?"

"Um...what?"

Probably not the response he was looking for, but I was kind of shocked. This wasn't something we'd discussed. I loved him, and I knew he loved me. To be honest, I'd been hoping he would ask me to move in with him, but we'd never discussed that, either. I was confident we'd be together forever, but I was only twenty-two.

On the other hand...

"I said, will you marry me?"

I started crying and said, "Yes. Of course."

"Soon."

"Okay..."

"I want us to have a family."

"Me too."

"What kind of ring do you want?"

"I have no idea."

"Where are we doing this?"

"No idea. None. Open to suggestions."

And then came all the things you hope to tell your grandchildren someday: how we sat there for another forty minutes of tears and *I love you*s, and that Mama was staying in the hotel and came to my room, and we sobbed our heads off, and my makeup was beyond smeared, and that put another monkey wrench in the press thing on the roof, but *who cares*, because I'd never been so happy in my whole life. Absolute, optimistic, hearts-and-flowers joy. That's what I would have told our grandchildren on a front porch somewhere in Minnesota.

Oh, I want to believe we're out there, somewhere in the universe of all possible paths at all possible times, holding on to all that joy with a beautiful grandbaby in my arms and an acoustic guitar in his. I want to believe that this sudden proposal was because he felt a sudden rush of "absence makes the heart grow fonder" and not because he was struggling with guilt or whatever. And maybe that's just the old insecurity talking, because if it was an impulse, the idea must have grown on him. He certainly never tried to backpedal. Quite the opposite. He couldn't wait.

By the time I got home from the press junket, he had a grand scheme in full swing—not so much for the wedding, but for married life—including renovations at the house and at Paisley Park. He didn't want me to see any of that before the wedding, especially the bedroom, so he'd had a big round bed put in the living room by the piano downstairs. On an impulse, I'd bought him a wedding band in Milan, and he immediately said, "I want it."

"You can't have it until the wedding," I said. "It hasn't been fitted."

"I'll get it fitted. I want people to know that in my heart and mind, we're already married."

I didn't argue with that. A few days later, he was wearing the ring, and other than during the first part of the wedding ceremony, I didn't see him without it. I guess he thought he was being super sly having Wardrobe call me. "Hi, Mayte, we're getting ready for this photo shoot with a new designer and new additions to the look, and we lost some of your measurements. What's your shoe size?"

"It's 7½."

"And your hat size?"

"I have a big head. Like—*big* big. Plus a lot of hair."

"And your, um . . . ring size?"

I laughed partly because it was so see-through but also because I honestly had no idea. I'd never had a fancy ring before. One afternoon in October, he called my apartment and told me to come over. I parked in the garage, came in through the laundry room, and found a series of notes on heart-shaped paper.

The first one was just an arrow pointing down the hallway.

The second one said, *Message 4 Mayte on Kitchen Table.*

The third had an arrow pointing to a glass of port wine. *Pour a little, take a sip and then look on "the bench."* I poured a little port and pretended to take a sip. I could hear him spying on me from the loft over the living room. By this time, we were both giggling.

The note on the bench said, *Just relax. You'll smile a thousand smiles.* An arrow pointed me in the direction of the big round bed by the piano. The note on the bed was just a smile with an arrow pointing to some flowers and a blanket, and under the blanket was a box, and in the box was a ring, and it fit perfectly. Laughter. Tears.

He was right. I smiled a thousand smiles.

I'm smiling a few more right now just thinking about it.

We toured Japan for two weeks in January 1996, and early one morning, I woke up in the hotel room and heard him playing piano on the other side of the door. I dragged the sheet off the bed and went to sit beside him. He was so content, so sure that he was exactly where he was supposed to be, and the music he played was full of that feeling. I didn't know it at the time, but he was working on *Kamasutra*, the music that would be played at our wedding. It flowed so easily from his heart to his hands to my ear. I rested my head on his shoulder, and he kissed my head, both of us wise enough to cherish that moment.

On the airplane as we flew home, he ripped pages from *Vanity Fair* and *Vogue*.

"Look at this dress for your sister."

"Oh. Okay. Um—"

He decided he wanted us to get married on Valentine's Day in Paris. We couldn't make that happen on such short notice, but he was fixed on that date and wanted me to find a wedding planner who could figure out a way to make it happen in Minneapolis.

We decided to get married in a small ceremony at a church in Minneapolis, followed by a private dinner for family and close friends at Paisley Park, and then move to the soundstage for a huge party that would include over a thousand friends, coworkers, and devoted fans.

When I got home, I interviewed wedding planners and hired the one who stressed me out the least. When she asked me about my vision for the wedding, I said, "Well, I always wanted a long train. And for my dad to wear his uniform."

"Good..." She looked at me expectantly. "And..."

"And...wow. That's all I got. Never thought about it."

Apparently, my fiancé had thought about it a lot. He chimed in with specifics for everything from flowers to flower girls—there would be seven. We had a casting call. Yep, you're reading that correctly: we had a casting call for our flower girls. And yeah, I get the rock-and-roll fantasy over-the-topness of that, but I was moved by how much he cared about every detail of this wedding. It was a work of art, not a show for an audience—there were very few people there; he wanted us to have this beautifully orchestrated memory in our own heads. The rich visuals were important to him, because the memory of it all was a gift he wanted to give me, along with music he was working on. He kept the songs closely guarded so I would hear them in the perfect setting. The reveal. The audience he was playing to was me—the me of that moment and the grandmother me. The old woman who would look back and tell her granddaughters on their wedding days how she was greatly, artistically, lavishly loved by their grandpa.

He'd come home from the studio, all excited, like a kid, singing, *"Wait till you heeeear."*

"What? I'm going over there."

"Noooooo, you're not."

"Yes, I am."

He'd go up a third—*"No, you're not"*—and then go higher and higher—*"No, you're not, no, you're not"*—until we were both laughing.

While all this was going on, work went on as usual at Paisley Park, including my album project *Child of the Sun*. This wasn't something I asked to be involved in. It came about because of a show we had done in Spain the year before. After a long, crazy concert of amazing songs, dances, and love, he was preparing for the encore while I went out and worked the crowd, tossing out tambourines and saying hi to fans. They started chanting, *"Mayte! Mayte! Mayte!"* and they didn't stop, even when he came back out onstage. After a minute or so, ♀ looked at them, looked at me, and then leaned in to shout over the noise.

"You need to do an album."

"No, I don't," I shouted back.

"You're doing an album."

That was the whole discussion. Within weeks, it was in the works. I loved him all the more for being so supportive, but my calling was to dance, and as I evolved as an artist, I was getting more and more interested in directing and editing—which strikes me as a very natural progression, because it's all about rhythm and motion and technical precision. Just like dance, it transforms the emotional into the visual.

The album, *Child of the Sun*, was released by NPG in Europe later that year. It was actually a lot of fun.

We did a duet, "However Much U Want," which was the first song I ever sang in the studio and was written with me in mind. I did a gender-bend version of "The Most Beautiful Girl in the World"—"The Most Beautiful Boy in the World"—and he came in to put a new spin on the Commodores' "Brick House." The cover has me in full-on golden Egyptian goddess mode, though we didn't discover the hidden significance of the title track, "Children of the Sun," until years later.

Just before the album dropped, he wrote to me:

Dearest Darling,

👁'm listening 2 a re-mastered version of your album. It's deeper and louder. Much better. Kirk did it in L.A. U have the cutest voice! It's your album now. Anything u don't like or wanna fix u can. 👁'll give u the $$. Forgive me 4 being so distant, 👁'm just burnt on the studio & the routine of record-making. 16 years of it, 👁 guess. 👁'm ready 4 a change—World tour, new clothes, new money, hairstyle, car, house. 👁'm ready 2 be ♀. 👁'm sure u understand.

Every rain storm passes. Every earthquake stops. Every night brings morning. Please don't ever doubt my love 4 u. 👁 love u with my soul! No one has ever or will ever get close 2 my soul the way u have. Other women want my babies. 👁 just find it funny! My future's all arranged. If they're not your babies, 👁 *ain't havin' none!* 👁 *wouldn't want 'em. 'cuz they were never supposed 2 be here! Patience is a virtue.* 👁 *trust God with everything now. Even u. If u stay with me, it's because (*👁 *believe) he wants me 2 be married (a huge extravagant wedding) and have 2 angels for him...*

He put together a beautiful program to hand out at the wedding and included some of the things I'd said in the hypnotic state. He wanted to share a few of the little coincidences and parallels that made us smile. There was the unlikely way we met; he never, never took random tapes from people and immediately watched them like that. There was the prophetic little joke he made to Rosie, and how both our fathers are named John. My mother, Nelly, and his middle name Nelson—Nel's son. His mother, Mattie, so close to Mayte. When I met John Nelson, we stood in his kitchen, and he told me that I reminded him of Prince's mother. I told him that my birthday is November 12, just one day off from hers, and he grunted out a brusque, "Damn it. Of course."

After a few years, the coincidences began to feel more like fate.

He asked me to marry him on July 25, 1995, while I was in Barcelona. I didn't connect the dots until Daddy showed me a ticket stub and pointed it out to me that the first time Prince and I saw each other was at the concert in Barcelona on July 25, 1990. Another moment of fate and coincidence that took our breath away for a moment.

There was a rehearsal the day before the wedding, and I went back to my apartment so we wouldn't see each other before the ceremony. In the wee hours of the morning—I could barely sleep from the excitement—I woke up and found Mama crying. When I asked her what was wrong, she said, "I didn't get to do anything! I never had a wedding of my own, and now—all this, and I didn't help with anything. I didn't even cook or make rice or my Puerto Rican wedding cake. There's nothing for me to do."

"Well, that's not true, Mama. There's..." I racked my brain trying to find something the wedding planner hadn't already covered. "You know what? I have some almonds. I was thinking, we should do little, like, little—you know, do them up in little bags. You know how much he likes almonds, so I got them, but I haven't had time to put them on the table and make them pretty." This calmed her for the moment, and the next morning, I called the planner and begged her, "Please, please, find something for my mother to do."

My husband-to-be called and said, "Hi."

"Hi."

"How are you?"

"I'm great. Excited," I said.

He said, "Me too."

I went over to the church to get dressed, and while I was having my hair done, I heard helicopters overhead. Nervously, I asked Daddy, "Do you hear that?"

"Yeah, that's for you," he said.

"The groom asked for a police escort," said the planner. "The press caught on."

My fiancé called me and said, "Don't worry about it. I have a way to get there. They won't see me."

A vision of him being wheeled into the church in a roadie case crossed my mind.

"I'm having a limo come over," he said, "but I'm riding in the back of the van with the flowers."

That made me laugh, because he was wearing a clean, crisp, tailored white suit, and I had a hard time picturing him squatting in the back of a van among the gardenias and orchids. You can see half of his wedding suit on "Holy River"; it's the bolero jacket. On the back is his symbol with an *M* superimposed on it. I'd never seen this combination of his new name with my initial. I didn't know that he'd had it monogrammed all over our home—the china, curtains, napkins, and towels. When I walked down the aisle and saw it for the first time, I was overwhelmed.

Also a bit overwhelming were the flowers. I'd ordered what I thought was a lot of them, though I did tell the wedding planner, "These columns for three hundred bucks a whack? Not happening. We're only occupying the first couple of rows in the church." Without telling me, my husband-to-be had ordered an additional half million dollars' worth of flowers and had them flown in the day before the wedding. White and gold orchids. Gardenias on the railings. Roses and huge arrangements on pedestals. The flowers I'd budgeted with the wedding planner were pretty much a joke next to all that. After the wedding he asked me under hypnosis if I was upset that we didn't have a big church wedding, and I told him, "I'm glad there were only a few people in the church. More room for angels."

Kirk's brother officiated at the ceremony, which went off perfectly, and afterward there was a private dinner at Paisley Park. I was astonished when I got there. The sleek corporate white and gray walls were painted sky blue with puffed white clouds. The purple carpet was decorated with signs of the zodiac. A kaleidoscope of colors and murals made every corner beautiful. The wall above the elevator was lettered boldly:

ELEVATE

I loved that and a million other small, perfect details. There was nothing dull about Paisley Park before, but this was like opening the door to Oz—if Oz was serving a vegetarian meal with edible flowers.

Our first dance as a married couple was one of the songs he'd been working on: "Friend, Lover, Sister, Mother/Wife."

friend lover sister mother wife
air food water love of my life

After dinner, we went back to the house to change clothes for the big party on the soundstage. Gianni Versace had generously sent me a selection of dresses for the big reception, and I chose a white strapless number with the greatest turn-around skirt ever made. It was gorgeous.

We got out of the car, and my husband carried me over the threshold on his shoulder like a sack of coffee beans. The house had been completely redone to make it *our* home. He took me by the hand and showed me every room. The foo foo magicians had been to my apartment, packed up all my stuff, and had everything put away neatly by the time we arrived. Upstairs in an anteroom outside the master bedroom, there was a crib. My husband went in and cued up the other song he'd been working on: "Let's Have a Baby."

Too bad that gorgeous Versace dress never made it to the party.

nine

The next morning, I found that my bags were
packed.

"Where are we going?" I asked my husband, and
he just smiled.

When we got to the airport, we went to the gate
for Hawaii. We were both ridiculously happy. Never
before or since have I experienced that particular level
of being *in love*. It was so strange and wonderful to
look at this beautiful man and think, *Husband*.

"We're married," we kept reminding each other.
"How insane is that?"

And then we'd go off giggling again. He always
laughed about the fact that people often mispronounced my name like "my tie," so when the flight
attendant leaned in and said, "Mai tai?" we both
cracked up laughing till we had tears in our eyes. We
asked for virgin mai tais, because we were trying to
get pregnant, and spent the rest of the long flight giggling, napping with our heads together, and making
out under a blanket.

In the limo on the way to the hotel, my husband was doing his best to tease and distract me, but I saw a billboard over his shoulder:

✚ Feb 16, 17, 18

"Seriously?" I said. "We're working?"

"I figured we'd get bored and want to play."

Lord help me, he was right. I couldn't even be mad. Michael, Sonny, Tommy, and Morris were waiting to meet up with us at Eurasia, a nightclub in Honolulu. For the rest of the week, we were booked to play the Blaisdell Center, an arena that held about eight thousand people. We rented a boat one day, and he kept me giggling by pretending to be seasick and impersonating people and sneaking video of some guy's janky old penny loafers. We spent an afternoon communing with dolphins at an aquarium—petting their snouts, imitating their nickering voices, letting them splash us with their tails—and that was amazing, but we didn't really hang around the beach or do tourist stuff at all.

We did go to see a local band one evening, and my husband blew their minds by getting up and jamming with them for a while. I loved that he did that. It was very rare for him to play someone else's guitar, because he hated using a whammy bar. He was very particular about using foot pedals and having them situated just so. I'm not sure what made him jump up and join in that night. I guess he was feeling happy and light and wide open in a way that was brand new to him.

Mostly, we spent our days the way we spent all our days on tour: sleep in as late as possible, head over to the venue for sound check, hair, makeup, warm-ups, go time. If we had any free time, one of us would nudge the other and suggest, "Let's try to have a baby."

The second day, my husband started saying, "I wonder if you're pregnant."

"Maybe."

"I think you're pregnant."

"It's possible."

"Do you think you're pregnant?"

"I don't know! The only pregnant girl I ever knew dropped out of high school."

"I need to know. We need one of those tests."

He was going to call home and have someone FedEx us a pregnancy test, but I reminded him that they do have drugstores in Hawaii, and we now had the whole entourage in tow, so there would be someone to go get it for us without anyone knowing who it was for. This happened and the test was negative, but he thought maybe it was so early we would need a blood test. Off we went to a clinic to see a doctor. I felt like an idiot asking for the test.

"We're newlyweds," I told the nurse. "Pretty excited."

"It's too soon. You'll have to wait just like everybody else," she said.

When I got back to the hotel room, he sighed. "Okay. I guess we'll keep trying."

"Fine by me," I said, crawling back into bed with him. This aspect of it was a joy, but honestly, if we'd had any more downtime, he would have driven me nuts with the pregnancy questions.

It ended up being the perfect honeymoon for us. Hard to imagine having more fun than we had when we were onstage together. We were doing a lot of music from *The Gold Experience*, including "The Most Beautiful Girl in the World," which sent fans into a fit of ecstasy. We performed it the same way we'd been performing it for the past year and a half, with exacting choreography we worked out together for the World Music Awards, but it was different somehow. He kept referring to me as "my wife, Mayte."

Ah, I thought. *That's why it feels so different. Because it is.*

When we got home, we were right back in the swing of things at Paisley Park. There was a lot going on that winter, which left little time for obsessing over the pregnancy question. We had booked some tour dates and one-off shows and aftershows. ♀ was working on music that would become his *Emancipation* album, celebrating his separation from Warner Bros. The Spike Lee movie *Girl 6* was about to come out with a soundtrack album featuring music by Prince with The Family, Vanity 6, and New Power Generation. There was a movie about Selena in development, and I had been asked to screen test for it.

On a day-to-day level, there wasn't a huge difference in my life. We had worked hard before we were married and kept working hard after. We were still doing what we loved, but now we had a real partnership. Before we had been driving down the same road; now we were on the same bus. He talked to me about finances and asked my opinion about decisions, and I started thinking about things like utility bills and taxes. I was still performing with him, but he was feeling less comfortable with some of my costume options, not loving that his wife was out there in hot pants and bikini tops.

Thinking ahead to what I'd do when I did get pregnant and couldn't tour with him for a while, I went to the office and said, "You can take me off the payroll since I'm his wife now."

A year before that, not in my wildest dreams could I have imagined myself saying the words "take me off the payroll," and looking back now, I just sigh and shake my head. *Baby girl, what were you thinking?* I wanted to stay involved, stay productive—I was still on my standing mission to always prove my worth— but it seemed odd to me that I would be paid a salary when I could have anything I wanted. We were in this together. A partnership.

We didn't do much sleeping in those days. I

remember a lot of work, but it was the kind of work that breeds joy. I heard the piano a lot, at all hours of the night and into those creative hours before dawn. I wish I'd had a camera phone back then. It was such a luxury to be sleeping and hear his lavender piano being played just on the other side of dreaming, and then slowly wake up to realize it was him, and he was creating something. He spent most of the time recording and jamming, and through the jamming came songs and more songs. I started cooking for us—mostly what I called Love Soup—garbanzo beans and lots of veggies, which we eventually started growing in our own greenhouse. I felt like a wife and wanted to be a mother, so I started rethinking my hot-pants-wearing, stage-diving lifestyle. I knew I wanted to get behind the camera, directing and editing music videos, and my husband was totally on board with that idea.

"You have that eye," he told me. "You have that sensibility."

One night we made plans to go to the Philharmonic and then to see Alanis Morissette afterward. During the symphony I suddenly felt this strange surge of sleepiness. I rested my head on my husband's shoulder and drifted with the music while he breathed against my temple and played with the ends of my hair. During intermission, he made me laugh, doing little sound effects in my ear to illustrate what the people around us were thinking. In the car afterward, I took an Advil, and he asked me if I was all right.

"Just feeling a little off."

He gave me that Scooby-Doo look, ears perking.

"Don't get your hopes up," I said. "I think I'm getting my period. First one since going off the Pill, so it'll probably be hard core. But it's good, because then I'll be on a predictable cycle."

I hated to bail on the Alanis thing, but I could hardly keep my eyes open, so he suggested we go home and watch TV. I went up to the bathroom and was surprised to find I didn't have my period. And my boobs looked...bigger? Yes. Definitely bigger. I felt a surge of excitement, but I didn't want to get ahead of myself, so I called my friend and asked her, speaking in Spanish, if she would pop out to the drugstore and get me a pregnancy test. She came back with four different tests. I did the first one, and didn't even have to wait. The little doodad showed a bright blue plus sign almost immediately.

I went to the doorway and called out, "Um, hey."

No response.

"HEY!"

He muted the TV and said, "What is it?"

"Can you come over here?"

"I'm watching this."

"Come. Here. Now."

He turned away from the TV, and I held up the stick.

"It's positive?" he said. "Are you serious?"

I laughed and hugged him, but he wanted to do all the tests, so he set them up like a science experiment on the counter. He looked at the four tests, each with their bright distinctive positives, and said, "We gotta go to the doctor right now." The limo driver was on call, just in case we changed our minds about going out again, so by midnight we were at Urgent Care. They did blood work, and the doctor offered to do one of those *down there* ultrasounds with the wand, which we politely declined. The nurse came back with the blood work, and she was smiling ear to ear.

"You're pregnant," she said.

He hugged me hard, and we laughed for pure joy.

"I'm gonna get fat!" I said.

"Yes! Good!" He dropped to his knees and whispered something to my belly, then got up and took me by the hand. "Who should we tell?"

It was almost three in the morning by this time, almost four in Miami where Mama was living. He got on the phone with her and said, "What's up, Grandma?" It took her a minute to catch on, but then she was shrieking and crying. We went home, and I made him come in and look at my boobs in the bathroom mirror. Understand, people—I was never a well-endowed woman in that area, and he was always dead set against the idea of me getting my boobs done, so this was a spectacular development, so to speak.

He nodded appreciatively. "Huge."

"I know! Right?"

We huddled together in bed, living this perfect moment, knowing we were going to be parents, talking about all the things that needed to be learned and done and prepared. We were in those still, creative hours before dawn. The whole house felt full of love and joy and expectation. In the morning, I woke up wanting orange juice.

"I need to start eating breakfast," I said. "I need to start research and planning and I don't know what all."

He was on the phone conducting business, telling people, "Cancel the tour. Mayte's pregnant." I could hear their happy voices on the other end of the line. When we walked into Paisley Park, it had become the joyful place in the song. Just happy, happy, happiness everywhere.

At my first appointment with the obstetrician in Crystal, Minnesota, the receptionist kept sticking her head out the door and calling, "Mrs. Nelson?" I finally jumped up and said, "Oh, shoot! That's me!" They did all the first appointment things and calculated my due date: November 6. Just a week before my birthday. The best birthday present I could ask for, every birthday for the rest of my life. And this confirmed my suspicion that I may have gotten pregnant on our wedding night. The OB flipped through my chart.

"I see no reasons to worry," she said. "You're twenty-two. Healthy. Blood work looks fine. Next time I see you, we might be able to hear a heartbeat."

I don't know what compelled me to do it, but on the way home, I impulsively stopped off at a pet store and purchased a puppy: a little female Yorkie. I was trying to decide what to name her and suggested to my husband, "You should put me under and ask me."

He stroked my face and whispered me into that deep, meditative space. When I woke up, he told me, "You said her name is Mia."

I smiled and said, "Of course. That means *mine*."

At the following appointment, there was the heartbeat, chugging like a little choo-choo. I called my husband at work, hoping he might be able to hear it over the phone, and he said, "I need that machine."

"What—the heart monitor? It's like a doctor's equipment thingy. It's not for sale."

"I want to record it," he said. "Put her on the phone."

Half an hour later, I walked out of the doctor's office with the heart monitor and went straight to Studio B. I slathered the goo on my belly, and moved the monitor around while he bounced impatiently on a chair. When I caught the exact right location, and he heard that little choo-choo chugging away, his face lit up like a neon sign. Thrilled. Amazed. Scared, but in a good way. He recorded the sound, and people told me for years that he walked around with that tape, playing it for anyone who would listen. You can hear it blending into the percussion track on "Sex in the Summer."

Can't U feel the new day dawning...

We were so elated, so thrilled, but looking back I see this strange undercurrent of—I don't know. Fate and coincidence have their dark sides. Remember the dear old cat Paisley, who'd been around since Paisley Park was built? When I was just a couple of months along, she died. My husband was so sad about that, but we got a kitten and named her Isis, and that seemed to cheer him up.

We spent a lot of time driving around the lake and arboretum listening to music, just like we did the very first time I visited Paisley Park, and somehow the car always steered itself toward the shore of Lake Riley where the Purple House stood. Back in the '80s, with the money from his early success, Prince had built the Purple House (not to be confused with the Purple Rain House) in Chanhassen, and he'd had it painted dark purple. Later on, after he built the house where he lived when I met him, his father, John, moved into the Purple House.

Every time we passed by, I'd gently nudge, "So...
your dad lives there now, right?"

"Yeah," he'd say and keep cruising right on by.

He'd been estranged from his father for a long
time. They hadn't really spoken for five or six years. It
was unusual for my husband to talk about his childhood, but one day while I was pregnant, he was feeling introspective. A conversation about music led to
him reminiscing about his father, and I impulsively
said, "I'm gonna go see him."

His eyes got wide. "What? You are?"

"Yes! This is ridiculous. You're just two people
who—you love each other—but you let your egos
keep you apart." I grabbed my car keys and started
toward the door, wondering if he would stop me. Kind
of hoping he would. But he didn't. So off I went. I
wanted to unify the family because we were creating
one, but all the way over there, I was thinking, *Crap.
What did I just do?* I was certain John wouldn't be
mean to me in any way, but I had no idea what I was
going to say when I pressed the buzzer on the gate.
There was a long pause. I decided to count to 30 and
then drive away.

...25...26...27...28

I jumped when I heard a gruff voice say, "Hello?"

"Hi."

"Who's this?"

"It's your daughter-in-law."

"Oh."

There was another pause, and then the gate creaked open. As I pulled up in front of the house, he came out. Feeling both butterflies and the baby in my midsection, I got out of my car and hugged my father-in-law. I didn't care if he hugged back, but after a startled second or two, he did. He was clearly taken aback. I knew I had to smother him with love or this was going to go all bad.

"I'm holding your grandchild," I told him.

He invited me inside and made me a cup of tea. We talked for a little while. Small talk. Nothing too intense. Everything that wasn't being said was intense enough. I didn't want to add to it. When I got back in the car a little while later, I called my husband, and he picked up immediately.

"What happened?"

"He was sweet," I said, playing it cool, like we were buds now, though that might have been stretching it. "He said he'd come to visit."

"He did?" His tone had an unmistakable note of *I'll believe that when I see it.*

But a few weeks later, John showed up at Paisley Park. He drove up outside, and my husband did that thing you do when you're trying not to run, but you have to run, and so you end up kind of trotting very fast. He hustled out to the parking lot where his father stood leaning against his car. He was not much taller than his son and only a little less stylish. I saw the way they hugged each other. That made me hang back so they could talk privately for a few minutes, and then I went out to say hello.

John smiled as I approached. "So ya got married, huh?"

The small talk was a little stiff, but not bad, considering how long it had been since they'd seen each other.

"I'm gonna go inside," I said, rubbing my arms, pretending I was going in because it was cold. As I walked away, I could hear them laughing and bantering, and it sounded warm and hopeful, but less than fifteen minutes after he arrived, John was gone.

"What happened?" I asked my husband as he came back to the door.

"He said he's gonna come by another time."

"Well...yay!" I said. "Right?"

He smiled and nodded. But it didn't happen. I never saw John again. The Purple House is gone now. I heard that Prince had it demolished after his father's death, but when I peeked inside Studio B during my last visit to Paisley Park, I saw John's picture there, and it broke my heart a little.

Things started to go sideways not long after that brief visit from my father-in-law. I woke up early one morning and realized my husband hadn't come home. I called the studios, the office, every number I had. He didn't answer. It was an ungodly hour, but I called one of the security people to go check on him. I laid down again, but I had this vaguely off feeling. The security person called me a little while later, speaking Spanish so my husband wouldn't know what they were telling me. They were taking him to the emergency room. They'd found him passed out. There was vomit on the floor. He was saying it was because he took aspirin with red wine, which made zero sense to me.

I ran to the garage and drove to the hospital. At the ER reception desk I said, "I'm his wife. What's happening?" A doctor came to take me inside. He told me they pumped his stomach and gave him the charcoal treatment they give a person for an overdose. The moment I got inside the room, I threw my arms around him. "What happened? Are you all right?"

He jumped off the gurney. *Jumped.* Like, *sprang.* Full of energy, like always.

"Let's go," he said.

I followed him to the car, peppering him with questions. "What were you thinking? Why would you—"

"I had a migraine," he said. "I took too many pills."

"Too many *aspirin.*"

"Yes."

"Why? How is that even possible?"

"I don't know. My head hurt." He turned and said to his security person, "Go back and get those records. This is private."

On the way home, I sat in the back of the car with my heart pounding, my hands spread protectively over my stomach. I kept saying, "I don't understand this. I don't get it."

He kissed my hands and told me not to worry.

"It was a stupid mistake," he said. And I accepted that.

Yes, it's lame. I look back now, and I see a dozen moments like this one, and I want to go back in time and shake this girl by the shoulders and say, "Wake up! *Aspirin*? Girl, please!" If this had been a daily or monthly or even yearly occurrence, of course I would have been all over it. I would have insisted that he get help, but on a daily basis, during the years I lived with him, this seemed like an isolated incident. I was pregnant and vulnerable and hopeful and young, so I accepted his word that it would never happen again. He promised me it wouldn't, and it didn't, so I didn't question him any further.

We didn't mention it the next day—or ever.

My husband was determined to be clean and healthy and fully present for his family. He went on one of those cleanse regimens where you drink psyllium husk smoothies and colloidal silver. We planned to do a home birth in the big bathtub upstairs. We watched educational videos on natural childbirth and circumcision and nursing. How to bathe the baby.

How to burp the baby. How to change the baby's diaper.

We both read *What to Expect When You're Expecting*, but there's really no way you can know what to expect when you see that first ultrasound. We craned into it, fascinated at the murky image of our baby's body, waiting to catch a glimpse of a hand or little toes. We took home a videotape and watched it over and over.

"Wait! Rewind a little," I said. "Is that what I think it is?"

"No. Umbilical cord. That's all."

We had agreed we didn't want to be told the baby's gender, but I was certain I could see a little you-know-what between his legs.

By the beginning of my second trimester, I had a nice little pooch going. I had a dress with *BABY* printed on it and an arrow pointing down at my belly. He had a shirt that read *BABY MAKER* on the front and *BAM* on the back. We had them in every color. He also loved wearing my big baggy maternity sweaters. I didn't get morning sickness, but I was tired all the time.

"Your body is making a human being," he reminded me daily.

I said, "I want to listen to all your music and watch all your movies."

He leaned in and whispered to my tummy, "Your mama's crazy."

We bought a scale, and I made him get on first. He weighed 118 pounds. I got on the scale and weighed exactly the same.

"It's okay," he said. "All muscle."

"I'm going to weigh more than you by the end of the week."

And I did. I packed on several pounds before my next visit to the doctor.

"You need to slow that down," she said, and I didn't know how to tell her I was eating healthier than a Tibetan monk. My husband was making sure of that. He was urging me to drink soy milk and get my fruit servings and be a vegetarian again. He noticed every change going on with my body and loved it. He couldn't stop kissing and touching and whispering to my belly.

When it came time to talk about names, he put me under, and asked me, "What is our baby's name?"

"Amiir," I said.

"Amiir?"

"It's Arabic for 'Prince.'"

"Amiir," he whispered to my belly. "Perfect."

Oh—excuse me? What's that?

You saw on the Internet that my son's name was "Boy Gregory"? I hate to be the one to tell you, but a lot of what you see on the Internet is fiction.

When you're a famous person—or a famous person's wife or son—you can't check into a hotel or a hospital under your real name, because tabloid journalists get wind of that. So when my son was born, I was checked into the hospital under the name "Mia Gregory." When you have a baby in the hospital, until the birth certificate is filled out, there's an ID on the baby's bassinet or incubator that says "Boy" or "Girl" followed by the mother's last name. This is how the "Boy Gregory" thing got started. Someone who had no right to share any information about my family tried to sell a photograph of my son to a tabloid journalist, who saw that label on his incubator and stupidly reported the baby's name as "Boy Gregory." To this day, it gets repeated over and over, and it offends and hurts me, because every time I see it, I'm punched in the throat with the betrayal of our privacy on top of the devastating loss of our precious child.

While I was pregnant, ♀ gave an interview to *Forbes* in which he said that he intended to keep the names and genders of his children unknown to the public. He frowned when celebrities sold baby pictures to *People* or whatever, even if they were giving the money to charity. Fans had stalked and intruded on him in the past—fans as in "fanatics," not the music lovers and concertgoers he referred to as "friends." He wanted to keep our children physically safe and well away from the craziness of celebrity, and he wasn't playing.

Early in the pregnancy, I bought a charming old-fashioned baby carriage—a "pram," they'd call it in the United Kingdom—and the next day I found it up in Wardrobe. My husband had instructed them to cover it with a black tarp.

"The baby needs sunshine," I said gently.

The tarp was not happening, but I did understand his fears about the damage that could be done to a kid by privilege and being in the public eye. We wanted to be normal parents whose normal kids grow up healthy, hardworking, respectful, and kind.

At the time, that didn't seem like so much to ask.

This next part of my story is very difficult to tell, so please bear with me. It's something I've never shared before, because my husband was extremely protective of our child, and I honored his wishes as long as he was alive.

In May, when I was almost four months along, we flew to New York for a premiere. Jan came with us, and Mama was flying in so we could all get together for her birthday, which also happened to be Mother's Day. When ♀ and I arrived at the *Girl 6* after party, the club was thick with cigarette smoke. My husband and I looked at each other and shook our heads.

I said, "I don't want to be here."

"I don't want you to be here," he agreed. "Wait for me in the limo. I'll say hi to my friend and be out in a minute."

I knew he did want to be there, though, so I was surprised when he came out in less than thirty minutes—and not so surprised when he said he was going to drop me at the hotel and go back. But surprised again when he returned to the hotel room fairly early.

The next morning, he told me, "I'm heading home."

"What—now?" I said. "This was supposed to be a family day. It's Mama's birthday. She's expecting you to be there."

I was hormonal. Vulnerable. Insecure. Whatever. I didn't take it well. I got angry and cried. After he left, I lay back down and fell into a deep sleep, dreaming strange, dark dreams. We were staying in the presidential suite at the St. Regis in New York, a place we'd stayed many times, and the foo foo folk had been there to make it feel like home for us, so the windows and the French doors out onto the balcony were sealed shut and covered with foil to keep the room dark enough for sleeping during the day.

I was jolted awake by a sudden burst of air and light.

I sat up, instantly wide awake, my heart hammering out of my chest—morning sun in my eyes, cool wind in my face—gradually putting it together that a gust of wind had blown the French doors wide open. Daylight, spring air, and distant traffic noise poured into the dark, silent cocoon. It took me a minute to get my bearings, and then I went out to the balcony and stood there in the midday sun. Below me, Central Park was spread like a bright green blanket. It was a beautiful day. I put my hands on my belly, imagining Amiir's tiny body inside mine.

I called Mama to come up to the room with Hena.

"He left," I told her. "Come up and we'll go get something to eat."

When she came up, I was sitting on the sofa. We chatted for a while, and then I got up to go get dressed.

"Mayte." Her voice was odd. As if she was out of breath. "You're bleeding."

I looked at the back of my robe and saw a red stain. I ran to the bathroom. Blood was running down my legs. There was no pain. No contraction. Only blood and intense fear. I tried to call my husband, but he was still on the airplane. An ambulance met me at the back door and whisked me to the hospital without a siren. They put me immediately into an exam room, and I waited there, crying. The doctor came and did a *down there* ultrasound, and I didn't object.

"The good news is, the baby's still alive," he said.

"What's happening?" I asked.

"If the placenta tears away a little, sometimes it can reattach, sometimes not. If it's a miscarriage, you'll know within a few days."

"Am I okay to go home?"

"Don't travel today. See your doctor as soon as you get home."

When I finally got my husband on the phone in the studio, he said, "You'll be okay. You just need rest. You need to come home."

The next day, I flew home, and we went immediately to the obstetrician for another ultrasound.

She said, "I can see where the placenta is starting to tear away."

"It's in God's hands," said my husband.

I squeezed his hand and said, "Exactly."

"We should do an amnio to make sure there's nothing wrong genetically," she said. "Sometimes the body is trying to release the fetus for a reason."

She explained what that meant: long needle, aspiration of fluid, risk of miscarriage.

He said, "No. We're not doing that."

"The upside is that you know," she said. "You won't sit there and worry."

"We won't worry," he said. "We have faith."

I wanted to agree. I hated the idea of the test causing a miscarriage, but I was terrified of everything we didn't know. My faith wasn't like his. He had conviction and certainty. I had doubts and questions. I wasn't sure I could live without the answers.

When we got home, he got down on his knees and prayed, and I got down on my knees and prayed with him.

"We have faith," he said. "We have faith in you. Please, bless this child. He's in your hands. I have complete faith. You are everything. We give it all into your hands. We know you won't allow this child to be harmed."

We did this every day from that hour forward. His prayers were better than mine. I tried hard to be strong, but sometimes mine went off in the direction of, "Don't you hurt this man who has this great faith in you. Don't you take our baby away. We want this child. We prayed for this child. We'll do anything. We'll be good."

Every night, I rubbed vitamin E oil on my belly, and he moved the heart monitor over it until we could hear the comforting sound of Amiir's steady heartbeat. We still felt joy every time we heard it. We kept preparing for the baby's arrival. Weeks went by, and everything seemed to be all right for the moment. I had terrible headaches, and I continued to swell bigger and bigger, but I was basically okay. I stayed quiet, reading and planning, working on video editing with a private instructor who was teaching me. Every night we prayed on our knees. Every day we listened to the baby's heartbeat. He'd lean in, moving his lips against my belly.

"Hey, how's it going?"

Whenever he came close, the baby would roll over inside me. We'd burst out laughing at every kick and hiccup. Sometimes my stomach would get elongated and taut. We loved when that happened.

"Look. It's stretching its legs. See how strong it is?"

A few more weeks went by. My husband wasn't going to LA much anymore, and frankly, I preferred to avoid the place as much as possible. Most of the girls he'd slept with—or who'd wanted to sleep with him or thought that sleeping with him would do something for their careers—ended up there. I didn't want to be bumping into those girls, and LA itself had always intimidated me. He'd bought a house that wasn't like the pleasant rental houses where I'd first visited him. Maybe because I was pregnant, I was even more sensitive to it.

"This is a single man's house," I said.

He nodded. "I'm gonna get rid of it."

We talked about how our priorities would have to change now that we were parents. I told him I wanted to help support the family. It was important to me, and I was excited to be learning something that could be important to him.

Back in Minnesota, he made arrangements to unload the house and ultimately sold it to Raquel Welch, which made us both laugh, because he'd always worshiped her and even went through a phase of wearing the fur boots like the ones she wore in *The Legend of Walks Far Woman*. My Raquel moment—the fur bikini from *One Million Years B.C.*—seemed very far away now. I was swelling like a beached whale. By September, my back was killing me. I switched from kitten heels to sneakers and followed a strict diet, but my body kept bloating bigger and bigger.

The OB told us, "These ultrasound measurements are off. It's possible that we're seeing a form of dwarfism."

My husband and I looked at each other and shrugged.

"And?" he said.

"I'm totally fine with that." I laughed. "That's the least scary thing you've said in months."

Of all the possible outcomes that had been offered to us, this was the first one that didn't terrify me. The OB urged us to reconsider the amnio. "There are other genetic abnormalities that can be life-threatening. We need to be prepared."

"No," my husband said. "We're leaving it in God's hands."

The next day, I told Mama, "These cramps are kicking my butt. I feel like I'm getting my period."

"Go to the doctor right now," said Mama. "It sounds like you're in labor."

I grumbled and complained, but with a bit of persuasion, I went. As the OB prepared to examine me, I stopped and said jokingly, "I'm gonna stop wearing underwear when I come in. All you ever do is feel me up."

She seemed grateful for the opportunity to laugh.

I was dilated two centimeters, which wasn't that alarming.

"Braxton-Hicks," she figured. "No need to worry, but let's stay in touch and start checking in more often."

But suddenly my stomach went taut. I said, "Oh, look! He's stretching his legs."

The doctor looked down at my stomach then looked up at me and said, "No. That's a contraction." She hooked me up to a monitor and determined that I was in labor. "We need to stop this. We need to check you into the hospital. You're the size you should be at nine months, but it's too early to deliver, and since we didn't do the amnio, we have no idea what we're dealing with."

"If there's something wrong," my husband said, "it's God's will. Not because we didn't prepare."

"I told you months ago—there's something wrong."

"I'm taking her home."

"Sir, you're not letting me do my job. She needs to stay in the hospital."

I lay there trying to breathe as their voices got angrier and louder. I wasn't in pain, exactly, but there was a tightness that wouldn't stop.

"Let's go," he said to me.

She was right behind him saying, "She can't go."

"She's free to do whatever she wants!"

"That's right. Mayte, this is your body. You don't have to go."

"Please, let's not—"

"If you take her," the OB said to my husband, "she'll need to sign a release saying that she's going of her own free will—against my advice—saying that you understand she's in danger."

"I'll sign," I said, in tears because I didn't want to upset my husband who clearly needed me and our unborn child out of that room. He wasn't used to someone standing up to him like that, and the more disrespected he felt, the more scared I was of the jangling, negative energy swirling around us in that little box of a room.

I signed, and we left, but in the car, I begged him to take me to another doctor. We went to the closest ER. He waited in the limo so there wouldn't be a scene. I walked in alone and checked in under the name Marlene Gong and said as little as possible.

"I'm seven months pregnant. I'm having cramps."

They hurried me back and hooked me up to the same machine with the same results. I asked for a second opinion. Another doctor came. I asked for a third opinion. My husband came in. He knew people would see who we were, and it would raise a hassle, but he couldn't stand waiting out there any longer. He wasn't happy because they weren't telling him what he wanted to hear. I wasn't happy because he wasn't happy, but the third doctor was a petite red-haired woman who had a better way with him. She seemed to have an instinct about how to deliver information and make recommendations in a way that didn't make him feel that he didn't have a voice in all this and his faith wasn't being disrespected. She didn't just tell him, "There's no way she'll deliver vaginally." She showed him the measurements and said, "This is why it will have to be a C-section."

"The body can do remarkable things."

"Yes, but sometimes it needs help."

He must have been well and truly terrified by now, because he agreed to have me stay in the hospital on a magnesium drip. I checked into a room under the name Mia Gregory. My husband stayed with me for a long while, singing to Amiir, watching for kicks and hiccups. He put his cheek against my stomach and whispered, "You'll be okay." I drifted off to sleep, and when I woke up, Mama was there. Then she left, and I was alone with Amiir and the soft pipping and beeping of the monitor. I stroked my belly and sang to my baby.

> *. . . You are my sunshine, my only sunshine, you make me happy . . .*

Days turned to weeks. Weeks stretched to a month. I'd forgotten how hairy my legs could get—not to mention the unmentionable bits that require landscaping. I tried to go take a shower and ended up on all fours in the bathroom. I watched with longing as other mothers checked in, delivered healthy babies, and checked out again. Lying there like a beached whale, I saw on TV that Madonna had a brand-new baby.

A nurse had to come and help me struggle to my feet. I don't remember her name. I'll call her Angela, because she always brought this positive, loving energy into the room. She came in every day and said, "How's our sunshine?" and then she'd put her stethoscope on my belly and smile when Amiir kicked at the pressure of her hand. Every day, she tried to get me out of bed and into a wheelchair so we could go out and get some air. She tried to coax me into the pool, but she only ever convinced me to leave the room once, and it was such a weird feeling. I didn't want to do anything but hibernate and sustain the child inside me. I felt fate balanced like a sword on top of my head. I didn't want to do anything to tip it one way or the other.

My husband came every day and tried to be supportive, but he was horribly uncomfortable with the idea of me being there week after week. It was actually a relief when he had to go to Japan for a few days. He called me several times a day, and we talked for hours sometimes.

I told him, "I like this. It's just like when I was sixteen."

He laughed and said, "Yeah."

Those hours were an oasis in all this. A reminder of who we were to each other.

While he was gone, the doctors came and told me that there was an injection they could give me to help the baby's lungs mature faster.

"We know your other half won't approve," they said, "but it would be safer if you deliver early, and at the rate you're going, you will most likely deliver prematurely."

I felt rotten for doing it without telling my husband. I was crying when I did it, but I did it. He came back, elated with the response to his international promotions for *Emancipation*, which could now live up to its name. The C-section was scheduled a week later on October 16. Thinking like a protective husband and a seasoned showman, he arranged for a plastic surgeon—someone who'd understand that I was a belly dancer whose life and livelihood were in his hands—to come in and oversee the procedure and close me up afterward.

The night before the Cesarean, my body roared into full-blown labor. They kept trying to drug it down as I lay in agony, hour after hour. My husband sat beside me, gripping my hand. The only relief was when he stroked my face and put me under, talking softly in my ear. "We're going to get through this, and everything will be fine. I love you. I'm here for you. Nothing bad is going to happen."

I had requested that Angela be the OR nurse. I needed that positive, loving energy. I laughed when she told me, "That man of yours is gonna have scrubs on. I told him, 'You're not in charge here, I am.'"

"No way," I said.

"Way," she assured me.

They shaved and prepped and carted me in, and I burst out laughing when I saw him in those scrubs with the booties and puffy hat.

"You look really cute," I said.

"I know." He asked the doctor, "Do all these lights need to be on?"

"Unfortunately, yes."

A burly nurse introduced herself to me and said, "You're going to hate me." It was her job to hold me in a headlock while they did the epidural.

"Tell me when it feels like a sore tooth," said the doctor.

I said, "What do you mean—*oh!* Oh, God. Okay. Yeah."

"Do you feel this? This? How about here?"

"Yes. Yes. I feel everything."

"Okay, she's ready."

"I feel it! I feel everything!"

"You will," she said. "You'll feel it, but it won't hurt."

My husband gripped my hand as they cut me open. He kept his face close to mine, speaking softly, comforting and encouraging me, clowning around like he couldn't breathe behind the mask until I begged, "Oh, don't make me laugh."

It seemed to take a very long time. There was this weird tugging sensation. Like the unzipping of a dress that's too tight. There was soft music playing—harps, guitars, spa-type music—but I heard a liquid sound. Suction. The clinking of instruments. I felt them pull the baby out of me.

"It's a boy!"

I don't know how to describe the look on my husband's face. Pure joy. Pure love. Pure gratitude. I'd seen his face when he stood in front of a stadium filled with forty-eight thousand screaming fans. I'd seen his face as he scored platinum albums and received the highest awards in his industry. I'd seen him experience the ecstasy of creative genius. None of that compared to the look I saw on his face in this moment, when he became a father.

And then they held the baby up in the glare of those harsh lights.

For a suspended second, I saw nothing but my son's beautiful soul. I heard nothing but his perfect silence. He made no sound. My heart called his name.

Amiir.

The pure elation on my husband's face turned to pure terror.

On the cold white page of a medical text, Pfeiffer

syndrome type 2 is a genetic disorder that causes skeletal and systemic abnormalities. Craniosynostosis is the premature fusing of the bones in the skull, sometimes resulting in "cloverleaf skull," in which the eyes are located outside the sockets. Brachydactyly is the fusion of bones in the hands and feet, causing a webbed or pawlike appearance. Anal atresia is the absence of an anus, indicating life-threatening abnormalities in the colon and bowels. I learned all this later. I became fluent in a language I didn't want to speak. But in that first moment, I couldn't understand what I was seeing. It was as if we were at the center of a whirlpool, and the room around us was turning in on itself, contorting, twisting everything.

There was only an instant of fear. In the next instant, we became parents. Our love for him embraced everything he was. And then—chaos.

The OR nurses swooped in and took him. Everyone was talking at once. I heard my husband saying, "He's not crying. Why is he not crying?" He wasn't breathing. They whisked him to a table and began frantically working on him. Everything inside me said, *Let him go*, but someone told me later that they were required by law to revive him.

Suddenly my husband's face was close to mine. He gripped my hand and said, "It's going to be okay. He'll be okay."

"Oh, God…oh, God…"

We heard him cry. My husband disappeared for a moment. Then he was there again. "It's a boy. It's a boy. They got him breathing."

"Let him go."

"No. No, we're going to make it, okay? He'll be okay."

They brought our baby over to us. He was curled on his side, gasping shallow little goldfish gulps of air. Because there were no lids to blink, his eyes looked startled and dry. I caught hold of his tiny hand, saying over and over, "Mama loves you. Mama's here. I love you so much, Amiir. Mama loves you."

When they came to take him, my husband said, "I'm going with him."

"Yes. Yes. Go."

He left. The plastic surgeon came. Someone told me I might need a transfusion. I didn't want to be away from my son a moment longer than necessary.

"Please," I said, "unless I'm gonna *die* die, don't let them do it."

There was talk about my mother giving blood, but I didn't want her to, because I knew she was about to have surgery herself in a matter of days.

I kept pleading, "I need to be with my son. Please, let me go to my son."

Angela was there with her positive energy. "You'll see him soon. First, we need to get you stabilized."

"Is he alive?"

"Yes. Mayte, I'm giving you something for the pain. You're going to get a little sleepy."

When I closed my eyes, I could feel the plastic surgeon dragging meticulous sutures through the skin on my belly. When I opened my eyes again, I was in the hospital room, and my husband was there, still in his scrubs. He looked so tired, so beaten down, but to me, he'd never been more beautiful. He was Amiir's father, a protective Papa Bear thinking only of his son. From the first moment of our son's life to the last, my husband thought nothing of himself. His vanity, his ego, his needs—all that had been stripped away. All that remained was a solid core of unconditional love.

My throat was dry. All I could say was, *"Amiir."*

"He's in surgery again." He described the procedures one after another. They'd sewn his eyes shut. Intubation. Ventilation. Feeding tube. Colostomy. Exploratory...something. It was impossible to take it all in. "They want you to pump milk so they can feed him."

"I want to come and nurse him."

"I don't want you to see him like this. I don't want you to see him till they get him stabilized so he can come home with us." He waited while I pumped and then took the bags of milk. "I'm going back. I'll stay with him."

I hit the button for the painkiller drip and closed my eyes again. When I woke up, Daddy was there. He said, "He's beautiful. Don't worry."

Two days later, my husband briefly went home to take a shower. While he was gone, I had someone wheel me down to see my son. I could see that Amiir was crying, but there was no noise, because they were feeding him my breast milk through a tube in his nose and there was another tube down his throat for ventilation. I stood up from the wheelchair and pulled my IV with me over to the incubator. When I reached inside and took his hand, he immediately became calm, and I suddenly felt calm myself. I'd cherished this child when he was inside me, and then he had been ripped away. Pain. Craziness. But now we were breathing the same air again, touching each other.

"I need to hold him," I said. "Can I hold him without hurting him?"

They took me to a chair. There were so many needles and wires and tubes attached to every part of his body, it took two nurses to lift him into my arms.

"I'm here, Bebo. Mama loves you. I'm your mama."

His skin was indescribably soft. The joints of his fingers were fused, so he couldn't grab my finger, but he found a way to fold his little hand around the side of mine, hanging on for dear life. My husband came. I worried that he'd be angry, but he wasn't. He sat on the floor with his body against my knee, humming and whispering to Amiir, and we stayed that way for hours. I was in pain and fighting to stay awake, but I didn't want to leave. Finally, the nurses gently insisted.

They took the baby, and I let my husband wheel me to my room and help me into bed. Then he went back to be with Amiir. There were more surgeries. He didn't want our son to be alone through any of it.

Every day something new went wrong or collapsed or presented itself, some new problem was discovered, some existing problem got worse. We spent all the hours we could in our little family corner in the NICU, humming and telling stories, and taking in the softness of his skin and hair, the soft smell of his warm little body, the beauty of his spirit, the shape of his lower lip that was just like Jan's lower lip.

After six days, he was struggling to breathe, and I said to the doctor, "He's not leaving here, is he?"

He avoided answering my question. Instead, he talked about more invasive measures, including a tracheotomy.

"No. No, you're not doing that to him," I said. "He is *suffering*."

He quietly explained to me that if we didn't allow him to insert this permanent pipe in Amiir's throat, we were making the choice to let him go, and the more he talked on and on in this cold doctor way, the more hysterical I got.

"You're torturing him! He can't live like this!"

My husband pulled me into the next room and tried to calm me down. "Mayte. Mayte, maybe if they do this—if they can get him breathing with the machine—"

"Then what? What else?"

We stood there in the empty room, coming to the same terrible place.

"We have to let him go."

I wanted to grab the words back as soon as they were out of my mouth. Letting him go meant carving a piece from each of our hearts, but now I was the protective Mama Bear alongside the weary Papa Bear. I wasn't going to let anyone hurt my baby anymore, and I told myself that if we loved him enough to let him go, maybe he'd come back to us. Maybe he would find us, the way we had found each other.

Holding each other tight, we agreed: "If they take him off the machine and he can breathe, we keep fighting. If he can't live without the machine...maybe he's not supposed to be here."

We went back in and spoke quietly with the doctors. They tried to reassure and comfort us, tried to tell us this was the right thing to do, but the rightness of it didn't make it any less bitter. We signed papers and agreed on a time when life support would be removed the next day. They sent me home with painkillers and Valium, and I crawled into a dark sleep. I woke up every three hours during the night to pump breast milk, and I wanted to go to Amiir, but I was terrified to go there again. When we did, it would be over.

When I woke up again, I heard a phone ringing. A

moment later, my husband came and said, "It's done. They took the tubes out."

"What? No! I'm supposed to be there!"

"I didn't know if you could handle it."

"I'm going. Right now. If no one wants to take me, I'll drive."

He put his arms around me. Made me stop. In less time than it would have taken me to get there, the phone rang again. He answered it, and then he hung up and said, "He's gone."

I lost it. I went in our room and cried and cried. I don't know what my husband did. A few hours later, our son's ashes were brought to the house in an urn with three dolphins on it: mama, daddy, and baby. We spent most of the next day huddled together on the couch, crying, touching each other, expressing complete wonder at this beautiful creature who'd just drifted into our lives and then away again. I kept getting up to pump milk.

"You should stop," he said.

"I can't."

My breasts ached, heavy with milk. My hormones were screaming. Every fiber in my body craved the smell of my baby.

I don't know how long I lay in bed with Amiir's ashes. All I remember is the hot, hard pain in my breasts and grief as airless and dark as the bottom of the ocean. Sometimes I was aware of my husband lying next to me or sitting in a chair, staring at the television. The next day—or maybe it was a few days or a week later or in another lifetime—he came to me and said, "I can't be here. I have to go."

He went to play a few gigs and promote the *Emancipation* album. I stayed in the hollow house, wishing I could die. My breasts felt raw. My nipples started to burn and chafe. The stitches on my belly felt like they were crawling with spiders. I lay on the bed, sweating from fever, shaking from shock and chills. I had an infection. A doctor came. I heard her talking to my husband. Their voices were quiet but tense.

"She needs to go back to the hospital."

"No. God's hand is on her. She'll be fine."

"If we don't take care of this, it could cause infertility."

I sat up and said, "I'm going."

He didn't say anything else while I dragged myself up and pulled on pajama pants and a clean shirt.

"Will you come with me?" I asked.

He shook his head, staring straight ahead.

In the hospital, they hooked me to another IV and pumped antibiotics and painkillers into me. The nurses came and put ice on me every two hours. They put salve and compresses on my breasts. After a few days, the pressure subsided, and the milk stopped seeping through the front of my hospital gown. I was sent home.

I sat on the sofa with Mia near the bookshelf that housed the dolphin urn that held Amiir's ashes. The ashes were everything. Everything was ash.

"Where's my Vicodin?" I asked.

"I don't know," he said. "I'll send someone to get you some more."

Days passed in darkness.

He shook me awake. "Mayte. You have to get up."

"Why?"

"Oprah's coming to Paisley. Today. She'll be there with her crew."

"No…"

"Yes. You have to do this. You have to get up."

"Tell her I'm sick. Tell her I can't."

"I need you to do this. I told her you'd be with me."

"I can't. I can't. I can't."

He had me on my feet, steering me toward the bathroom, but I was sobbing, stumbling. My body felt like it was made of quartz. People came. Lights were turned on. A mask of heavy makeup was applied to my face. A cream-colored suit was put on me.

This must be what it feels like, I thought, *when they pretty up a corpse in a funeral parlor.*

While I was being prepared, my husband took Oprah on a tour of Paisley Park, and her mission was clear. She'd come to find out if our child was dead or deformed like people were saying, and in retrospect, this would have been a good way to share the truth in a dignified way. Later on, with not much else to fall back on, the producers cut in screenshots of ugly tabloid headlines:

DELIVERY ROOM TRAGEDY FOR PRINCE
Rock star's baby has horrible birth defect

I think Oprah could have handled it better if we'd let her. God knows she tried, gently prodding my husband for some kind of information as they toured Paisley Park without me. In Studio B, he tried to steer her toward the album that had just dropped, but she said, " 'Sex in the Summer'...the song featured the ultrasound heartbeat of your baby."

"Yeah," he said, and he smiled at the memory of that intensely happy day. "What we did was take a microphone and place it on Mayte's stomach and move it around with the gel till we get the right sound and..." He beat-boxed the sound of Amiir's chugging little heart. "You know, you start to hear that, and then we put the drums around that." He played a little snippet from the cassette tape. "That's the baby."

"When you heard that sound for the first time," she said, "what did you think or feel inside yourself?"

"I was pretty much speechless. It really grounds you, makes you realize that things you thought are important aren't really."

While I was in the hospital, he had installed a lavishly equipped nursery and playroom at Paisley Park. I hadn't seen it yet. In fact, I didn't know anything about that or the huge playground that had been installed outside. He wanted all this to be a surprise for me when we brought Amiir home from the hospital. Oprah saw it before I did. I have to wonder why he took her in there. I suppose it's possible that on some level he wanted to tell her the truth or at least hoped she'd figure it out on her own and understand why he didn't want to make a direct statement. They stood in the middle of this colorful paradise of toys and ramps and murals. It had everything a perfect nursery needs, except for the only thing a perfect nursery needs.

"Oh...wow," she said. "Wow."

"Here's my favorite room."

"For the children to be...the children to come..."

He nodded with great certainty. "Yes, ma'am."

"The child in you? Or just the children?"

"Oh, the children, yeah."

"It's been rumored that your baby boy was born with health problems," said Oprah. "The reports have fans concerned."

It was a tactful way to phrase it. Respectful. Compassionate. He just couldn't go there.

"It's all good," he said woodenly. "Never mind what you hear."

A journalist at heart, she finally asked him directly, "What's the status of your baby?"

"Our family exists. We're just beginning it."

A cryptic answer, but he wasn't lying. This is what we believed to be true. Believing that was the only thing keeping us going.

I sat on a sofa at Paisley Park, smiling a pretty ballerina smile.

Lights. Camera.

Oprah smiled, too. We both knew our choreography. I sensed her frustration; she had a show to do, but I'd been instructed by my husband: "Say *nothing* about Amiir."

She asked about when we met, and my husband told her how he said to Rosie, "There's my future wife." That's such a good story, isn't it? I giggled and nodded and kept my eyes away from Oprah's. The woman is no fool. I was clearly no longer pregnant. There was no baby in my arms. The obvious questions seemed to hang in the air, but she was patient. She asked me how I had felt when we met.

"I felt calm. I felt at peace," I said, and I tried to feel that again in the moment with his arm like a steel safety rail behind my back.

I was surprised to hear him say something about how we'd known each other in past lives—that I was his sister or possibly the same person. These were things I'd said to him while I was in his arms, under his hypnosis.

"Isn't this all kind of weird?" Oprah said.

I giggled and shrugged, thinking, *Girl, you don't even know.*

"Well, it depends on how you look at life," he said.

She looked at me and said, "When he talks about you, there's a thing that happens in his eyes."

I smiled and looked at my hands.

My husband said, "I do feel like I've come closer to who I aspire to be by being with her."

"Really?" said Oprah. "And what does she do for you that you didn't—that you didn't have alone?"

"She makes it easier to talk to God."

"Really?"

"Yes."

"I could cry," she said.

But I couldn't. If I'd let a single tear drop down my cheek, I would have dissolved like the woman in the Bible who turns to salt. I concentrated on my hands. My smile. My ballerina mask while he told her about our small church wedding, how there were only a few people there, adding, "She said she was happy it was empty because it left room for the angels."

Another private moment. Something I had said while I was under. On our wedding night. Why would he give that little moment away? I felt it cost me something. Just a penny or so, but...something.

"Is he romantic?" she asked me.

I giggled and nodded. "He's romantic."

"I'm thinkin'," Oprah mugged, "if he ain't romantic, who is?"

"He's—he's very romantic."

"Like...romantic how?" she nudged. "Like, rose petals in the bed and...?"

He smiled a teasing smile and started to raise his hand to my face the way he always did when he hypnotized me. I gracefully but firmly took hold of his wrist and brought his forearm down to my lap.

Not that. I was not giving that away for a penny. Not today.

We were here to do business. Fine. Keep it about the business. I laughed lightly and said, "For me, the most romantic thing he's done is write all these beautiful songs for me."

"Mm-hmm?" She raised her eyebrows, pleased that I was finally saying something. And maybe there was something I wanted to say. Maybe this was the moment to stop choking it down. Honestly, the whole thing is a foggy mess in my mind now, but maybe I wanted to offer him that opportunity without kicking through his need to control the information.

"You know," I said, " 'Let's Have a Baby'—because of that—I mean...I got pregnant."

He smiled a tight smile, his lips clamped shut.

After the interview, I left them at Paisley Park to

do B-roll or whatever they were going to do. I didn't want to hear about it and never watched the show until much later. During part of it, he's wearing that "Holy River" bolero he wore at our wedding. He wore it for me, I understood later on, but at the time, I didn't notice.

I went home, took Amiir's ashes from the shelf, and crawled back into bed. I cried until I slept and slept until I woke up crying. I remember staring at myself in the bathroom mirror. I didn't recognize my own skin. My eyes were the empty eyes of a plastic doll. In my hand was the bottle of Vicodin. I filled a glass with wine and tapped the pills into the palm of my hand. First one. Then three. Then the whole bottle. I studied them, planning how to swallow them all without the bitter taste making me vomit. I decided to move to the bedroom. I didn't know how long it would take. Better to lie down and not be found on the bathroom floor. I sat on the edge of the bed and raised my hand to my mouth.

And suddenly Mia was there, pawing my bare leg, scratching me with her blunted claws.

"Go away," I whispered.

She yipped and spun in circles. She knew she wasn't allowed on the bed, but she wouldn't leave. She kept scratching at my knees and ankles.

"Mia. No!"

She wouldn't take *no* for an answer. Dancing with

urgency, demanding to be noticed, she kept throwing herself on her back like she wanted me to pat her belly and pick her up. She insisted that I receive this love she was determined to give me. She pawed and licked and rubbed her face against me until I put the pills back in the bottle and sank down on the floor and held her, shaking like a leaf. She licked the tears streaming down my face and badgered me with affection until I was laughing and crying at the same time.

When people ask me where my passion for animal rescue came from, I can trace it directly to this moment. Mia saved my life. If Mia hadn't been there, I wouldn't have been there the next day or the day after that. Or months later, when I finally started to feel like myself again. Or years later, when Gia finally found me.

Amiir's gift to me was motherhood. He taught me what a privilege it is to love someone more than you love yourself. He showed me that I was capable of sacrificing my own heart to protect my child. Amiir made a mommy of me.

That was his gift to Gia.

So now you know what happened. To me, anyway. What happened to me and my son. I can't speak for my husband or describe what this experience was for him. I can only tell you what I observed through the haze of my own pain:

Imagine a skydiver leaps from an airplane. He has

the best equipment and does everything right. At first, there's euphoria. He sees so clearly—blue sky, green earth, beauty without limit, a higher perspective. He has absolute faith that he'll land safely and be a better man than he was before. But it turns out his parachute is tangled. He struggles to fix it, but the chute tears away and disappears into the sky. Panic grabs him by the throat, but still—faith. He has his faith. In free fall, he flails, trying to pray, but the force of gravity takes his breath away. He sees the hard ground coming at him, and he knows that if he survives this, he will never be the same.

ten

My husband wrote many songs inspired by or dedicated to our son. One that still wrecks me after all these years is "Comeback." It's the voice of Amiir's daddy, alone with the echoed versions of himself, accompanied only by the quiet acoustic guitar I love.

sweet wind blew not a moment 2 soon
I cried when I realized that sweet wind was you

In the unresolved chords at the end of this song, you can hear this man's love for his child. It was bigger than him. We loved each other, but this child—we *loved* this child. He was everything to us. We would have done anything for him.

"I smell him," I told my husband.

"Do you?"

"Yes. In the air when I wake up. I smell him. Like my senses can't accept he's gone."

"Don't say gone. He'll come back."

"He will. I know he will."

as sure as the candle burns
every soul must return

I begged him to put me under and talk to me about it, but he wouldn't do that anymore. The deep connection created a door he was afraid to open now. We clung to our faith in eternal life and the great journey of the soul. We lay in the dark, talking about where Amiir might be now and how we could bring him back.

We didn't wait to try to get pregnant again, but this ordeal had left my spirit so empty, it didn't surprise me at all when my period came each month, my body telling me it wasn't time yet. My body was doing everything a woman's body is supposed to do after she gives birth to a baby, but nature designed all that with a baby in mind. My hormones were speedballing, and my breasts ached, even after the milk was gone—and the milk wasn't completely gone for a long time. I'd wake up from a dream about Amiir and find it soaking my shirt and the sheets.

I'd been around the military all my life, so I knew about post-traumatic stress syndrome—shell shock, they used to call it—but it never occurred to me that there are all kinds of battlefields in this world. Now I see so clearly that we were both scarred and suffering for years, because we didn't know how to deal with it in the moment. I was a zombie for months. It was hard for me to see past my own pain long enough to understand what was going on with my husband. Even if I could have, he was not the type of guy you can bring chicken soup to when he's sick. He wasn't accessible that way. As his wife, I could get closer than a girlfriend, but even after I had the phone numbers, there was a point of *Do Not Enter*. There were times when I knew better than to intrude. As cliché as it is for sexy older men to date younger women, I think his preference was more than physical; it was about the power balance. He didn't like to be argued with. He wasn't used to someone banging on the door and saying, "I'm coming in! I don't care what you say."

Before we were married, he wrote to me:

A secret—when 👁 have a disagreement with someone—it's usually only one. Then they're gone. 👁 don't mind them (disagreement) with u because 👁 know we'll always be 2gether. Although 👁 hate 2 fight, 👁 hope we are both better souls from the exercise. That's how 👁 look at it—as exercise... The toning of the heart muscle so it's strong and able 2 withstand anything when I'm a father!

I'm going 2 be one u know. When 👁'm ready! 👁'm glad u're young cuz u can wait 4 me. Well 👁 hope u do. 👁 only want your kids! We're so much alike, it's inevitable.

If fighting was "exercise," the last year of our marriage was a Spin class from hell, but there was a long stretch before that when I truly believed we'd be all right.

At first, the best we could do was pretend to be all right. We didn't know how to do this, so we just kept trudging forward, walking wounded, trying to look like everything was normal. Everyone has their own way of mourning, and my husband's way of dealing with anything painful was work. Creating music and playing it for people—that was the only solid ground he'd ever known. A few days before the Oprah interview aired, "Betcha by Golly Wow!" was released. He had recorded the song while I was pregnant and started working on the music video in the aftermath.

His vision for this video involved children, as many of his videos did, dancers in white alphabet unitards that spelled out "betcha by golly wow," a gymnast, and this whole very charming dance, all cut into a storyline about ♀ hurrying into the ER, where I'm sitting on an exam-room gurney in a hospital gown. At the end, when he finally gets to me, we embrace with joy, and you get that we've just learned I'm pregnant. It's beautifully done. Incredibly sweet. People loved it, and everyone has always naturally assumed that this sentimental moment was captured while I was pregnant.

It wasn't.

It was done in early November 1996, only a few weeks after we lost Amiir.

When he told me about this idea and said he wanted to shoot the scenes at the hospital where Amiir had recently died, I wanted to shake him. I wanted to slap him and say, "Are you serious right now?" The idea of going back into that hospital made my legs feel weak. But he was so earnest about this vision. He wanted to return to a moment when he felt complete joy, complete faith, complete love, and he wanted to take me with him.

I can look at it now and see the sweetness of it, but for a long time, I couldn't look at it at all. I did it for the same reason I did Oprah: I didn't know what else I could do to help him. If nothing else, I wanted to be in the same room with him. If that room was Studio B, fine. If it was our bedroom, even better. This man was my family now, and I was his. If he'd asked me to drive off a cliff with him, I would have done it.

Mama had put off the surgery to remove a large tumor from her uterus as long as she could, but I urged her not to postpone it any longer. Having gained a whole new appreciation for Mama, I was determined to be there for her. I arrived at the hospital to find that, because the surgery was gynecological, they had her in the maternity ward. The hospital was hard. This was too much. My husband found me sobbing about it and said, "We'll get her a nurse. She can go home, and you can be with her."

The official release of *Emancipation* was also happening in November, and a huge part of the PR push was his live appearance on Oprah, so my husband went to Chicago to do the live portion of her show. He went on to do as many performances as he could wedge in for the next several weeks. I was relieved to see *Emancipation* quickly climb the charts—to number eleven in the United States and Top 20 in the United Kingdom. I knew it would do his heart good. So much of his vision for the future was riding on that release and the independent distribution deal he'd struck with EMI.

He left on tour, which was a form of escape for him. *Now it'll hit him*, I thought, and I worried about him riding alone on the bus and brooding in a hotel room in the dark hours before dawn. In mid-December, he canceled two shows, which is something he never did. When I went to talk to him about it, I found wine spilled on the rug in the hallway and vomit on the bathroom floor. I knew he was struggling. I knew he was in pain. But I was struggling myself. I never told him about my thoughts of suicide or how close I had come to actually doing it. The moment Mia saved me from myself remained a secret between her and me. I didn't want my husband to worry about me, but I started to think he knew, because my Vicodin kept disappearing. The prescription would be filled, and a few days later, most of the pills would be gone. I assumed he was hiding them to keep me from hurting myself. In retrospect, I don't know what to think.

At that time in our life, he alienated a lot of people. As I got back into the business of living, I'd go to New York to visit Jan or I'd go to Miami to hang out with my mother, but it was unusual for them to come to Minneapolis. We rarely had guests unless it was work-related, and my husband was gone a lot of the time. It felt so strange to not be working, to be sitting there alone.

The tabloid coverage of our loss rubbed salt in the wound. While the celebrity news cycle hadn't yet reached the frenzied fever pitch of today, it was still in overdrive—and as one of the biggest pop stars in the world, my husband—and our tragedy—got a lot of play in some of the sleaziest media out there. One day at the grocery store, I was standing in line trying not to look at the twisted headlines, and some well-meaning idiot said to me, "Did you have your baby yet?" I left my tampons and Advil on the conveyor belt and cried in my car. The tabloids were full of speculation and ugly rumors. I'm not even going to address all that here. It was devastating.

Creating music was my husband's solid ground; dancing was mine. It's not like I could just slide back into my skinny jeans like nothing had happened. I'd gained over eighty pounds while I was pregnant. Forty of that disappeared immediately, because extreme fluid retention was one of the symptoms that indicated serious problems with the pregnancy; it had been the first real warning sign that something was terribly wrong. The rest of that weight came from the normal weight gain of pregnancy, combined with months of inactivity. I refused to beat myself up about it, but I had to work it off.

I'm built like my dad, with a body builder's musculature. It served me well when I was dancing hard seven days a week, but as I lay in the hospital, I could feel myself getting softer every day. I had planned for this, but my plan was to go to work out with a personal trainer while Amiir giggled in his bassinet nearby. I planned to hike with him on my back and teach him to swim and play, play, play all day. Instead I was alone, trying to rebuild my body like a house after a hurricane.

Christmas came and went, but we hardly noticed it. I told Mama, "Sometimes couples need a break. So this is going to be our break, and we'll get strong again. We'll find each other."

He wanted the same thing. On our first anniversary, February 14, 1997, he released *Kamasutra*, the music he'd composed for our wedding with the NPG Orchestra. I listened to it over and over and felt myself coming out of this thick fog of grief I'd been trying to find my way through. I listened to the new music he was working on, and it was full of love for me and

Amiir. We agreed that we needed to go somewhere, make a place for just the two of us, far away from the business and the tabloids and the demands—a place we could retreat to and have another baby surrounded by peace and music and privacy. We considered Hawaii, but they said I'd have to leave Mia in quarantine for six months, and that was not happening.

"What about Egypt?" he asked, and I was into that idea right away. My memories of Egypt—going all the way back to my childhood—were filled with mystic connection, more beauty than a pair of eyes could take in, and the rich scent of dreams coming true.

"There would be a bit of culture shock," I said, "but I would love to live there. And maybe we could do some good, you know? When I was a kid, the first thing was this culture shock. I'd never seen such poverty. The children run around, and their hair is light brown with dust. They're out at midnight, because they swap times in the house. They rotate times to be out on the street. I mean, I'd come home and kiss the soil, grateful for what we have, and I do have a problem with the way women are treated, but I've always felt a connection to the music, the architecture, the people. There's an energy there that I've never felt anywhere else."

He'd been soul-searching, reading books on various religions, consuming one thick tome after another on Christianity, Buddhism, Hinduism, Judaism, and

Islam. He wanted me to read with him and discuss all the different types of scripture, and that was a conversation I was into. I was curious to learn about the world beyond the boundaries of my grandmother's strict Catholic faith.

He asked me about the Muslims in Egypt, and I said, "There's something about it that appeals to me. I hear the music and the prayers, and it seems natural. Comforting. I never felt out of place there. You hear this amazing singing, and everything stops, and the people pray. I've been stranded on planes because it was prayer time."

"They stop to pray," he said. "To observe that practice—to prioritize that in your life—it would change everything."

We decided to go house hunting that spring. While he continued touring, I went ahead to make arrangements. When he arrived, I took him everywhere. We bought oils in the marketplace, visited the musical instrument shops on Mohammed Ali Street, and sat in the nightclubs watching the belly dancers. We got henna tattoos on our hands and walked around the Great Pyramids. We looked at houses and visited mosques and ruins.

At the Egyptian Museum in Cairo, we stood for a long time, looking at Akhenaten and Nefertiti, listening to the tour guide's short version of their great love story. Akhenaten had desperately wanted a son, but Nefertiti gave him six daughters, so he had a male child with someone simply known as "The Younger Woman." But his undying love for Nefertiti overcame her wrath. He raised her up as an equal, and together they revolutionized Egypt and changed the world.

We stood there for a long time, taking it all in, fate and coincidence swirling around us. It wasn't just that we looked like these people or the fact that they were called Children of the Sun by some. We felt connected to them in a way we couldn't explain or speak about to anyone but each other. It was profound. It was real. We didn't want to leave that room, and when we finally did, it was because we needed to be alone together in private.

When we came home, it was as if we'd started a new life together, reborn to each other. We'd found each other again, and the miracle of that made us laugh and love each other even more. He had created a beautiful office for me right next to his office on the second floor, and I loved occupying it along with Mia and a tankful of tropical fish, all of whom had names, including Larry the Starfish. Outside the door, the doves were always billing and cooing softly.

I went in every morning feeling loved and creative and energized, and I started tracking my temperature with a basal thermometer. My spirit felt ready to have another baby, and I wanted to make sure my body didn't miss any opportunities.

In April, EMI/Capitol shut down, which pretty much screwed my husband's distribution deal, and that was a bitter disappointment, but he was already on to the next thing—the *Newpower Soul* album and rehearsals for the Jam of the Year Tour—because moving on to the next thing was always his defense mechanism of choice. He had another batch of songs he'd pulled from the vault, and those were coming together on a project called *Crystal Ball*. He was also hanging around with Clive Davis, the president of Arista, engaged in the early stages of *Rave Un2 the Joy Fantastic*, and I have to say, Clive had the best take on the never-ending question, "What do you call him?"

"It's like when you get married," said Clive. "You can't call your father-in-law 'Dad'—that's awkward—so you run around, looking for substitutions, and then you end up just saying 'Hi.'"

For a long time I'd wanted to do a major project of my own, and I felt ready. Ever since I saw the Joffrey Ballet interpret some of his music, I'd been thinking I'd like to form a dance company and take that idea to the next level.

I told my husband, "I want to do something like the Joffrey did, but I want to make it even better."

"I've been waiting for you to say that," he said. "Tell me what you need."

"Just give me the music."

I sat dancer style on the floor in front of my fish

tank with thirty Prince, ⚥, and New Power Generation CDs spread out on the carpet in front of me. This
was only a fraction of my husband's enormous body of
work. In addition to all this music and everything still
on the shelf and in the vault, he'd written a play and
an opera, and he'd created the NPG Orchestra to do
the music for our wedding. He'd always wanted to do
something on Broadway. And then there was *Kamasutra*. I looked at the image of myself dancing on the
cover. My shadow was the symbol that was now his
name. This music was moving and told a story about
a love affair between a rock star and a ballerina.

I went next door and said, "I want to do *Kamasutra*."

I developed a script with a three-act structure. The
first act was the hits, because Mama gotta pay them
bills. The second act was *Kamasutra*, because—wow.
It was classical instrumental, and with a darkness and
sexiness that a dancer would drool to move to. The
third act was all new music, because our long-term
vision was to eventually come together in one spectacular show we could take on tour together. It meant
a lot to me that he treated me with such respect, never
second-guessing or selling me short. From the early
years of our friendship, he made me feel that my
endeavors as an artist mattered as much as his did,
but this was something beyond that; he was prepared
to invest in my vision. I was absolutely in the driver's
seat, but I welcomed his input.

"Everybody should look different," he said. "Like their hair should be purple or electric blue or shocking pink."

This was before shocking pink hair was popular, so I was into that and figured I could run interference if anyone objected. After a few months, these dancers were like my kids. They trusted me. The advance press was going well. Booking was a challenge, because he was going through a period of being very anti-agent, anti-promoter, anti-everybody. He did all this himself. He'd pick up the phone and say, "Yeah, I'd like to come and play at your place for a couple days next month." Whoever was on the other end of that phone call was instantly falling all over themselves to pay him whatever he wanted to be paid and make sure he had the right brand of bottled water backstage.

He expected me to do the same thing and couldn't understand why it didn't really work that way for me. I was pretty good at a lot of things. By this time, I had experience directing music videos, editing, and being the company director. I was choreographer, stage coordinator, stage director, lighting—all that. But booking a company of forty dancers was a bit more complicated than booking myself at a Turkish restaurant. We had some choice words about it, but these arguments felt like Akhenaten and Nefertiti in a joint effort to rule the world, not like Mama and Daddy in a jealous rage. It felt like the soul exercise Prince wrote about in that letter so long ago. We were finally there.

Mama says she knew the minute she was pregnant with me because she was monitoring her temperature every day with a basal thermometer. My basal thermometer was a super-fancy digital version of that, accurate to a millionth of a degree or something, so when it showed a slight shift three days in a row, I checked my calendar and realized I was late. I hopped in my pink BMW and dashed to the grocery store for a basketful of pregnancy tests. I went to my office at Paisley and held the first box between my hands, saying a prayer before I opened it. I took that one in the office, then went home to take the rest.

The little plus sign wasn't as bright as it was the first time, but it was positively positive. Excitement and fear tangled up and tied a knot in my stomach. My hands were shaking when I called my husband and said, "Can you come home?"

"We're rehearsing," he said. "I'll be there soon."

"No. Come now."

I sat on a kitchen chair, willing myself not to freak out, waiting for the sound of the big garage door and that distinctive jingling step in the hallway.

"Hi."

"Hi."

"I'm pregnant."

Everything that I'd been feeling—excitement, fear, hope, caution—it all flashed through his eyes, before he took a deep breath and said, "You are?"

I held up the little stick, but he already had me tight in his arms, laughing for joy, kissing me, kissing my belly, shifting into Papa Bear mode.

"What are you going to do with the dance company?"

"Not dance."

"Maybe we should cancel."

"No, they've worked too hard for this," I said, "and I want to stay busy so I don't obsess on every little thing with—with everything. But I won't dance. I'll take it easy, I promise."

"I'll step up and help however I can."

It was the end of August. My OB calculated the baby's due date: May 10, 1998. Mother's Day. Mama's birthday. It felt like a good omen.

"Let's not tell people right away," I said. "Let's get through the first trimester and make sure everything's okay."

All we had to do was make it to November 19, I told myself. Then we could breathe again. We could open the door to that big playroom at Paisley Park, turn on the lights, and give ourselves over to the sheer happiness.

He flew with me to the dance company's opening night in Chicago. All the band members came, so I felt wonderfully loved and supported. And I was proud of what I'd created. During dress rehearsal, I felt a surge of pride and a capable *yeah, I got this* handle on life. The baby growing in my belly made me feel like a creative tour de force. One of the guys in the dance company came to me fussing about his wig, and in full-on Nefertiti mode, I said, "Wear the wig or go home. Don't stress me out."

On opening night, I sat in the audience with a headset, giving lighting cues as the performance came off without a noticeable hitch, and my husband sat next to me, looking smug and comfortable. I did him proud, and he liked feeling proud. We went home and after some heart-to-heart discussion, we disbanded the company, promising to come back to it after the baby was born. It would take a lot of time and energy to turn a profit. For now, I wanted to focus my energy on the baby.

I also worried that it was an expensive production to put on the road, and while I wasn't super involved in our family finances, I knew that distribution deal had gone bad, and that was not a good thing. I had never asked a lot of questions about money, but one day he sent me along with one of his bodyguards to buy a new Jeep Cherokee—white with a cream interior and every option known to automobile kind. He sent me along to pay for the $46,000 vehicle with an American Express card.

I remember when I was a little girl, the very first check I wrote (one of those fake checks you get in your junk mail) was made out to Daddy for a million dollars. This felt kind of like that.

At the end of that summer, my husband played the Pyramid Arena in Memphis, and he noticed that Larry Graham was playing a small venue nearby that same night. There was an aftershow at Music Mix Factory in Nashville. ♀ called Larry and asked him if he wanted to come over and jam. He was elated when he called me afterward. He said that he and Larry had an unspoken rapport—they didn't even have to look at each other to know where the music was going. Larry's psychedelic soul/funk pedigree was stellar—he'd come up with Sly and the Family Stone—and he'd innovated his own particular style called "thumpin' and pluckin'," which involves slapping the strings and creating a whole different sound.

But the connection my husband felt with Larry was spiritual, not just musical.

"This man's faith is so certain," he said. "There's no room for doubts or fears."

I was happy for him. I thought this friendship would be a healthy, positive influence. He told me Larry was a strong family man and a brilliant musician. He'd had a handful of R&B hits, one that crossed over to Billboard's Top Ten in 1980. After that, his experience in the industry was more typical than my husband's. He worked hard and toured hard with genuine passion for the music and genuine faith that he would be led in the direction God wanted him to go. When Larry and his wife, Tina, came to Minnesota to hang out with us, I was impressed with their daughter and their obvious bond as a family. Tina was a personality-and-a-half, with a great laugh and church-lady grace. Larry had kind eyes and a broad, easygoing smile, and he was unabashedly crazy in love with his wife, which I found charming.

The only thing that made me a little uncomfortable was that Larry sometimes went off on these long sermons about—I don't even know. I can't even tell you what they were about. These long-winded teachings were like no brand of Christianity I'd seen before. The more I heard about the Jehovah's Witnesses and *The Watchtower* and Armageddon and the pagan root of birthdays and Christmas, the less it appealed to me. There was so little room for celebration and even less for doubt. This was not a problem for me. I respect the belief systems of others, but I didn't feel that mutual "whatever peanut butters your jelly" vibe coming back from them. It just didn't sit right with me.

"I'm not judging. I'm just not feeling it," I said to my husband after sitting through another mind-numbing evening. I smoothed my hand over my belly. "I don't know what kind of medical treatment this little one might need. And when he gets here healthy and strong, I'm not going to tell him his birthday's been canceled. We're celebrating. Balloons, acrobats, those inflatable jumping things, petting zoo—the whole nine yards. You'll think you died and went to Glam Slam heaven."

In September, he went out on the Jam of the Year Tour and took Larry with him. As fall went by, he worked on *Newpower Soul*, staying late every night in the studio, and I was determined to stay by his side. Sometimes by three or four in the morning, I was sleeping with my eyes open, but I sat on that studio sofa, my head bouncing to the beat.

We welcomed every little sign of a healthy pregnancy. If I got light-headed or sleepy, he'd be there with his arm around my waist. He'd spread his hands over my midsection, measuring the little pooch that was starting to be noticeable. This pregnancy felt very different from the first one, and we agreed that that was a good thing. My weight was on point. My belly wasn't growing much, and my symptoms weren't nearly as visible. My boobs grew, and I got dizzy, but nothing else. We wanted to wait until the three-month mark to listen for a heartbeat and start getting ultrasounds, but we were confident that this baby was healthy. *Come on, November 19*, I prayed silently. *We can do this, little one.*

On November 19, I woke up, prepared for a busy, joyful day. I went into the bathroom and found blood seeping out of me. It felt like a long walk to the telephone.

"I'm bleeding."

He took a short, sharp breath. "Okay."

"I'm going to the doctor."

"Okay."

"I'll call you."

"Okay. Bye."

Click.

I went to the doctor's office and got an ultrasound.

"The good news is that there's no heartbeat," she said. "There's placenta, but no fetus. Your body is trying to naturally expel the products of conception."

I remember thinking, *Thank God.* I was intensely, selfishly grateful for every minute I had held Amiir in my arms, but to prevent his suffering, I would have been willing to suffer anything—including the heartbreak I was suffering now. I sat in the car sobbing, trying to find the strength to go inside and tell my husband what I had to tell him. When I was finally able to face him, we stood in my office. I told him what the doctor had told me, but the words weren't even necessary. The reality of another crushing loss hung in the air between us. It was impossible to read the expression on his face.

"Are you—"

"I need to get back to the studio." And he walked toward the door.

I went down to stay with Mama for a few days, and she was concerned when the bleeding didn't stop. I'd done the research on miscarriages and hoped it wouldn't be an issue, but after several days, it seemed to be getting worse, not better. I was trying to go out on tour with my husband as much as I could, but I was miserable and still bleeding. As soon as we got home, I went to the doctor.

"She says I need a D&C," I told my husband. "Dilation and curettage. It removes the lining of the uterus so you don't hemorrhage."

"Nature will take its course if you let it."

"But nature isn't always—"

"Either we have faith or we don't. Larry is always saying—"

"Larry has a child! He should thank God for that and stay out of other people's business."

It came out sharper than I meant it to. This isn't how I'd seen the conversation going. I looked at my husband, searching for something that felt like the protective stance that used to make me feel safe and sure of the world. There was only that same off-putting certitude that had troubled me about Larry—along with a solid refusal to place my physical well-being over his own self-righteousness.

"I'm not going to risk my future fertility for something I don't even believe in," I told him. "I'm going to do what the doctor says. I'm going to the hospital."

He looked at me, and there was a flash of…something. Concern. Grief. Or maybe just fear. He said, "Do you want Tina to come to the hospital with you?"

"No, I want you!"

"I don't believe in what you're doing."

"I have to do this. I could bleed to death. Maybe God is taking care of me by sending me a doctor."

He called his limo driver to take me to the hospital. A compromise, I guess. The D&C was done, and a biopsy of the tissue they removed showed XX chromosomes.

"It's called a partial molar pregnancy," my OB explained. "The egg is fertilized and implants itself, but it doesn't develop for one reason or another. It can be genetic or inadequate nutrition."

"Like a vegan diet?"

"I can't say without genetic testing. You and your husband would need to be tested. That's really the only way to know what's going on with you."

"Would it work if I did the testing myself?"

"To some extent," she said. "If you test positive for certain genetic issues, that could be the answer, whether he's positive or negative. If you're negative… do the math."

I knew my husband was not going to participate in the testing, but I needed to know. I tried not to feel like a traitor as they drew the blood for it. *Fine. Whatever*, I told myself. *I'm just a birthday-loving pagan.*

Nothin' wrong with that. I said nothing about it when the test results came back. There was no abnormality in my DNA. I didn't see any need for him to know that at the time. I figured I'd let him play and let myself heal, and then we could go somewhere private and talk about our options. I counted my Vicodin every morning and tried to keep an eye on it at night. I tried to get back on track, tried to keep up. I sat in a public restroom at a stadium in Fargo or some such place, feeling like my body was being turned inside out, but I was determined to keep going until I couldn't.

One day, he surprised me with a trip to Versace. He wanted to buy me a gorgeous gown to wear to some upcoming event, but this thing cost more than my first car. I went back the next day and returned it. I didn't tell him. It was a sweet gesture, and I didn't want him to think I didn't appreciate it.

In the spring of 1998, my husband asked me to direct a music video for a song called "The One." The lyrics he'd written for me described both the man he didn't want to be—

a man who'll treat you like anything but a queen
I ain't the one

—and the man he did want to be—

treat your every step . . . like you're walkin' on holy
 ground
I am the one

It spoke so powerfully of how hard he was trying to find his way back to me, especially when he
mixed an alternate version in which he sang, *"My my*
my my Mayte tay tayyyyy, I'm the One." The arrangement, a lavish background by the NPG Orchestra, is
an intoxicating blend of jazz and Arabic vibe. I danced
the lead with my husband and cast members of the
NPG Dance Company as the women of the harem.
The choreography felt natural and sensual, taking us
back to everything that had brought us together in the
beginning.

We created a story within a story: Dressed as
a Charlie Chaplin hobo, he comes to the door of a
shabby house where a girl (me) and her mother bicker.
He sees her open a book that transports her to a harem
where they dance with all the beautiful young odal-
isques. They try to distract him, but he always returns
to the woman he loves, and by the end, we're literally
bound together. We return to the real world on the
shabby front porch, and I open the door to find him
standing there. In the colorful dream world that exists
parallel to that gray place, The Prince puts his arms
around The Princess, and they are one.

He gave me carte blanche to do this short film however I wanted, so I reached for the moon and got it: Rita Moreno was cast to play my mother. The first day on set, when I saw her in the flesh, every little Puerto Rican girl's triple-threat dream, I had to go in the dressing room and sit with my head down for a minute. My husband came in to see if I was all right, and I said, "Do you know who that is?"

He laughed and said, "Breathe. Get it together, and go do it."

I knew what I wanted, but I questioned myself. It meant a lot to have him show me such respect and approval, and to have Rita Moreno asking me for direction—I can't even. Hyperventilation. She was alert to everything going on around her and willing to try anything. We went over the storyboard and discussed the scene where we're arguing with each other, and she came up with some hilarious bits—blowing dust in my face and smudging my blouse with dirt—which had my husband in stitches. He laughed and listened and asked questions. Never once did he say, "Hey, you know what would be cool…" I couldn't have asked for two actors I loved and looked up to more than these two. They both recognized how important this little film was to me and gave me everything I needed to make my vision a reality.

From the first rehearsals through the last cut of the editing process, I kept my hands around this piece.

My husband came and went from the studio while I was working on it. He asked me to thread a secret message around the vignette scenes on the pages of the book, and he wanted the opening words of the story to be "In the beginning..." but beyond that, he left the whole thing up to me. He loved that I sensed the beats—of the music and of the eye—in a way he'd tried to explain to other editors without success.

"The One" is the truest work we created together. When you look at it, even if you don't know the backstory, the love between us is tangible. There's a shadow of sadness in the music, but the sensuality overwhelms it. There's tension in the choreography, but it's overcome by grace. I saw it as the story of us: two souls that drift apart and come together again, over and over, just like the story of "7." In keeping with my belief in our eternal love, the video ends with a black screen that reads *THE BEGINNING.*

And for a while, it was.

Working together on "The One" brought the fresh surge of tenderness and connection I'd been longing for. We decided to buy a house in Spain. Something in Marbella, looking out over the sea. While he went out on tour again, I went to Spain and put wheels in motion. It felt like I looked at a hundred places, and finally, he circled one in a Realtor's catalogue and told me to buy it. It was a big mansion on the coast, not a normal person's house like our house in Minnesota.

From the balcony, you could see the Rock of Gibraltar and the distant coast of North Africa. The plan was for me to go to Spain and buy this house after I did some media. I went on BET for the world premiere of "The One" in June 1998, but after that, I stuck around long enough to go on *Vibe* with my husband, Chaka Khan, and Larry.

My husband loved the details of the costuming in "The One," including fine curls sculpted on my forehead instead of bangs. "You should do that for *Vibe*," he said, so before we went on the show hosted by Sinbad, I had his hairdresser Kim carefully create them. She's a true artist when it comes to curls.

During the first part of the show, Sinbad was a big, adorable teddy bear, Chaka was her fabulous self, and Larry was the coolest dude you'd ever want to sit next to. I'd been waiting backstage with my husband, not expecting to go on the show itself, but when Sinbad introduced "the Funkateer Himself" with the iconic opening chords of "1999," he caught my hand and wouldn't let go.

"What—am I doing this? I'm not hooked up with a mic or anything," I said, but he was already pulling me toward the stage manager who held a curtain aside. The stage manager and I smiled and shrugged at each other, and my husband and I walked down the stairs together and sat on the sofa next to Chaka after a quick hug from Larry. Things started out great. My husband cracked everyone up, talking like Mickey Mouse, and then he said something very sweet and heartfelt about how "being married did help a lot, opening me up to be more comfortable with speaking in public." He went on to speak intelligently about the cause he'd been fighting for the past three years:

"What a lot of artists, I think, don't recognize," he said, "is that when they get into the business and they sign away the rights to the master recordings, it in fact makes you a slave, in the sense that the proceeds from those master recordings, for all of time, will go to whoever owns them."

"Some cat who can't play," Sinbad said. The audience hooted for that, and we all laughed and nodded.

"Well, you said it, I didn't." My husband smiled. "What we've been trying to do with New Power Generation, what it stands for is a creative freedom and financial freedom to run and operate your own Genesis, so to speak, so that you reach a much brighter Revelation."

There was a round of applause, and I was part of it. I was incredibly proud of the way he'd stood up for his rights as an artist, and he was finally starting to get people on his side. Not record people—music people. The people who loved and respected him and wanted to work with him, and the massive audience who just wanted to see and hear him do his thing.

"Now, when is this thing hitting?" Sinbad asked, holding up the *Newpower Soul* CD.

"Bam," said ♀, and the audience loved that, too.

He talked about "The One" and *Crystal Ball* and about how albums had drawn him to Chaka and Larry in the 1970s. Sinbad brought up the name thing and talked about why he himself picked the name Sinbad—for the daring dude in the old movies.

"That's sort of a precarious situation for me," said my husband, "because to people who love me"— this made the crowd go nuts and call out, "We love you!"—"to people who love me, I get off on the fact that they think of me as a prince. So I'm pretty much cool with that. It's when they don't respect the fact that I've adopted a name that has no pronunciation that it gets to be troublesome."

Sinbad broke for a commercial. Tina, Larry's wife, was not about to remain offsides after I came out, so she came and sat with us, which confused me a little, but okay—Tina was great, and Larry and Tina together were great as long as they didn't start—

Oh, God. It started.

"Originally, when I had written this song," said my husband, "I must admit, I was a little fearful to call it 'The Christ,' and my good friend Larry hit me to some things, and it woke me up to . . . or maybe—Let him explain it."

Larry was already on the edge of his seat, more than willing to get in there and explain it.

"Well, actually we've had a number of, uh, very

good Bible discussions," he said, "and we do this on a regular basis, the whole family of us, and—"

"Well, that's a different artist tour," Sinbad quipped, trying to keep it light.

"Yeah, we do a lot together, and each day, each time you have these deep discussions, you enlighten to various things, and you make various adjustments in your life. You make various adjustments in a lot of areas."

I sat there with a frozen smile, thinking, *Whoa, whoa, whoa. Hold up. Please.*

"In this one particular Bible discussion we were having had to do with *stauros*, which is an upright stake or pole..." Larry went off on one of the arcane scripture lessons with which I'd become more familiar than I ever wanted to be. I squeezed my husband's hand, but he was looking at Larry with rapt attention.

"...and come to find out," Larry finally seemed to be wrapping it up, "Jesus actually died on an upright stake or pole."

"He was impaled," my husband said, and Tina echoed, "Yes, impaled."

"Like this." Larry demonstrated with his arms above his head. "He was impaled, as opposed to like this." He opened his arms to demonstrate a crucified Jesus.

Something that felt like a fire alarm went off inside my head. *How is this happening right now?* Observing my husband from the corner of my eye, I felt my heart sink. No way would he have allowed Larry to go off on a ramble like that without agreeing in advance that that's how this was going to go down.

"So then the question was, well, then, why is it then that, you know, people do this and people choose this or that, and, uh, so he chose to wanna make it clear..."

The audience sat there, silent and confused. You could almost hear the eyes glazing over. They were here to see the Artist Formerly Known as Prince. They were here for the music. Now the studio was heavy with that feeling you get when the Jehovah's Witness knocks on your door and you know he already saw your car in the driveway. You don't want to be rude, but—dang.

"...and sometimes the truth—it may hurt a little bit sometimes—various things—if a person finds out, 'Well, I was thinking this or thinking that the whole time,' and now all of a sudden, you need to make an adjustment in your thinking, well, that's not on me. It's written. It is written..."

He went on like that for another three minutes until Sinbad smoothly intervened and said, "Looks like we're about to go to church!"

Big laugh.

There was another commercial break, thank God, and then ♀, Chaka, and Larry performed and blew the doors off the place, because that is what the funk they were born to do.

Alone with my husband that night, I could see he was so proud. He knew he was pushing the envelope but thought it went great. I didn't have the heart to ruin it for him, so I kept my opinion to myself. I was just happy to be with him. I told myself he was grieving. Everyone has to grieve in his own way. I was certain he'd work through this difficult phase. Larry would have his collaborative role in the music and then disappear. On to the next thing. I'd seen my husband go through plenty of other creative phases. He loved learning and needed a friend. Larry was a good teacher and had a perpetually inviting energy. How could that be a bad thing? I seemed to be the only one who had a problem with it.

As the study sessions expanded, I felt less and less like a part of the group because my beliefs so clearly didn't fall into line. Now whenever I mentioned Akhenaten and Nefertiti, he explained to me how idolatrous and misguided they were. He kept encouraging me to hang out with Tina, and I tried to participate in the study sessions, but it simply wasn't my truth. Men and women studied separately, and I believe faith should bring people together. I believe birthdays are beautiful. I believe all good people will be rewarded in the end.

We went with Larry's family to meetings on Saturday morning, and I was certain I smelled alcohol as we made our way to our seats. Either some of these people got tore up drinking the night before, or they were drinking first thing in the morning. Since we were married, we could sit next to each other; otherwise, men and women were segregated. People recited scripture, interpreting it with a strained logic that seemed to have a lot more to do with what they wanted it to say than what it actually said. "Judge not, lest ye be judged"—something as straightforward as that—could be morphed to some kind of diatribe, and then everyone would nod and agree, stricken by this profound truth. After an hour or two of that, I was yearning for a shark tank to dive into.

I kept comforting myself with the memory of another celebrity trying to win him over to Scientology years earlier. "It's intriguing," he said, "but I don't need somebody telling me how to believe in my God." He was always a spiritual seeker, I told myself, fascinated enough in all possibilities to integrate the signs of the zodiac and third eye and reincarnation into the Christian beliefs his Baptist mother and Seventh-Day Adventist father had exposed him to. He was way too smart to be sucked into something just because he was vulnerable in that moment.

There was a brief tour to raise money for our charitable organization, Love 4 One Another, and though

I was too beat down to go with him, I needed to see him, so I showed up to surprise him one night. In the craft service area, I saw this girl who kind of looked like me but...earthier, wearing jeans and flat boots with no makeup. She was youthful, easygoing, like a kid fresh out of school. My husband had been spending a lot of time in online chat rooms. Someone told me she was a superfan who'd connected with him on one of the sites dedicated to all things Prince. I looked at her and got a bad feeling in my gut.

Listen to your gut, girls. A woman's intuition is no joke. I casually asked a few people, "Who's that girl? Why is she on the tour?" and someone introduced me to her.

"Mayte, this is Manuela. We hired her to do some charity work and merchandising."

"Really?" I said, looking directly into her dark eyes. "Because I'm in charge of merchandising and Love 4 One Another, and I've never met you."

She laughed. I smiled my ballerina smile. And that's when my husband walked in and shook her hand. Just as he'd shaken my hand years before, when we were both so much younger.

When we were alone on the tour bus later, I said to him, "I'm not stupid. I know something is going on."

"There's nothing going on," he insisted. "Why would you even think that?"

"I know that handshake. I remember it from when

I was eighteen years old and Carmen Electra was standing there next to me, thinking she was the only woman you'd ever love."

When I got the handshake in front of Carmen, he and I weren't intimate yet, but we both knew it was going to happen. With Manuela, I could feel the "coming attraction" energy like the moment the lights go down in a theater before the main act comes onstage. He hadn't been intimate with her yet, or so I've been told, but the overture was playing. And this time, he was a married man. In my mind—and in his, I know—this made a huge difference.

The hailstorm of harsh words—jealousy, betrayal, denial, indignation—it was all sickeningly familiar. I'd listened to my parents have this same fight a thousand times, and so had my husband. We were just keeping up the family tradition, it seemed. He was terribly offended, denied everything, and sent me home to Minnesota. And I didn't cry all the way home. I never saw this as a deal breaker. My husband was a complicated man. I knew what I was signing up for, and along with the tradition of waging war on each other, my parents routinely strayed, then got past it and stayed together. They had children. They made a life. Their complicated marriage lasted decades, because even when they couldn't stand to look at each other, they still loved each other.

I told myself I just needed to be with him. I had

to prove my strength as a performer and a wife and a friend and a partner who brought to the table something meaningful of my own. I thought that if I performed with him again, it would bring back that energy we had.

One night he wanted me to go to a basketball game with him, but I was feeling so wrung out and depleted, I just couldn't. Somehow my "no thanks" turned into a giant blowout—the first and only time in all our years together that he looked me in the eye and said, "Fuck you."

"*What?*" I was instantly at code orange. "What did you say to me?"

"You know how many people want to go to this basketball game with me? How many women exhaust themselves trying to get my attention?"

"Oh, I know," I promised him. "Believe me, I know."

Larry and Tina were now living in our guesthouse. They were touring together, working on an album. I had a hard time understanding what the business arrangement was between him and Larry. I sat through a lot of blather about how contracts are hostile, but Mama had brought me up to know that "good fences make good neighbors," so the idea of working that way made little sense to me.

I kept reminding my husband of our decision to go somewhere far away from all this. He suggested we could open an orphanage in Spain, but I had no idea how such a thing would be accomplished. I still don't. I tried to talk to him about adopting a baby, but he stuck to the company line about God's will and the superior wisdom of nature. But what's more natural than loving a child?

Manuela was now diligently studying with the group, he told me, and she always looked so comfortable in jeans and boots, her hair naturally wavy.

"You should stop straightening your hair," said my husband. "Keep it natural."

I was starting to feel desperate. I just wanted to get him to Marbella so we could start over. I went to Spain to buy the house, and the money for the down payment wasn't there. I panicked, and thinking about the Cherokee purchase, I said, "Do you take American Express?" They didn't. After two anxious days, the money appeared. I bought the house and started the complicated process of moving us over there.

I made frequent trips home, not wanting to leave him with Manuela too long. If I'm to be totally honest, I have to accept that I'd left him alone too much already. I wondered if I could have tried harder to understand what he'd been through. I thought about the many days and nights I spent locked inside my own pain, not knowing or particularly caring where he was, other than to note that he wasn't there for me. Trying to shake off the fog of depression, I'd spent time with Jan in New York. I'd taken refuge at Mama's house in Miami. I went to Hawaii alone. When we were in bed together, if I was able to come home or he'd let me meet up with him on tour, I spooned up to him, wanting to be close, but I could feel the silence, and the coolness, and the tension growing.

Finally, he did come to Spain, but he had the whole entourage with him, and I noticed Manuela was wearing a gold chain with his symbol encrusted in diamonds. Not exactly the kind of thing you get from the merch table at a concert. He didn't even bother trying to explain to me why it was important for an administrative person from the charity to be at every concert, including this appearance on my own stomping ground. Conveniently, the extramarital relationship didn't conflict with the "study" crew dogma, I guess.

We went back to Europe, and on a chartered flight she sat directly behind us. I sat there feeling sick to my stomach. Onstage in Marbella, we performed "The One," and I wondered, What kind of woman could watch a man she cared about onstage with his wife, professing their love like that? Did that bother her at all? Later on she told me that they weren't physical until sometime after that, and I thought, *Yeah, whatever.* The timing doesn't seem all that important to me.

Several times while I was in Spain overseeing the renovations on the house, I got phone calls from people saying, "Hey, I saw you and Prince in New York at such and such a restaurant. I didn't come and say hi because I saw you guys walking into the private room." I stood there shaking, left with two options: humiliate myself by saying it wasn't me or pretend it was me and be humiliated later when they heard it through the grapevine.

My husband never went anywhere without the little black bag stuffed with the cash he'd give people when he sent them off to get things. With the growing distance between us, I was no longer certain what people were fetching for him, and that scared me. He asked me to meet him in LA one night, and as soon as I saw him in the hotel room, I could see there was something seriously wrong. He was still in bed, horribly sick to his stomach and on the verge of weeping. He gripped my hand and asked me not to go away again.

"Not without you," I said. "Do you think you can do this?"

"No." He said he wanted to check out of the hotel and cancel the show.

"Okay. We can do that. We can go home."

He got dressed, and we went to the tour bus. I helped him get in bed and stroked his face and tried to talk to him, but he was beside himself. He told me there were pills in the hotel room. He didn't trust anyone else. He wanted me to go back up there and flush them down the toilet.

"Okay. Okay, I will." I kissed his cheeks and rocked him in my arms. "And then you're coming to Spain with me. We're stopping. We're resting. We're going to figure out how to be a family."

He told me to take over. He said whatever I thought we should do, he would do that. I ran up to the room and found the pills exactly where he'd told me they'd be. I sat next to the toilet and cried for what felt like eons. Sorrow surged through me—for our son, our pregnancy, the loss of connection to the love of my life. *What would I do if I lost him?* No answer came. I flushed the pills down the toilet, pulled myself together, and went downstairs. We stayed on the bus all night and went to the airport the next morning, but I flew back to Spain by myself.

"I just have to do these last two shows of the tour," he said. "Then I'll meet you there."

Several weeks later, I was still waiting. It comforted me a little to see his clothes in the closet and his piano in the living room. Eventually, he did come for a few days, but then he left again. This became a dance we did. He'd say, "I'll be back Monday. Just wait here for me." A few weeks later, he'd pass through again. Between visits, he'd call me almost every day and talk and talk and talk about what the study group was studying. I was more than irked by the Manuela thing, but I figured that would pass. I'd seen my parents survive affairs and infidelities. It didn't surprise or threaten me.

This religion thing was another story. He was hard core into it and had gotten it in his head that God was displeased with the life he had lived when he was younger, and Amiir's death was part of the price he had to pay for that. He talked about David and Bathsheba and how David's sin had cost him the thing dearest to him, his son Absalom.

This was a place I couldn't go to. I could not go there with him, no matter how hard he tried to make me see that path.

"There was a time when you said our love was your salvation," I reminded him, thinking of the seven versions of himself he kills off in "7"—*and together we'll love through all space and time.* The man who once wrote to me, *"U are my Jesus... Ur love is my salvation,"* now saw those words as blasphemous and ugly. But now, if I expressed any disagreement with the teachings of the study crew—well, I'll quote their own literature, *Watchtower*, October 1998:

> *Opposers try to hinder this work by mocking.*
> *Sometimes individuals interested in the*
> *Kingdom message give up because they cannot*
> *endure the ridicule... Jehovah's people long for*

the time when God will triumph over all his
enemies. This will start with the destruction
of "Babylon the Great"—a figurative city that
embraces all forms of false religion.

I had disobeyed my husband when it came to my
health care decisions and refused to embrace the Gospel According to Graham. I was the enemy now, the
opposer, who wanted to drag him back to the sinful
ways of Babylon.

I missed my husband with all my heart, but I had
hope, because this was also the man who wrote this
to me:

> ... 👁 *am married 2 my music. It never frowns*
> *at me.* 👁*t's the one thing* 👁 *know* 👁 *can depend*
> *on. My music has proven itself—time and time*
> *again.* 👁 *shouldn't be asked to compromise...* 👁
> *write what comes to me. U've seen the process. U*
> *know it comes easy 4 me.*

Spirituality had always played a role in my husband's music, and this new path was no different.
There are moments where it seeps into the lyrics.
But creating music was, for him, a spiritual experience. Never had a spiritual path come in such conflict
with the sexual nature of his music, and I felt certain
the music would win out in the end. He would never

compromise that, and no one was going to oppose it, because that's where the money was. I believed that if I just waited out the Manuela thing, if I stayed steadfast and faithful to our marriage vows, we'd return to that place where we were at the end of "The One"—bound together, on this plane of existence and all others.

During his brief visits to Marbella, we'd sit up at night and talk and talk and talk, but the long, soul-searching conversations we'd always enjoyed took a dark, baffling turn. I'd fall asleep trying to make sense of it and wake up to find he was gone again.

In October 1998, as he began the Newpower Soul Tour in Europe, my husband came to Marbella for a press conference at the Plaza de Toros. He looked weary but well enough. He held my hand as we walked in, but we started out with a measurable gap between our chairs. It started with the usual questions and answers. I answered some in Spanish, which every-one in the room loved. Someone asked about a rumor that we'd purchased a house in Marbella, and he was evasive.

"My residence is the world. I'm happy anywhere."

Someone else asked how he balanced his profes-sional and personal lives, and he said, "For the past twenty years, I consider work my personal life. Being married has taught me a lot about taking better care of time and realizing that recreation means re-creation of self, so I think I may take a vacation soon."

I smiled when I heard that. I felt a surge of hope when he moved closer to me, took my hand, and wove his fingers through mine.

There's a tragic aria in *Madame Butterfly*. The soprano sings, *"Un bel di..."* as she looks out over the sea, waiting for her lover. *One beautiful day.* I looked out at the sea from my house in Spain with the same heart full of longing. And at some point in my waiting and longing and wondering, it occurred to me that I'd forgotten a lesson I learned my very first year at Paisley Park: The girl in Minneapolis is the girl on her way in. The girl who leaves Minneapolis is the girl on her way out.

I guess I shouldn't have taken it so hard. Carmen Electra was replaced by a sixteen-year-old belly dancer. It took God Almighty to get me out of Minnesota.

eleven

Here's another Internet fiction alert for you: For almost twenty years, I've been reading that our marriage was "annulled" in 1998, but in fact, a legal marriage is not annulled just because an eccentric rock star says it in a press conference. That's like you saying your marriage was annulled because you took off your ring before you hit on someone in a singles bar. That is not a thing.

This press conference—at which my husband and I were wearing our wedding rings—took place in Spain in mid-December 1998, while he was on the European leg of the Newpower Soul Tour. In the car on the way to the Santo Mauro Hotel, where the conference was being held, he enlightened me on his "revelation" about contracts. Everyone knew that he was against them when it came to record companies, but now he had been contemplating the contract we had signed when we were married, and he was against that, too.

This was baffling to me. He was the one who'd asked me to marry him when I had been perfectly happy with the way things were. He was the one who wanted the traditional vows and the half million dollars in flowers and the whole church wedding experience. But I already felt estranged and didn't want that rift to grow, so I sat quiet and confused.

When we walked into the press conference, I had my game face on, hoping it would turn out like the press conference a few months earlier; when pressed to think about what truly mattered to him, he had admitted that our marriage made him a better man. My husband talked about his vision for NPG and how he was working to elevate and empower other artists. He gave his spiel about masters and slaves and not believing in contracts—something they'd heard before but knew the importance of—and then he announced that he and I were going to have our marriage annulled so we could renew our vows and "continue our marriage in a less traditional fashion."

I felt my eyes go wide. I sat with a frozen smile on my face as the assembled press tried to climb over the language barrier to make some kind of sense of what he was saying. I willed him to look at me so he'd see the questions in my eyes: *What are you saying? How do you expect me to sit here and listen to that?*

I played Princess Mayte for the rest of the press conference, but in the car, I was hurt and furious. "Why would you do that to me? You made it sound like our marriage is a mistake—like it doesn't mean anything!"

He went off on a long, alarming rant that lasted late into the night. Hour after hour, as I cried and argued and tried to reason with him, he quoted scripture and dragged me through the minutia of the Biblical teachings he'd been wallowing in. He wanted us to declare our marriage annulled and then renew our vows on our anniversary, February 14. He wanted us to be baptized the same day. He wanted me to sign a paper that said I agreed to all this, that our vows were annulled, and we were free from the chains of that contract.

Now, stay with me here, people: I refuse to be cynical about this. I don't believe this was him trying to avoid divorcing me so he could get out of a financial settlement. I think this is proof that he loved me and didn't want to lose me. I think he was struggling with the whole Manuela flirtation. She tells me now (and most days I believe her) that they still weren't intimate until much later. She says they were friends. But I was familiar with the "friendship" choreography; it wasn't so much a platonic buddy relationship as it was an elegant sort of tantric delayed gratification. In any case, it was well beyond the boundaries of okay for a married man. I think he was looking for something—anything—that would make him feel less guilty about betraying me, and the "annulment" concept allowed him to feel like he was still *The One* guy as opposed to the *not the one* guy.

I tried to read that stupid paper, my eyes blurry

with tears and exhaustion. It wasn't anything official or legally binding, but just on principle, I didn't like the implication with regards to Amiir. Even if it meant nothing legally, it was saying that Amiir's parents were never truly married. Frankly, I wouldn't have fought him over money, but this? Now you're messing with Mama Bear.

"What—are you saying he was born out of wedlock? Is that what you want to say about our son?"

"No! I want to say I love you, and you love me, and we don't need this piece of paper telling us how to live. I want us to be baptized and renew our vows and be newly married in the eyes of God."

"It's your eyes I worry about. You can't seem to keep them off Manuela."

And so on and so on, hour after hour. The words coming out of his mouth seemed coached and contrived. I don't know if he believed it any more than I did, but he bullied me until four o'clock in the morning. I was desperate to lie down and even more desperate to make him shut up and lie down with me. Eyes burning, ears ringing, I let him put the pen in my hand. Defeated, numb with weariness, I scribbled my name on the paper. He was calm then. Before we fell asleep, he talked again about renewing our vows with a baptism in February. Maybe we should do it right here at our beautiful house in Spain, he said. When I woke up, he was gone.

New Year's Eve was the moment Prince fans had been anticipating for sixteen years: time to party like it's 1999. I was with him in LA, and for a moment we let go of everything that had been going on. On New Year's Day, he played the MGM Grand in Vegas for a couple of days, and then we all went back to Paisley Park.

Over the course of the following year, there was never any mention of the annulment or a renewal of our vows. He continued to refer to me, publicly and privately, as his wife. I kept flying to wherever I had to go to meet up with him for red carpet and press events, and he kept promising to take time off to be with me in Spain. I continued to wait and hope, traveling back and forth, from one continent to the other, from happiness and hope to disappointment and despair.

Sometimes I'd show up after a performance and sit with him while he sat up discussing scriptural minutia and rambling philosophy with Larry and Tina and others from the Jehovah's Witness crowd, all of whom seemed thrilled to be hanging out with the mysterious and wonderful ♀ at three in the morning. I wasn't willing to chime in on these conversations. I didn't believe any of it, and I wasn't willing to pretend.

I would have been thrilled to be hanging out with him myself. I got lonely sitting there in Spain. As soon as the Witness crew clued in to the fact that I wasn't buying it, I felt a steady campaign to separate and alienate me. When Larry and Tina first came to Paisley Park, my husband asked me to direct a music video for Larry, and I was excited about doing that. The guy's a brilliant musician, and we came up with a great idea, and had a roller rink rented out and—I don't know what happened. It just never materialized.

I want to be clear: I thought Larry and Tina were wonderful people. Their daughter is a lovely person. Everyone in that crowd—including Manuela—I'm sure they're all just wonderful, wonderful people at heart. I respect their beliefs. But as the year went by, I felt less and less welcome in my own home, and I saw changes in my husband that worried me. Every once in a while, he'd ask me to meet him somewhere, and I'd race to wherever that was. Sometimes it would be like a breath of oxygen; we'd connect and make love and laugh and talk about sane, meaningful things. Other times, it was as if I were meeting a stranger.

Once he called me to meet him in Paris and took me to Le Crazy Horse, which is the classiest, most upscale strip club you can imagine, but a strip club nonetheless. I know it sounds odd, because my husband's music was largely about sex, and I'd done some pretty out-there stuff as a performer, but not like this. This was full-frontal, nipples-in-the-wind stripper stuff that reminded me of the scary, sad Joel Grey parts in *Cabaret*. I sat there with tears in my eyes, thinking, *How are you bringing your wife to a strip club?* He was acting loopy and strange. I felt like I had two choices: drop dead or start drinking. Three hours later, I was throwing up drunk in our hotel room, and he was on his way back to Minnesota.

In September, I met him for the MTV Video Music Awards in New York. He was introducing TLC, so we were expected to make an appearance on the red carpet and at a number of after parties. When we were planning what we should wear, he said, "You know what would be cool? You should wear that red belly dancing outfit."

"What?" I laughed, thinking he was joking, but it became clear that he wasn't. He wanted me to wear the costume, and his eyes went wide when I said, "No. That would not be cool. It would be stupid."

It crossed my mind to tell him what I thought of his corny little braids with blue ribbons, but I wanted to make peace and please him. As a compromise, I wore the belly dancing getup to the after parties, but I was horribly uncomfortable, and when we got back to the hotel, we started fighting about whether he would come to Spain with me and what was going on with Manuela and how angry I was to be locked out of my own life. He was feeling guilty and defensive and kept coming back with all this claptrap about me not being an obedient wife, refusing to wear the belly dancing getup on the red carpet, refusing to drink the study group Kool-Aid.

Finally, I pressed my hands against my face and screamed.

"What is it going to take to get through to you?"

I picked up a wine bottle and hurled it against the wall. It smashed and dribbled, and it did surprise him, but the feeling wasn't nearly as satisfying as I had hoped.

The next day, we went to our separate corners, but we talked on the phone. He'd call me when he felt low, and most of the time, I tried to listen without saying anything I'd already said a thousand times. We kept talking about spending quiet time together in Spain, but for the most part, I was there by myself. Sometimes I'd go to Miami to visit Mama, or I'd fly her over to visit me. I continued the family tradition of outrageous phone bills, talking to Mama in Miami, Daddy in Texas, my grandmothers in Puerto Rico, and Jan in New York.

Jan was going through some heavy stuff. She'd been with her partner, Myra, for about three years. They were very much in love and totally committed to each other. (They still are. They were married in California as soon as it became legal in 2008.) Jan and Myra were the best thing that ever happened to each other, and I was so happy for them, but when Jan came out to our parents, Mama practically had a stroke. I don't think she was completely surprised, but she wasn't ready to have her friends know that her daughter was a lesbian, and she was terrified when she thought about how her own iron-clad Catholic mother was going to react. She basically turned her back on Jan, and that made me furious.

It was a glorious, sunny day on the coast of Spain, so I took my phone and paced the patio outside my office, calling Mama out for how she was treating Jan.

"This is who you are as a mother? Do you understand what I would do to have one hour with my son? But you're going to shun your own daughter because she found a good woman to love? I do not accept that! This is your baby! You call her on the phone right now, and you beg her forgiveness! You tell her that you are her mama and there is nothing—*not one thing*—about who she is that you do not love. You do not *accept* her, like you're doing her a favor. You *love* her. Unconditionally. Because you are her mama."

In tears, Mama agreed that I was right, and we hung up the phone so she could call Jan. I was ready to take on anything, so I called Grandma Nelly. Standing in second position, feet apart, ballet legs strong, I kept my eyes fixed on the Rock of Gibraltar and said some things I'd been wanting to say to her since I was a little girl.

"You are a terrible mother. You belittled and criticized and humiliated my mama all her life, and she is one of the most magnificent women you could ever know. She was your perfect little baby—gorgeous girl, amazing dancer, amazing woman—but you made her feel unworthy of love and incapable of showing affection. You tried to make her a judgmental witch just like you. Well, she's *not*! She's a beautiful, loving soul who would do anything for her daughters. She's a better mother than you even tried to be!".

I clicked off the call and stood there feeling my anger running through me like an electric current. I allowed myself to feel the sear of everything I'd put up with and smiled through and danced over. No more. Things were about to change. I pocketed my cell and turned to go back into the house.

My office was engulfed in flames.

"Oh, God! Oh, God!"

I'd been standing in the hot sun, raging at Grandma, so I hadn't felt the heat on my back. The swiftly spreading fire went up the drywall behind my desk and licked at the heavy drapes. A layer of thick smoke billowed in a tornado around the ceiling fan. I started to run toward the house. Realized that was crazy. Then ran to a patio wall.

"Fuego!" I screamed in Spanish, *"Fuego! Fuego! Ayúdame!"*

The gardener, God bless him, came running with a hose. He had things basically under control by the time the fire department came. They told me the American adapter on my computer had started an electrical fire that quickly crawled up the wall. It was a little too symbolic: the curtain monogrammed with our family crest was now a sooty, blackened rag.

The first swing of a one-two punch came with the release of my husband's single "The Greatest Romance Ever Sold." The lyrics about *why Adam never left Eve* were clearly about me and might have given me another pang of hope, if not for that bitter little twist in the refrain—*the greatest romance that's ever been sold*—though I wasn't sure who sold it to whom. The accompanying music video featured my husband getting down and dirty—and I mean *very* down and *very* dirty—with a girl I later discovered was a stripper from Le Crazy Horse. This was pushing the envelope, even for him.

Mama had blood in her eye after she saw that video. "Who would humiliate his wife in public that way? No good man! No son of mine!"

I was angry when I saw it, but more than that I was worried about him. It wasn't like him to be so cynical.

In November 1999, ♀ released his twenty-third album, *Rave Un2 the Joy Fantastic*. He'd been bartering tracks with several artists, including Ani DiFranco and No Doubt—you play on mine, I'll play on yours—which was such a cool development in the whole artist-empowerment-revolution thing. The song Ani played on (and this has nothing to do with her or her mad guitar skills) was called "👁 Love You but 👁 Don't Trust U Anymore." The lyrics are the bitter lament of a betrayed lover, and when people heard the lyrics, they leapt to the obvious conclusion that I'd been cheating on him. Because I was living it up over here in Spain, where the fun never stops, except when you're engulfed in flames. The truth is, the lyrics echo everything I said to him during that long, horrible night in Marbella.

I remember meeting you here in the good ol' days
I would never pick the flower of my favorite
*   protégé*

One. Two. Punch.

On December 31, 1999, the last of the contracts he'd signed as Prince Rogers Nelson expired, so early in 2000, he announced that he would be called Prince again. Apparently, he felt that the unpronounceable symbol no longer suited him. I'm sure that was a relief for everyone who'd been bending over backward to insert that symbol in font collections and figure out what to call him and asking me what I called him, but I was sad to see it go. It meant something on a plane beyond words, beyond fame, beyond the ordinary— and that's the plane where his soul recognized mine.

In all the years we were together, I never called him Prince. Now I did. I felt an era ending, and I knew our marriage was ending with it. He'd humiliated me, going around with Manuela and putting out a video of himself crawling up another woman's cooch. He'd drained the money I was supposed to be using to maintain the house in Spain, so bill collectors were banging down the door. He made me feel banished— and not just banished by my husband, but banished by God. It was as if he expected me to simply disappear, and in a way, I did. I felt myself slipping down the drain and didn't have the will to fight it anymore.

I woke up every morning in a fog of depression and spent the day pushing terrible thoughts out of my head. My love for this man had been the formative force of my entire adult life at that point. I was only twenty-six years old, but I felt like I'd lived ten lifetimes in the ten years I'd known him. I didn't know how to be a grown-up woman without him, and I didn't want to learn. No one had ever ignited my mind or body the way he had. No one had taken me to the heights he took me to, creatively, professionally, and emotionally. We'd given each other a child. We'd given each other the dream of children. We'd held each other in the darkest imaginable moments and in the brightest possible sun.

On March 20, 2000, I wrote him a letter and told him how enormously unhappy I was. Seeing the words on paper, I sobbed myself empty.

> *I have come to terms with the fact that you don't love me anymore.*

That was a lie I tried to tell myself. I hadn't come to terms with the loss of him. I never really did. And I believed that on some level—even though it was a level now lost to him—he did love me and always would.

> *...what you really want is to have me out of your life without having to go through the legal system. Regardless of my feelings for you, I do not wish to be humiliated anymore...*

I couldn't bear to write down the word *divorce*.

> *What do you suggest we do in order to resolve this matter legally, in a way that is not damaging to us? I'm sure we can handle this quietly and expeditiously as adults instead of making a spectacle out of it.*

I left my mansion in Spain and moved in with Jan and Myra, living out of a suitcase and sleeping on the couch in their one-bedroom apartment in Harlem. My attorney was a friend of Jan's from Jersey. I'd come to Paisley Park ten years earlier with more than $100,000 in my belly dancing account. I was ready to leave with nothing. Jersey Lawyer told me I was crazy. When Prince's high-powered attorney made an opening offer of settlement—I could keep the house in Spain, but I would get very little cash—Jersey tried to tell me, "That is a crap offer."

"Tell them we'll take it," I said. "I just want to move on."

I figured I could sell the house and live on that money while I took a moment to recover and start rebuilding my career, but it took years to find a buyer. When I finally got an offer I could live with, to sweeten the deal, I had to throw in a pink BMW my husband had given me as a wedding gift. By the time I unloaded that gorgeous albatross, the cost of maintaining the house and grounds had gobbled up every nickel of equity.

I'm not going to groan on and on about it, but I don't want to underplay the effort it took to come back from this heartbreak. I was seriously depressed. I would never want Gia to think that a woman's life is over if she loses her man, but that's how I felt. I'd lost the love of my life, my son, my songs, my job, my band, my home, my home away from home— everything from Larry the Starfish to the "Children of the Sun" master, which, ironically enough, was owned by NPG Records, to whom I was apparently a slave.

But in that whole purple foo foo world, only one small thing truly mattered to me: Amiir's ashes. It took me a long time to find out what had happened to the little urn with the dolphin family. I kept asking and badgering and getting no answer. Eventually, a compassionate friend told me that she'd heard about a troubling incident: Prince's assistant was upset that he had been asked to burn everything in the house that reminded him of me or the baby, including the contents of the nursery—Amiir's crib and toys and clothes and books—everything.

I stared at her, stammering in disbelief. "But—but surely, he—not *everything*."

"It's all gone," she said. "I'm so sorry."

I sucked in a deep breath. My whole body felt taken over with rage. It felt hot and toxic and lasted for a long, long time.

In May 2000, less than sixty days after I wrote that letter to Prince, Daddy drove me to my lawyer's office to sign the final papers. Jersey handed me a thick manila envelope and said, "You're divorced." Nothing but numb, I got into the car with Daddy, and we drove back to New York.

Somewhere along the line, I said, "This is bullshit."

Daddy was startled. He'd never heard me cuss. Not one time in my life. But then he smiled and nodded in agreement. "Yep. Bullshit it is."

All that summer, he and Mia and Mama and Jan and Myra patiently loved me back from the ledge. It sucked, but I couldn't wallow in it. I pounded the pavement in New York, hoping to get a recording contract or dancing gigs or anything short of the *Playboy* spread people kept suggesting. At one meeting, after viewing my demo, the suit told me, "We really dig that Latina-Arabic vibe. We just signed a girl named Shakira."

Contemplating a new direction for my life, I thought about what it took to get through that Oprah interview just days after Amiir's death and realized I was a lot better actress than I ever gave myself credit for, but to make a living at that, I'd have to start a new life in LA, the one place that had always intimidated me.

twelve

Right away, I accepted one hard fact about getting over my ex-husband: I would never get over him. All I could do was move on to the next thing. I hooked up an agent and started acting classes. I started forging a circle of good friends. Wade Robson asked me to choreograph a music video with Britney Spears, which was a lot of fun and got my name into circulation as someone who was still in the biz, good behind the camera, and making something of myself. I was still struggling emotionally, but I worked hard to stay in great shape, continue learning my craft, and keep my chin up. I wasn't looking to meet anyone or get into another relationship, but Tommy Lee's drum tech and longtime friend Viggy spotted me at a club one night and introduced us. Prince always said that if he ever had a real rock band, he'd want Tommy Lee and Dave Navarro to be in it, so it's kind of hilarious that Carmen Electra ended up dating Tommy Lee and married to Dave Navarro, and I ended up dating Tommy after I moved to LA in 2001.

Tommy understood what it was like to marry—and unmarry—a pop culture icon. Neither one of us ever bad-mouthed the other person's ex. On the contrary: he was in awe of Prince, and I thought Pamela Anderson was the bomb. I loved her attitude, her openness, and the fact that she'd given birth at home. I heard through the grapevine that Prince was unhappy about my seeing Tommy Lee. I guess he thought I'd see someone "normal" like an accountant or a software developer or, better yet, stay celibate the rest of my life.

But Tommy was the perfect rebound romance. He was unfailingly honest. Could not tell a lie. He was a great cook and consummate gardener, who loved picking flowers and knew the name of every plant under the sun. He was thoughtful and deeply considerate of others. When he met Mama for the first time, it was ninety degrees outside, but he wore long sleeves so she wouldn't be confronted with all his tattoos.

We hadn't seen or spoken to each other for over a year, but in late August 2001, I was stunned by the news that Aaliyah had died in a plane crash, and then I saw the news that Prince's father had died that same day. My heart ached for him, and I was surprised to find that the hard ball of rage in my gut had softened a bit. It had been about eighteen months since we last spoke, and I was almost ready to hear his voice again, so I left him a message.

"It's me. I just want to say I'm so sorry to hear about your dad. I hope you were able to make peace with him before he passed. I hope...I hope you're well."

He called me as I was driving home after some MTV-related bash not long after that, and we talked for a long time as I drove through the LA traffic. We talked a bit about his father, and he seemed remarkably okay with it. Somehow, seeing his father's life in its entirety now, he was able to keep the music and let the rest go.

He asked me a question about his taxes, and I reminded him that it wasn't my problem anymore. He asked me if I'd been able to sell the house, and I said I was working on it. We talked about Aaliyah's music and about the music he was working on at the time. That summer he previewed his album *The Rainbow Children* at a weeklong festival at Paisley Park. Musically, it's Prince and therefore extraordinary, but the storyline is a thinly veiled parable about Jehovah's Witnesses, and in that scenario, there's a beautiful unbeliever who gets banished to a foreign land. Meanwhile, the "Wise One" hooks up with another woman conveniently sent to him by God. When I heard it, I fought the impulse to roll my eyes, but he didn't ask me what I thought of it, and I didn't volunteer an opinion. It felt so good driving along and talking with him, I didn't want to say anything that would tip the mood in the wrong direction.

After about an hour, I was almost back in Wood-land Hills, and the conversation was winding down. He said, "I should let you know . . . I'm going to marry Manuela."

"What?" I almost rolled the car over. "No. Not her. Go ahead and marry anyone else in the world, but this—no. I do not bless this. You do not have my bless-ing." I went off on him, and he hung up on me, which was jolting. He'd never cut me off like that before.

I don't know why I was surprised. I was the "Ban-ished One," and she was part of the Bible study crowd, which was apparently God's own *Good Housekeeping* Seal of Approval. On New Year's Eve, they were bap-tized together and got married in Hawaii. Again, I fought the eye roll. I fought it hard. I didn't want to admit that the real reason it hurt so deeply was that I had assumed we'd eventually get back together. Like Mama and Daddy. As a little girl, I learned that mar-riage is forever, and divorce is just a bump in the road. It was tough for me to grow up and accept that we were *over* over.

On 9/11, I was in Laughlin, Nevada, with Tommy, visiting his dying father. I was trying to be there for him, but I was emotionally wrecked and drinking, which was very unusual for me. Through a haze of grief and alcohol, we stared at the TV in disbelief, like everyone else in the world, and then we flew home in a private plane. It was eerie; it felt like we were the only plane in the sky over LA. I was so grateful to have his strong hand in mine.

Not long after that, Tommy asked me to marry him. He proposed with a gummy bear ring with my parents sitting there and a cascade of silly string and applause. How was I going to say no? But the next morning we woke up, and had a mutual moment of *Oh, God, what did we just do?* The media picked up on it right away. I heard through the grapevine that Prince was distraught about it. He called one night and left a message when I didn't pick up.

"Hello?" It was strange to hear his voice. And we never said "hello." We always said, "Hi." In our vocabulary, "Hello?" meant "WTF?"

"Hello?" he said again.

And after a brief silence, he said, "Hi." And then he hung up.

Tommy and I worked at staying together for a few months, but we never talked about actually getting married. At the end of the day, Tommy and I were each exactly what the other person needed in the exact moment we needed each other, and for that, I'll always be grateful. We had *fun*, and I was in serious need of some fun after what I'd been through in the previous two years. The same was true for him. During the two years I was with Tommy, he and Pamela were in a fairly gloves-off custody thing, but despite that, their kids—people, these kids were adorable, smart, good-hearted, grateful little people. Their mom had a pretty freakin' great résumé there, because children don't just fall off the plum tree like that, especially in Hollywood.

I loved those kids. Still do. But they had a terrific mom, who was not me, and ultimately, that was a problem for me. I still wanted to have a child of my own, and Tommy was good with the kids he already had. We were honest about it, with ourselves and with each other: it was a deal breaker. We parted with some sadness, but we remain good friends to this day. When Prince died, Tommy e-mailed me: *Don't know what to say. I am so sorry.* I got a lovely note from his fiancée as well.

I didn't speak with Prince again for several years. I saw him, of course. It was hard not to. I still loved his music, and so did the rest of the world, so I saw him on TV and heard him on the radio. We ran into each other one night at the Green Door, and he actually seemed happy to see me at first, but I was feeling spicy, so I said, "Hey, Prince. How's it going, Prince?"

"Why are you calling me Prince?" he asked.

"Isn't that your name now, Prince? Nice necklace, by the way."

He quoted some scriptural teaching about covering one's chest.

"Typical Gemini," I said. "Bring your religion to the club."

He was irritated by that and went off on a toot about how he wasn't going to vote in the upcoming elections. I finally had to turn away and say to my friends, "We're gonna need another bottle of champagne."

In March 2004, the first year he was eligible for it, Prince was inducted into the Rock & Roll Hall of Fame. People are still talking about how he ripped the place apart with an incredible guitar solo on "While My Guitar Gently Weeps" as part of a tribute to George Harrison. *Rolling Stone* said, "It could be the single greatest moment in any Rock Hall induction ceremony in its history." I sat at home watching with tears in my eyes, partly because it truly is a mind-blowing guitar solo, and partly because I was thinking about the night we were there together, honoring George Clinton. That night, I linked my arm through my husband's and said, "We'll be back for yours in a few years."

I heard that he and Manuela had bought a house in Toronto. I knew that choreography, too. It didn't surprise me at all to hear that they'd split up shortly after that, and their divorce became final in 2006. What did surprise me was that Manuela reached out to me and said that there was some stuff of mine in storage at Paisley Park, and I should go get it. I was skeptical at first, because this message came to me on social media. Assuming it was someone pretending to be her, I replied: *Tell me something so I know this is actually you.*

She shot back: *Tubesocks.*

I burst out laughing. Yeah. Only someone who really knew him would know what that meant.

I didn't hold back when I replied: *I have no respect for you. I dreamt of ways to beat your ass if I ever saw you.*

She surprised me again by saying: *I'm truly sorry.*

We ended up having a very long, interesting conversation, which confirmed what I always suspected: she's a pretty cool girl. Being gorgeous was one thing, but to maintain more than passing interest from Prince, you had to be smart and strong and kind, and now that I've gotten to know Manuela, I know she is all those things. Sadly, that doesn't change the fact that she crossed the line with my husband, so I can't pretend I've never had another unkind thought about her. Let's just say the relationship status is "Complicated" and probably always will be, but I give her credit for reaching out to me and apologizing. Ten years later, she's a wonderful mom and still a natural knockout beauty.

In November 2006, I wrote Prince a long letter and told him that I was ready to forgive him. He called me, and we talked for a long time.

"We're bound to run into each other," I said. "I don't want it to be weird."

"No, no. It's not weird. Not on my side."

"Good. I'm glad," I said. "I've actually been talking to Manuela."

"What? No. Why? Don't do that."

"She's a cool girl. It's fine. I'm over it. It's been a long time."

He sighed heavily. "What is time?"

"A magazine."

"Oh, so you're still funny."

"Yep."

"I don't believe in time. It doesn't exist unless you believe in it. It has no power over you unless you grant that power."

"It has power," I said tartly. "Take a look at my butt."

He roared at that, and I savored the fact that I could still crack him up.

"You seem to be holding up pretty well," he said. "From what I see."

"Well, they do keep asking me to do *Playboy*."

"Ah, *hell* no!"

"Just saying."

We talked and laughed for a long time. He told me about his Las Vegas residency, 3121 @ Rio Casino, which was essentially a six-month tour with only one venue. I was thinking about what a luxury that would be when he circled back and started talking about time again, saying how he wanted to be like the Dalai Lama, always moving into the future, and that he didn't age because he didn't celebrate his birthday.

"Oh, shut up already," I said. "You're a human being. We all age. We all need to sleep and eat and breathe—everything in moderation—and what's wrong with celebrating your life if that comes from a loving place and makes you happy?"

"Hmm." He took that in for a moment. "So what are you doing for your birthday?"

"Vegas."

"Would you want to come to the show?"

"Of course."

"Okay."

"Well. Okay then."

We said good-bye, and I hung up feeling very glad that he had called. On my birthday, I sat in the audience, basking in that old familiar torrent of purple light and energy, and feeling that, for the first time in years, I cried. I realized how much I'd missed it. I was still in awe of what he could do as a performer, and the idea that this extraordinary man was once—*Oh. Whoa. What...*

He had come down from the stage and was walking toward me. When he got to the aisle seat where I was sitting, he took my hand and pulled me up into his arms and hugged me. Despite the lights and loud music and a thousand pairs of eyes in the room, I closed my eyes and let myself feel the muscle and bone of his arms. For a moment, he was that man I loved. The next moment, he was Prince again, and I found I was once again able to love him purely for that, the way I did the first time I saw him in Spain when I was sixteen.

I thought he might call me that night and ask if I wanted to come and hang out, but I was no longer the girl who waited by the phone. I went out gambling.

Over the next few years, I was happy to see him reconnecting with Wendy and Lisa and other people who'd been important in his life as well. He was always good at keeping track of the people he truly cared about. He'd have an assistant grab tapes of TV performances, appearances, articles, whatever they were doing. So I knew he was watching as I worked on movie and television gigs, some in English, some in Spanish, and one movie where I got to dust off my old German skills. Over the years, I did guest spots on *Nip/Tuck*, *Las Vegas*, *Psych*, *CSI:NY*, and *Big Shots*, and scored a nice recurring role on *Army Wives*.

In 2011, I agreed to do a reality show called *Hollywood Exes* on VH1. The opportunity to star in a series that could potentially last several seasons was a gift from God. It wasn't exactly the artistic direction I had dreamed of for myself, but I was grateful, because I really needed a steady gig at that moment.

I had been diagnosed with MS.

This is something I had to keep hidden at the time

and have spoken about very little in the years since, because it's difficult enough to be a woman over forty in Hollywood. I want to keep up the impression that I am vibrantly healthy—because I am. I work hard to maintain my belly dancer body, and I don't want people looking at me like I'm sick or wondering if I can hack it. When I feel the need to share my diagnosis with someone, I want them to be every bit as stunned and disbelieving as I was when I first heard it myself.

To this day, I've never experienced any of the typical large muscle symptoms of MS. I woke up one morning with a weird blurry spot in my vision. The optometrist referred me to an optic neurologist, who came in and casually said, "It's optic neuritis. It's a side effect of multiple sclerosis." Before I could even wrap my head around what he was saying, I was in the MRI machine—my new home away from home—and the scans showed several lesions on my brain.

Which brings us once again to the cold pages of a medical text: Multiple sclerosis (MS) is an abnormal response of the body's immune system directed against the central nervous system, including the brain, spinal cord, and optic nerves. The myelin sheath protecting the nerve is damaged and sometimes destroyed, causing nerve impulses to slow or even stop. There is no cure. The goal is to manage the disease and preserve remission as long as possible.

"This can't be right," I told the neurologist. "I'm healthy. I eat healthy. I work out. I'm a *dancer*."

"All that's working in your favor," she said, "but this is serious, Mayte. This is something we need to stay on top of for the rest of your life."

She started me on a regimen of interferon injections, which I gave myself three times a week in the beginning, alternating thighs to control the spread of huge purple bruises, which didn't exactly jibe with my work and life. One of my friends had been diagnosed with MS ten years earlier, and I sometimes gave her those injections. Now I was sticking my own leg and reading everything I could get my hands on. I quickly became fluent in yet another language I didn't want to understand.

So the first great gift I got from *Hollywood Exes* was a new circle of fabulous friends at a moment when I really, really needed good friends. The show featured several women who'd married A-list celebrities, including Andrea Kelly (ex–Mrs. R. Kelly), who was a dancer, so right away, she and I had a lot to talk about. If you haven't seen it, open a bottle of wine and watch it sometime. Right now, let's fast-forward again. Because we're getting to the good part. The best part. The life-changing part where everything that went wrong takes a hard right, because God is good and never banished me one bit.

In July 2012, I was managing my immunotherapy and had my MS in a symptom-free remission, which I hope to maintain for a good many years. I was making decent money with *Hollywood Exes*, and in this business, work begets work, so I was getting more one-off acting jobs as well. I was busy with Mayte's Rescue, a charitable organization that finds loving homes for abused and abandoned animals. I adopted Boogie, the dear old golden retriever, and together we had a really nice life going. But there was this achingly open space. Not in my schedule, but in my soul. In my heart. I'd been thinking about adoption for years. I finally felt ready—way beyond ready—to be a mother again.

My friend Diane had adopted a child, and she nudged me to take the first step: a seminar that educated me on the whole process and explained the legal requirements and procedures. I loved the idea of having a baby in my arms, but I would have been just as thrilled to adopt an older child with special needs. But with my MS diagnosis on the paperwork, I wondered if I'd even be able to make it onto the long waiting list. I filled out all the state-required paperwork, but something stopped me from sending it in. I knew they'd ask me to be a foster mom first, and it was terrifying to risk loving and losing another child, but I was ready to take that leap of faith. The paperwork was on my desk, ready to be sent out the next day, when God decided it was time to play some jazz.

Fate or coincidence? I'll let you decide.

Gia's birth mother (her name and identifying details will be kept private here) is tough but beautiful. She's a feisty, intelligent girl and she owns it. Her choices are inked into her skin, a personal manifesto that was in her bones long before tattoo needles brought it to the surface. She made the choice to have Gia and place her for adoption, and she was adamant about finding her a good home, but she didn't want to put her into the foster care system, so she asked a counselor to help her find someone and navigate the legal issues. In August 2012, Gia was nine months old, and the counselor still hadn't found anyone who wanted her—not anyone who measured up to the standards of Gia's birth mother, that is.

One day in August, this girl had a minor accident at her job. Some cleaning solution splashed into her eyes, and she was sent home for the afternoon to take care of it. As she lay on her bed, thumbing the remote control, she settled on a reality show about fabulous women formerly married to famous men. Rich ladies, she figured, with rich lady problems. Drama, drama, drama. Gossip about the drama. More drama. It made this girl roll her swollen eyes.

But she decided this one chick was different. She was Latina, like her and her sisters. Like Gia. In the midst of all that fake reality, something about the Latina chick seemed real. She displayed no bitterness toward the rock star she had been married to. She spoke of him with respect and affection. It was obvious she still loved him. This woman talked about devastating losses and about moving on.

"In a perfect world, I'd be pregnant right now," she said as the cameras followed her into a doctor's office. "I'm nervous but optimistic. Whatever works, right?"

The lady was so flustered when the receptionist called her name, she dropped a stack of papers and had to get down on the floor to pick them up. After some uncomfortable small talk, the doctor said, "Currently, you're thirty-eight years old, and you've been pregnant twice, correct?"

"Yes."

"And what were the results of those pregnancies?"

"They're not here."

"Did both pregnancies result in miscarriage?"

"No. The first one was to term."

"Was there a genetic issue?"

"Yes."

"And the second one?"

"The second one was a partial molar pregnancy."

The girl watching the show didn't know what that meant, and they didn't break away to explain it, so she figured, *Whatever that is, it must be bad.*

"I can't wait for this part to be over," said the lady in the doctor's office. "It's hard for me to talk about the past, especially when I'm here to talk about the future."

But the future she envisioned was fading by the minute. A stark conversation about ovarian function, daily injections, chromosomal anomalies, and surgical procedures basically boiled down to the harsh reality that her perfect-world pregnancy was not going to happen.

The girl clicked off the television and stared at the ceiling. Gia was in her crib, crying the demanding, full-throated cry of a nine-month-old. The depth of the woman's sadness resonated in a strange harmony with the sound of Gia's crying—a motherless child and a childless mother—their need for each other vibrated like the silver tines of a tuning fork. The girl picked up her cell phone and Googled the name of the woman in the doctor's office.

mayte garcia

Thousands of results spilled out, led by the Wiki basics: *Mayte Jannell Garcia is an American belly dancer, actress, singer, and choreographer. She is of Puerto Rican ancestry... On Valentine's Day in 1996, Garcia, then 22, married Prince, then 37, in Minneapolis.*

The girl scrolled through a cache of images. She saw me dancing with a sword on my head, diving from the stage to crowd-surf in Berlin, standing outside the soaring white walls and windows of Paisley Park, and walking a gauntlet of paparazzi with Prince in happier days. There was cryptic news coverage of our lost child, blunt reports of our divorce, snarky blog posts about the reality show, and a Realtor's desperate sales pitch for the rambling mansion in Spain.

The girl went to my website and saw my tattoos, my dogs, my dog rescue mission, and more dancing. She clicked on the *Contact* tab and filled out the form, typing rapidly with her thumbs:

> *This will touch your heart and change your life...*
>
> *Mayte I had a baby that ended up with father offering to pay abortion I am Mexican he is White he said I would be on my own if I didnt get abortion I agreed to figure it on my own and would rather pray to God to let me cross roads with someone who can adopt her she is now a 9 month old girl she is mixed with ginger strawberry blond hair and i dont want to be a Mom on welfare something about you touched my heart that u would be the right person to adopt her u can see pics of her on my instagram you can email me*

When I saw this message, my initial reaction was a sharp flash of skeptical irritation. This was someone pranking me in a very cruel way. The worst possible way. It couldn't be real, I told myself. Babies don't just drop out of Heaven into your arms. That's not how it works—as I had recently learned, sitting through many hours of a seminar, being told how the adoption of a healthy baby could be difficult, expensive, potentially heartbreaking, and often impossible. If this was real, it would be...it would be like two souls recognizing each other from opposite sides of the universe, simply because they were meant to be together.

How could a sensible person put her faith in something as unlikely as that?

I called my friend Diane for a reality check. "I know this sounds crazy, but I'm forwarding this message to you. It can't be real...can it?"

"Probably not," she said, "but let me call her and see what I can find out."

I sat there, clinging to Boogie for support, waiting for what seemed like hours. Diane finally called me back. She'd had a long conversation with the girl.

"She's legit," said Diane. "Her counselor has been trying to help her connect with a family. At the very least, you should think about meeting her."

Still feeling very cautious, I messaged the girl on Twitter, and we began a long conversation. She told me how she'd been struggling to provide and care for Gia, how she'd prayed for the right family to come along—a family that spoke Spanish and English so Gia would grow up knowing both.

When I asked the baby's age, she messaged:

Gia was born November 12, 2011

"Oh!"

Boogie looked up when she heard me cry out. I had to push my hand against my chest and breathe for a minute before I replied:

That's my birthday!

A moment later, she sent me a picture of Gia. I clicked on the attachment and started to cry.

I was looking at the most beautiful girl in the world.

There was a process, of course, and I made sure that it was all done by the book, just as I'd learned in that adoption seminar. I didn't want any mistakes to be made, so I was determined to stick to the protocol outlined by the caseworker, but the first time I brought Gia home for a visit, I couldn't bear to part with her when the time came. When I called to ask her birth mother if we could extend the visit a few more days, the girl knocked the floor out from under me.

"I've said good-bye," she told me. "I can't say it again. I need you to keep her."

"*What*? But that's—Is that even—I'm not sure we can do that."

"It's done."

She left me staring at the phone with baby Gia on my hip, smiling up at me with her angelic smile as if she knew already that there's nothing more terrifying than getting the one thing you've always wanted. I didn't know what I'd have to do next, but I knew I didn't want to miss out on another minute of my daughter's life. I knew that this and all the cascading challenges of motherhood were now mine to figure out and push through. I would figure this out and make it happen, and for the rest of my life, I would have this baby girl's back the way Mama always had mine.

And I wouldn't have to do it alone. Mama took on grandmotherhood with her usual energy. Aunties Jan and Myra were enthusiastically on board. My friend Dave, aka Uncle Dave, was always there for us when we needed a hand. Gia immediately had him wrapped around her little finger, and to this day, this tough-talking Jersey guy gets misty-eyed with emotion whenever he talks about her.

Not long after Gia's first Christmas with us, she was mine—signed, sealed, delivered—and life settled into a lovely routine. Daddy (aka Buelo) said I won the lottery. Actually, he said, "You won the fucking lottery," but we don't use that sort of language in front of Gia, who is whip-smart. By the time she was two and a half, she was articulate enough to parrot bad words she heard.

The first few years of her life went by in a blissful blur of creating, coloring, singing, storytelling, dancing, jumping, thinking, and asking questions. She filled my life with a specific brand of Gia-flavored joy I could not have imagined, piles of blessings I never even knew I was praying for.

She's four—almost five now—so she hasn't seen *Purple Rain* yet, but I showed her the "7" music video a few months before Prince died.

"Mama, what's this song?" she asked.

"It's called '7.'"

"Why?"

"Because seven mysterious assassins chased after Princess Mayte, and Prince *smoked them all with an intellect and a savoir faire.*"

"Mama, you're a dancer."

"Yep."

"Mama, who's that?"

"That's Prince with the guitar."

"Do you love him?"

"Yep."

"Mama, did you have a baby?"

Every once in a while, she stops my heart. I don't know where these things come from. Maybe that particular question was because of the children in the video, but I didn't shy away from it.

"Yes," I said. "Prince and I had a baby boy."

"Where is he?"

"He's in heaven."

"With Boogie?"

"Yes."

Thank God for Boogie, Gia's guardian angel.

Hollywood Exes ended after a couple more seasons. I was grateful to have it last as long as it did. A steady gig is a precious commodity in this town. You've gotta open a lotta clams to find a pearl like this one. I kept going out on auditions and developed a belly dancing seminar much like the weekend programs Mama and I used to do when I was a kid. I was working hard and loving it, but being a single mother—let's just say it has a way of clarifying one's priorities.

When the house in Spain was sold, I was left with the chore of packing and moving all the personal belongings left in it. Ever since then, I'd been maintaining climate-controlled storage for the ton of clothes my husband left in his closet there. He never asked for any of it back at the time or answered when I repeatedly asked him, "What am I supposed to do with all this stuff?" In the fall of 2015, I decided to pull a few pieces from Prince's wardrobe and auction them off online.

"I know I'll get a lot of blowback from people online," I said to Dave.

"So what?" he shrugged. "You ain't made it till ya been hated."

This I knew from years of celebrity life, and anyway, my alternatives were limited to:

1. Keep paying for storage. (Not.)
2. Donate the clothes to charity. (For all the size extra-petite rock stars living on the street?)
3. Dedicate 90 percent of the closet space in my house as a shrine to the Artist Formerly Known as the Artist Formerly Known as Prince. (See option 1.)

Bottom line: According to the divorce settlement, the house and its contents went to me in lieu of a cash settlement. In the beginning and at the end, all I wanted was my husband. Before we were married, I asked him if he wanted me to sign a prenup, and he said no. Naturally, his people tried to get him to do a prenup. He wasn't having it.

"This is my soul mate," he told them. "We're not getting divorced."

I walked away with my dignity and never regretted it.

But now I have a child to support. I loved my ex-husband, but I couldn't afford to be sentimental about his cast-off clothes. These were bell-bottoms and boleros, people, not sacred relics. I wanted to talk to Prince about it and ask him if there was anything he'd like to have back, but I wasn't the one with the private numbers anymore. I called and e-mailed several times but didn't hear from him. I wonder now if my messages ever made it past the front door.

In January 2016, I heard through the grapevine that he wasn't doing well. I kept hearing rumors that he was sick and had alienated several people who cared for him. I reached out to our mutual friend Randee—the one who shot all that amazing footage in Egypt—and told her, "I'm going up there. I want to see with my own eyes that he's okay. I just need to know if you think I should take Gia. I really want him to meet her, but if things are weird…"

Randee assured me that the rumors were just rumors. She said Prince was fine and there was no reason for me to come up to Minnesota. I accepted that reassurance the same way I had once accepted my husband's promises that the thing with the pills would never happen again. It was easier to postpone the visit when I thought about Gia's little legs in the unrelenting cold of a Minnesota winter.

"Maybe next summer," I said. "After school gets out."

I'll never forgive myself for leaving it at that. I don't blame Randee, and she says I shouldn't blame myself, but I'll always wonder—if I'd taken Gia to meet him, would he still be alive? Would it have made a difference if he'd seen that fate and coincidence were still on our side?

Pushing my gut instinct aside, I went back to my busy schedule. I selected a few items to sell and went ahead with the auction. These few items were the tip of a handcrafted artisanal iceberg, but the money was enough for me to plan a summer trip to Puerto Rico. It was also enough to make Prince's lawyer call me.

He said, "Prince might be interested in buying back these items."

"How is he?" I asked. "Is he—"

"He's fine."

"I would like to talk to him."

"Send me a list of the items. We'll be in touch."

A few weeks later, Vanity died. I knew that must have left him feeling gut-shot, and I wanted to reach out to him, but the tone from the lawyer's phone call had left me with the impression that he was angry at me. I figured I'd let that settle. *Wait till summer*, I thought, *and then take Gia to see him*. He wouldn't turn us away if we were at the door, and I knew for a fact that it was impossible to look at Gia and not smile.

In April, there was a flurry of cancelled and postponed shows, and then it was all over the news one day that a charter jet Prince was on had been forced to make an emergency landing in Moline, Illinois, because he was "unresponsive." An ambulance met them on the ground and took him to the hospital. There were rumors of a drug overdose, rumors that he had AIDS, rumors that he was suffering a mental breakdown of some kind, and rumors that all the rumors were just rumors, and it was the flu.

I called Manuela, and she said, "I was told dehydration."

But we both knew that Prince drank water like crazy. That story didn't pass the smell test. I was uneasy and frustrated. I had the distinct feeling that people didn't want me to have the full story or access to anyone who could give it to me. I knew what it was like to be inside that isolated circle, so I knew what it meant to be outside. I saw a notice on Kirk's Facebook that there was going to be a party that night at Paisley Park. I clicked a "Like" on the post, hoping he'd see my name and reach out to me, but that didn't happen.

At that party, I'm told, Prince acknowledged everyone's concern about the emergency landing and the hospital visit. He made people laugh about it.

He said, "Wait a few days before you waste any prayers."

Six days later, he died.

tears go here
tears go here

afterword

*spirits come and spirits go
some stick around 4 the aftershow*

Since the day Prince died, people have remembered him on street corners and in cathedrals. There were a number of memorial services, some of which I participated in. One of the most meaningful moments for me was standing onstage with Sheila E in June at the 2016 BET Awards, raising his guitar over our heads. In October, I went back to dance in a tribute concert put together by Prince's family. I think people were a little surprised that I could still do the whole "7" routine, including backbends with my sword balanced on my head. Two weeks later, I returned for Purple Philanthropy, Sheila E's benefit concert for the charities Prince supported.

I've reconnected with so many people from my NPG years. We laugh and cry and feed each other's souls with stories about Paisley Park at its happiest. Even the doves felt the difference. When Prince built Paisley Park, there were two—Majesty and Divinity—and he hoped they would breed, but they didn't for many years. Apparently, they just needed to feel some procreative love and energy in the air. Suddenly, while I was pregnant with Amiir, eggs appeared and hatched. The hatchlings matured, and then more eggs appeared. Eventually, we had to get their growing family a bigger cage. The constant murmur of the doves was one of the first things anyone noticed walking into Paisley Park, but there are only two left now, and Prince's sister Tyka says that in the days after he died, they were strangely silent.

"Play some of his music," she told the caretakers, and that was wise. They heard his voice and responded, engaging him in conversation.

I hear the doves now, as I enter Paisley Park for the first time in sixteen years. It's not exactly allowed, but Prince's brother Omarr takes me there, and Fred, the property manager Prince and I hired twenty years earlier, lets me go upstairs.

"The carpet is different," I say to Omarr and Fred as we wander the quiet space. "The zodiac signs have been removed."

"Oh, yeah. None of that back then." Fred shrugs, knowing I understand.

I nod and smile. "Whatever peanut butters your jelly."

I have to laugh, because I'm not convinced the suns

and moons that have replaced the signs of the zodiac had any less mystic significance to Prince.

The elevator where Prince's body was found has been tastefully sealed off. As I pass it, I feel sadness but no sense of his spirit lingering there. If anything, I feel the distinct *not there*-ness of him—the same vacuum I felt when I held the urn containing Amiir's ashes. I knew he was gone; I clung to it only because that was all I had.

ELEVATE

I smiled remembering how I felt the first time I saw that word on the wall. It was the perfect word for what he did to everything he touched, including me. It was the thing he desired most for himself: to elevate to a consciousness of bliss. Now there was no doubt in my mind that he had.

His office, which is now downstairs, has been left almost exactly as he left it, several style generations from what it was when he and I had our neighboring offices upstairs. It's very global, Afro-chic meets psychedelic with a circular desk and purple phone. There's a dinner table, because he liked to eat dinner without actually taking a dinner break. They left his stacks of CDs and papers and other items undisturbed, including an odd pair of shoes by a chair—like bowling shoes, but wedges—and on a credenza, there are several framed photos of family and friends, Larry's family, children of staff members. Looking at their smiling faces, I wish I'd sent him a picture of Gia. I'm touched to see that he kept a well-worn book about Egypt close at hand, and for some reason, the little pet carrier we used for our cat Isis is still sitting in the corner.

It won't be part of the tour, I'm told, but I have to insist on visiting the doves before I go. They spark a familiar conversation with me, cooing and bobbing as I approach their ornate cage. I wish I could take them with me. They love to be around people, so it's good to know that soon people will be coming and going, keeping the birds entertained.

Before I leave the doves—and leave Paisley Park, perhaps for the last time—I lean in and whisper, "Have more babies."

I've witnessed many beautiful things being created in the hours when everyone is asleep. At my house, it's the only time that's quiet. As I write this, it's been six months since Prince's death. For the most part, I'm finally able to keep it together when I hear his music, but some songs I'll never be able to hear without weeping. Others have taken on an eerie aftertaste.

. . . if the elevator tries to take you down
go crazy, punch a higher floor

I try not to invest his lyrics with more meaning

than he intended. Sometimes these were just words that rhymed. Some songs were written or pulled out of the vault to pay the bills. But most of the time, they were more than that. I feel a shiver of privilege whenever I get the private joke or hear a turn of phrase that originally came out of my own mouth. Sometimes, when I'm listening to a song I've heard a thousand times before, I hear him speaking to me as plainly as if he was lying next to me in bed.

To make you all smile:

Jan and Myra remain happily married, restoring my faith in love, marriage, and happily ever after. My parents remain happily *remarried*—for the third time, having divorced each other twice. Manuela remarried, has two adorable daughters, and works hard to improve the lives of children through her nonprofit foundation. Sheila E and all the amazing people I worked with in New Power Generation continue to rock the world. I'm a little surprised that I haven't bumped into Larry at any of the many events celebrating Prince's life. I haven't thought about him in years. And Larry...Larry is an amazing musician who's lost a dear friend. I hope his faith brings comfort to him now, just as my faith brings comfort to me.

Gia started pre-K this year with a crisp little school uniform and a backpack full of socially responsible school supplies designed by Pharrell Williams.

"Don't take my picture," she frowned.

"I'm taking it."

"Fine..."

I Instagrammed her little face and looked at it with tears in my eyes a hundred times before lunch. Yes, I am *that* mommy.

Late in the evening, Gia and I snuggle on the couch, watching TV. I've been meaning to show her *Under the Cherry Moon*. I still love the choice Prince made to have it be black and white. It didn't start out that way. He started it with a vision of bright colors and Gatsby fashions. In the middle of things, he fired the director and made the post-production people meticulously un-color it. The end result is so charming and romantic. In garish color, it could have gone a little cheesy at the end when Christopher Tracy is gunned down on the pier. The grayscale keeps it classy and reminds me of the hours we spent playing *Wuthering Heights* and *Philadelphia Story* on the roadie box VCR.

At the very end of *Under the Cherry Moon*, the camera zooms in on a note Christopher Tracy has left on a table in the hall.

With love, there is no death.

And then the credits roll, taking us up into heaven where Prince and The Revolution jam in living color, dancing in the clouds.

Gia has slumped over sound asleep on my lap. I kiss her soft cheek and stroke her bangs from her forehead. Her hair smells like summertime. It's an enormous truth I've had to wrap my heart around: If I hadn't lost my precious son, if the pain of that loss hadn't torn me away from the husband I loved, I wouldn't have my daughter now. And I can't bear to imagine life without her. I don't know what to make of that, other than to say that I've learned to trust God to sort it out. Someday when I'm in heaven with Boogie and Mia and Amiir at my side, I'll ask a passing angel to explain it to me.

I'm glad I took Gia to see Paisley Park that first week, because it's already changing. I feel a moment of sorrow every time I see some news item about another small piece of my memories slipping away. But when I start to get sad about it, I have to remind myself that Paisley Park was always changing. During the decade that I was with Prince, I watched Paisley evolve—inside and out—just as his music evolved, and the bands evolved, the colors, shapes, and faces always changing. We all saw our seasons come and go, and it's okay, because that's what life is: seasons turning, one after another, a spiral of birth and rebirth.

His fans have evolved too, from big-eyed kids hitting Record just in time to catch "Let's Go Crazy" on the boom box to grown-ups addicted to our iPhones. Those of us who love his music will never allow it to die. As the years go by, his music will take on new dimension for us, because we'll grow wiser. We'll get closer to the sun.

Those of us who loved the man will never forget him. I couldn't begin to scratch the surface of his story in this space—much of it will always be a mystery, even to me—but I've tried to speak to what was most important to me personally: He was my family. His love lives on in me, and in a strange way, our love lives on in Gia. Maybe someday she'll tell her grandchildren, "He fathered me, in a way." And they'll hear his music, and his love will live on in them.

"Never say gone, never say gone," my husband told me over and over during those terrible days after our son died. Alone in the studio, he sang:

when you lose someone dear to you never say the
     words "they're gone"
they'll come back

With Gia in my arms, I hear his voice in my heart, and I know as surely as I know my name that I will see my love again.

a note from the author

MAYTE'S RESCUE is a dedicated 501C3 nonprofit on a mission to save abandoned, abused, and neglected animals. My love for dogs started as a child at my grandmother's house in Puerto Rico. At the time, she was like the Mother Teresa of stray dogs and would take in every emaciated, sick, and homeless dog on the block. She would nourish them back to health, and they would immediately become her pets. Every summer, my sister and I spent three months at my grandmother's house with twenty-five strays that I considered my furry siblings.

A few years ago I stumbled on a post on Facebook—a series of pictures with oil drums full to the rim with euthanized cats and dogs from a shelter. Horrified, I decided to do some research on dogs and cats in the US shelter system, and my heart sank when I saw the sheer number of domestic animals killed each year. Motivated by these shocking statistics and my love for animals established as a child, I started Mayte's

Rescue. Please join us as we help find loving homes for shelter dogs.

MAYTE GARCIA
Contact me: rescue@mayte.com
Visit my website: www.mayte.com
Want a dog or cat or friend? www.maytesrescue.com
Watch for new arrivals on Instagram: maytejannell
Follow on Facebook: officialmaytegarcia

acknowledgments

This story is my truth as I remember it. Some events have been condensed and some characters have been composited for length. Dialogue was reconstructed for dramatic purposes, using letters, videos, and public records. I've done my best to stay true to the content of the conversations, the facts of the events, and the spirit of the relationships portrayed in this book. Others may remember or perceive conversations and events differently. Though my journey has taught me a great deal about Pfeiffer syndrome, partial molar pregnancy, multiple sclerosis, the music industry, and the adoption process, I do not consider myself a medical or legal expert, and no part of this manuscript should be construed or misconstrued as medical or legal information or advice. My opinions do not necessarily reflect the opinions of NPG, VH1, or any other organizations who've employed me or hosted me as a teacher or public speaker or any organizations who may employ or host me in the future.

My love and gratitude go out to:

All the animals who've come across my path and to the ones I have yet to save. Mia, my guardian angel, I love you. Boogie and all my furry angels in heaven, keep up the good work. Mayte's Rescue supporters, we've only just begun. Gail, you are family. We love you.

Mama, you're an amazing woman and the best mama I could have wished for. Gia and I feel the sunshine of your love every day. Thank you for always having my back. Daddy, I think we have 75 more years left! Thank you for being my daddy. Jan, I thank you for being my sister and for bringing Myra into our family. Your love is true. Stephen, Drue, Dave, and Jen thank you for being there through a lot of the ups and downs. I love you all—and that love extends to family and friends too numerous to mention here. Every one of you has a special place in my heart.

I'm so grateful to Team Beautiful, starting with Gladys Gonzalez, my manager, and Jennifer Gates, my agent, who helped me shape this project from the beginning. This couldn't have happened without you two. Thank you! Joni Rodgers, you are the light in the dark room I was in. Thank you for hearing and helping me with my story. Jerusha, the grid is real! Patrick Demarchelier, thank you for your beautiful photographs. Michelle Howry and Hachette staff, your respect for my story and for Prince's fans has meant so much to me.

To Prince's family, our NPG family, the purple army, Sheila E, Wendy, Sotera, Robbie, Randee, and all the beautiful ones—the many brilliant artists, musicians, photographers, dancers, and crew I've had the joy of working with: Your love and support has gotten me through so much. The love is felt, and I hope you feel my love and gratitude in return.

♀ my love for you is eternal.

Amiir, I love you. Thank you for letting me be your mama.

Gia, my angel! I dedicate this story—and the rest of my life—to you. Because it was you who brought meaning and light to all of it.

In your gracious name, thank you God.

Mayte Garcia
Spring 2017

image credits

All images are courtesy of the author, except as follows. All images are used with permission:

page 1 (top): John Garcia, (middle) Francisco Marquez, (bottom) John Garcia

page 3 (top) photo courtesy John Garcia, (middle) Sotera Tschetter, (bottom) Shutterstock

page 4 (top) Getty Images, (bottom) Randee St. Nicholas

page 5 (all) LeAnn Doescher

page 6 (top) Nicole Nodland, (bottom) Randee St. Nicholas

page 7 (top) Patrick Demarchelier, (bottom) Nicole Nodland